Emile Gaston Boutmy

Studies in Constitutional Law. France, England, United States

Translated from the 2d French ed. by E.M. Dicey

Emile Gaston Boutmy

Studies in Constitutional Law. France, England, United States
Translated from the 2d French ed. by E.M. Dicey

ISBN/EAN: 9783337188399

Printed in Europe, USA, Canada, Australia, Japan

Cover: Foto ©Suzi / pixelio.de

More available books at **www.hansebooks.com**

STUDIES IN
CONSTITUTIONAL LAW

.

FRANCE—ENGLAND—UNITED STATES

BY

ÉMILE BOUTMY

Member of the Institute of France; Principal of the School of Political Science

TRANSLATED FROM THE SECOND FRENCH EDITION BY

E. M. DICEY

WITH AN INTRODUCTION BY

A. V. DICEY, B.C.L.

Vinerian Professor of English Law, Oxford

London

MACMILLAN AND CO.

AND NEW YORK

1891

INTRODUCTION

MONSIEUR BOUTMY'S *Études de Droit Constitution-nel* has reached a second edition in his own country. It has both in England and America been recognized by all persons interested in the comparative study of institutions as a brilliant and original essay on the essential differences between English and French constitutionalism.

In introducing the book in an English form to readers unable to enjoy the French original, I can confidently recommend it to the attention of students. The work was originally composed for Frenchmen; hence the author occasionally insists upon features in the English Constitution which to Englishmen may appear to be too well known to require notice or explanation. But the fact that the essay is written by a foreigner for foreigners, though it may seem at first sight to limit the utility of the book for English students, is in reality one of its great recommendations. We all forget to note matters with which we are familiar. Hence the best descriptions of a country's institutions have been often, not to say generally, composed by foreign observers. A stranger who has carefully studied the policy of a nation which is not his own seizes the broad outline of its political system more easily than can a native. If he overlooks or mistakes a few details, he obtains a better general view of the whole constitutional fabric than can a man who looks at the institutions of his country from the inside. Monsieur Boutmy is no exception to this rule. He has indeed mastered all that can be learnt from the best English historians such as Freeman or Stubbs; writing before the appearance of Mr. Bryce's exhaustive monograph on the American Commonwealth, he displays a more intimate knowledge of the American Constitution and of American politics than is generally possessed by well-educated Englishmen. But his claim to attention does not depend upon erudition. The aim of his book is to criticize and explain the constitutional ideas which govern the action of the English people in the light thrown upon them by a comparison with the ideas which have guided the constitution makers of France. It is this comparison which constitutes the true value of Monsieur Boutmy's work. An Englishman learns from it no new facts about the institutions of his country, but he is taught to look at familiar facts from a new point of view.

Monsieur Boutmy further, with great ingenuity, carries over to America, so to speak, the contrast between English and French ideas of government. He shows that, marked as are the contrasts between the English Monarchy and the American Republic, the institutions of the English people on both sides the Atlantic are in essence though not in form the same, and that they stand in marked contrast with the institutions of France. All the characteristics, he suggests, which distinguish the Constitution of England from every one of the constitutions of France reappear, though in a curiously changed shape, in America. In the United States, as in England, custom has the authority of law. The constitutional history of the United States is as obviously as the constitutional history of England the record of an attempt to close political contests by means of treaties. The development of American no less than of English political institutions has been the result of a long conflict between powers which existed prior to the Constitution. The crown, the nobility, and the commons existed long before the English Constitution had even a name. The States, Monsieur Boutmy insists, created the American nation ; it was certainly not the American people which created the States.

Of the translation I have said little. Anyone who can read French should study the works of a writer so lucid and brilliant as Monsieur Boutmy in the author's own language. The object of the translator has been not to render the French original sentence by sentence, and still less word for word, but to give, as far as possible, the meaning, the effect, and the spirit of each of Monsieur Boutmy's pages.

An Appendix to the second edition of the *Études de Droit Constitutionnel* contains replies to some of Monsieur Boutmy's critics. This Appendix is omitted in the translation. The criticisms being for the most part unknown in England, the answers thereto have, it is conceived, little interest for English students.

For the few notes, enclosed in brackets and marked (D), I am myself solely responsible.

A. V. DICEY.

OXFORD. MAY, 1891.

PREFACE

OF the three following essays two have been published separately, the one in 1878, the other in 1884. In the first I have attempted to make a critical survey of the English Constitution, combined with as complete a classification as possible, of its sources. I trust that I have not omitted anything essential. I do not examine into the institutions themselves, nor do I attempt to describe them ; such a subject cannot be dealt with in a hundred pages. I am satisfied, first, to distinguish the different parts of the political compact ; next, to note the special characteristics of each according to its origin, and lastly, to define the general spirit of the Constitution in which these parts are merged.

The second essay, *à propos* of a question of method, opens a number of vistas and, so to say, side-views of the Constitution of the United States. These views are tolerably numerous ; they throw light over a considerable surface, so that the reader can form a fairly complete picture of the whole Constitution. A good

deal of the detailed information in this essay is new,
and if it does nothing more, it may possibly somewhat
shake men's confidence in certain prejudices of very
old standing.

Owing to the political circumstances of the day, the
actual information given in these two essays has excited
an unusual amount of attention; but I think the real
value of this work to the public is of a different kind,
and does not in the main arise from the information
which the essays contain. I have given great care to
fixing the rules to be followed in exploring certain
departments of public law which have been mapped
out, either badly, or not at all. l have dwelt at length
on the precautions to be taken against the pitfalls into
which any person may fall owing to individual bias and
the influence of national circumstances. I have pointed
out, above all—and this is a warning against the snare
most dangerous to Frenchmen—that constitutional
mechanism has no value or efficiency in itself, independently of the moral and social forces which support
it or put it in motion; though by this I do not mean
to deny that the excellence of the mechanism inten-
sifies the action of these forces and makes it more
durable and regular.

The third essay has not been published before. It
suggested itself to me from the juxtaposition of the two
which precede it; it constitutes in a measure the con-

clusion drawn from them. By a more rigid and continuous comparison with France, I have in this essay
tried to recapitulate and bring out the differences not
only in form and in structure, but in essence and in
kind, between the Constitutions of England and the
United States on the one hand, and France on the
other. These differences are connected with the fundamental notion of *sovereignty*, which differs in the three
countries.

E. BOUTMY.

MAY, 1885.

PREFACE TO THE SECOND EDITION

THE indulgence with which this little volume has been received by the public encourages me to bring out a second edition. The three essays in the original edition are untouched. To the one on America, I have made a somewhat important addition concerning the exercise of the legislative function by the Chamber of Representatives.

Though tempted to do so, I did not wish to enter into certain questions of extra-constitutional order in the United States which have arisen of late, and will certainly be some of the problems of the future. I should have been, to a certain extent, justified in yielding to this temptation; for, whatever be the solution of these questions, its effect will certainly be felt in the region of public law. The rapidity with which the growth of landed estates has begun and progresses; the immense extent of the *latifundia*; the approaching exhaustion of the available soil — that seemingly inexhaustible treasure—the increase of tenant farmers (a class hitherto almost unknown and now by degrees replacing the yeomen who work their own estates) ; the appearance of the agrarian question ; the radical and socialistic character of the remedies proposed—these things all show an alteration of the ancient basis on which the political fabric was erected.   But if it is certain that the United States will tend to enlarge and strengthen the action of the central government, in proportion to their advance in population and material civilization, one cannot say as yet whether this centralization will be for the benefit of a single Federation or of several.   The question of secession is not yet closed.   Will the government of Washington alone profit by the powers taken from the thirty-eight States, or will these powers be divided among three or four governments at the head of Federations, fixed by natural geographical divisions ?   These are serious questions, which I could not have entered upon without giving more space to speculative conjectures than was compatible with my original plan.[1]

E. BOUTMY.

MAY, 1888.

[1] [A short paragraph is here omitted.   It refers to the replies to critics which do not appear in this translation (D.).]

CONTENTS

PART I

ORIGIN AND SPIRIT OF THE ENGLISH CONSTITUTION

PART I

ORIGIN AND SPIRIT OF THE ENGLISH CONSTITUTION

THE English Constitution is undoubtedly the first of all free constitutions in age, in importance, and in originality. It existed, with all its main features, four hundred years earlier than any other constitution. It has served more or less as the model for all existing constitutions. It contains the explanation, and embodies the true meaning, of more than one provision which its imitators have not always understood or have knowingly diverted from its first intention. No general or enlightened study of positive constitutional law can be undertaken without an exhaustive knowledge of this capital example. But the course to be pursued in acquiring this knowledge cannot be compared to any ordinary path, and especially not to the broad highway which the French jurists have laid out by rule and line in the domain of their law. It ought rather to be compared in the words of Pascal to *un chemin qui marche*, or to a river whose moving surface glides away at one's feet, meandering in and out in endless curves, now seeming to disappear in a whirlpool, now almost

lost to sight in the verdure.   Before venturing upon this
river you must be sure to take in the whole of its
course from a distance, you must study the chain of
mountains in which it rises, the affluents which swell
its waters, the valleys in which it widens out, the sharp
turns where it gets choked with sand, and the alluvial
soil which it deposits on its banks.   The most fertile of
these preparatory studies, and that which should come
first, is the analysis of the sources of the Constitution.

Section i

In the year 1793 Hérault de Séchelles inquired at
the Bibliothèque Nationale for a copy of the laws of
Minos.   Any one would make the same mistake now
who hunted for the *text* of the English Constitution.
There is no *text* but there are *texts*.   These texts are
of every age and have never been codified.   Nor even
taken all together do they contain nearly the whole of
English constitutional law, the greater part of which is
unwritten.   On any question of importance it is necessary
to refer, in almost every case, to several different laws
whose dates are centuries apart, or to a series of precedents which go far back into history.   For example,

the constitution of the House of Lords is the result
of several different statutes dated respectively 1707,[1]
1800,[2] 1829,[3] 1847,[4] 1869,[5] 1876,[6] of an opinion of the
judges in 1782[7] and of innumerable customs. The
duration of Parliament is determined by two Acts, one
of the time of George I., one of 1867, without counting
the usage, in virtue of which about a year of the
statutory time is curtailed. Publicists and jurists have
taken the trouble to search out and compare these texts
and to write down their decisions, and the legislator has
left this work to them, for no legislator has ever stamped
any methodical digest of the constitutional provisions
with his authority.

This state of things is very far removed from the idea
that the French have of a Constitution. For eighty
years past French history shows us under this name
one single document conceived all at once, promulgated
on a given day, and embodying all the rights of government, and all the guarantees of liberty, in a series of
connected chapters. Such are notably the French Constitutions of the revolutionary period from which all
the rest take their form and origin ; they are like
mathematical demonstrations or scientific classifications

---

[1] [6 Anne c. 11 (D).]   [2] [39 & 40 Geo. III. c. 67 (D).]
[3] [10 Geo. IV. c. 7 (D).]   [4] [10 & 11 Vict. c. 108 (D).]
[5] [32 & 33 Vict. c. 42 (D).]   [6] [39 & 40 Vict. c. 54 (D).]
[7] [See Anson, *Law and Custom of the Constitution*, p. 185 (D).]
It is in virtue of this opinion of 1782 that Scotch peers, created
peers of the United Kingdom, are allowed to take their seats in
the House of Lords. Up to that time they were excluded. [See
as to statutes affecting the House of Lords, *Index of the Statutes*,
Tit. " House of Lords " (D).]

starting with an axiom as a heading ; they are all works of art and logic.

The French are accustomed to see nothing but the advantages of this system, and they are evident. The English have chiefly felt its inconveniences and dangers. Probably they have been influenced by two facts : first, that to publish a clear, methodical, and analytical work for all readers would be to invite perpetual competition in producing an improved version, to make one's self amenable to logic, *i.e.* to a tribunal from which the right of appeal is indefinite ; secondly, that every systematic construction is tantamount to a promise to produce something complete and perfect which shall provide for and guard against every contingency, and this is to attempt an impossibility, so that the energy wanted to make such a Constitution, and the enthusiasm which it excites when first made, are only equalled by the cruel disappointments which follow as soon as it is put in force. So the English have left the different parts of their Constitution just where the wave of history had deposited them ; they have not attempted to bring them together, to classify or complete them, or to make a consistent and coherent whole.

This scattered Constitution gives no hold to sifters of texts and seekers after difficulties. It need not fear critics anxious to point out an omission, or theorists ready to denounce an antinomy. The necessities of politics are so complex; so many different interests are mixed up in them, so many opposing forces run counter to each other, that it is impossible to get together all the essential elements of a stable fabric and put them in their proper places, if the work is carried on under the eyes of a people whose taste is for homogeneous materials and a regular plan. The way to meet the difficulty is to arrange so that an ordinary spectator shall not be able to have any general view, such as would be given by codification. By this means only can you preserve the happy incoherences, the useful incongruities, the protecting contradictions which have such good reason for existing in institutions, viz. that they exist in the nature of things, and which, while they allow free play to all social forces, never allow any one of these forces room to work out of its alloted line, or to shake the foundations and walls of the whole fabric. This is the result which the English flatter themselves they have arrived at by the extraordinary dispersion of their constitutional texts, and they have always taken good care not to compromise the result in any way by attempting to form a code.

Section ii

THERE are four principal sources of English Constitutional Law : (1) Treaties, or *quasi*-treaties, (2) Precedents and customs generally known as Common Law, (3) Compacts, and (4) Statutes. The first and the two last of these divisions are the written part of the Constitution, the second is the unwritten part. They do not always differ much in form. The difference is chiefly to be found in their essential characteristics, in the matters which they regulate, and in the spirit which has dictated them.

There are two Treaties :—the Act of Union with Scotland (1707),[1] and the Act of Union with Ireland (1800).[2] The characteristics of treaties in the general sense of the word is that they bring two nations and two sovereignties face to face. The special characteristic of these two Acts of Union is, that the two sovereigns appear on the scene only in order to be absorbed and melted into one : these statutes belong to international law for a moment and then take rank in constitutional law. The Acts of 1707 are two statutes, one voted by the Scotch Parliament, and the other by the English Parliament, and sanctioned separately by Anne, first as Anne, Queen of Scotland,[3] and secondly

---

[1] [6 Anne, c. 11 (D).]   [2] [39 & 40 Geo. III. c. 67 (D).]

[3] The sanction in Scotland was not given as in England by the French phrase *La reine le veut*, pronounced after reading the title of the Bill, but by the representative of the Crown touching the parchment on which the Bill was written with a sceptre.

as Anne, Queen of England. These statutes are only
the ratification of one and the same instrument or
treaty [1] drawn up by a commission composed of duly
authorized representatives of the two kingdoms. At
this time Scotland was as completely separated from
England as was Hanover at a later date, or even more
so. Her government, her laws, her system of taxes, her
trade, were all in a sort of rivalry with England, and
even the constitution of her official Church was in direct
opposition to the Anglican Church. The two countries
were only held together by the personal and dynastic
union which threatened to come to an end at that
very moment. Scotland had not, like England, passed
an Act of Settlement which eventually called the
Hanoverian branch to the throne, in case of Anne's
dying without issue; but reserved to herself by a
special Act the right of settling the reversion to the
throne, in a way different from that fixed by the
English settlement.[2] This separation of the two
nations, verging on hostility up to the last moment,
was finally overcome by able statesmanship in 1707.

The Acts of 1800 are the two statutes 39 & 40 Geo.
III. c. 67, and 40 Geo. III. c. 38. They did not pass
without difficulty. Ireland, long treated as a conquered
country, had shortly before contrived, under cover of the
American War, to force the English Parliament into
giving her almost entire independence. In 1782 it had

---

[1] The articles of union are described as a treaty in the Act
itself. [See preamble to 6 Anne, c. 11 (D).]
[2] Act of Security, rejected in 1703, passed in 1704. [See
Burton, *History of Scotland*, viii., pp. 92, 99-101 (D).]

been decided that Ireland should have her own laws and her own courts of justice, and that her Parliament should have the free use of its own initiative, which up to that time had been subject to the approval of the king's privy council.

These concessions might have caused most serious embarrassment to the Government at Westminster. The danger was manifest when during the short period of George III.'s insanity the question of a regency was raised. There was actually nothing to prevent the Irish Parliament from choosing a regent, and this regent need not have been the one chosen by the English Parliament. In this case there would have been two regents, one at Dublin and one in London. The transition from two regents to two kings would have been quickly accomplished. The union of the two crowns, the only union which existed between the two countries, was threatened, and the near neighbourhood of the French Revolution increased the danger. In 1798 there was a formidable rebellion. Pitt acted promptly; before a few months had elapsed, by means of money or honours he had bought over the majority of the Irish Parliament, and in 1800 [1] it solemnly gave up its national independence.

The objects and the consequences of the two Acts of Union are shown by their very titles. The first made England and Scotland into one State under the name of Great Britain. The second united Ireland to Great

[1] The Union with Ireland voted by the English Parliament, July 2nd, 1800, came into force on January 1st, 1801. The Union with Scotland came into force May 1st, 1707.

Britain, and thus constituted the United Kingdom. The practical form which this double consolidation takes is: (1) the adoption by each of the two kingdoms thus annexed to England and to Great Britain respectively of one and the same dynasty, together with the settlement of the Crown in perpetuity on the Protestant line of the House of Hanover; (2) the introduction of a certain number of Scotch and Irish members into the two Houses of the English Parliament.

The Parliament thus constituted legislates for the whole of the United Kingdom; but the special laws of Scotland and Ireland which existed previous to the union remain in force as long as they are not repealed. A considerable number of these statutes exist, and they differ so considerably that Parliament finds it necessary from time to time to make special Acts for each kingdom. This is the reason why the following phrase is so often met with at the beginning or end of a statute: " This Act does not extend to Scotland or Ireland." [1] This exception is not necessary for the Isle of Man and the Channel Islands which are not parts of the United Kingdom. These islands are bound only by statutes in which they are particularly named.[2]

The most important of the other provisions of the two Acts of Union relates to the Church.

The Episcopal Church in England is an Established Church, that is to say, the Church which is in possession of the parish, livings, benefices, tithes, and church-

---

[1] There are several statutes which apply to Wales only.

[2] [1 *Steph. Comm.* (9th ed.) p. 101.   Or which by necessary implication are intended to extend to the Channel Islands (D).]

yards : the law regulates and sanctions its dogma, its constitution, its liberties, its jurisdiction and its ritual : the Queen takes an oath to maintain it, the Government takes part in its administration by nominating high dignitaries and certain incumbents of benefices.   In Scotland the Presbyterian Church is the official Church recognized by the Act of 1707, consecrated by law, and put in possession of the edifices and ecclesiastical revenues.   There is, indeed, an Episcopal Church in Scotland, but it is a free Church,[1] just as the Presbyterian Church is free in England.   Great Britain has therefore two State Churches, the Crown is the legal supporter of two opposite systems of sacerdotal hierarchy on the two sides of the Tweed.

Per contra, Ireland has no official Church at all.   The Episcopal Protestant Church of Ireland, formerly one and the same with the Church of England, was disestablished in 1869, *i.e.* separated from the state and dispossessed of its property under certain reservations which protected the interests of actual incumbents.   It has now become a free Church.

The extraordinary diversity which is the characteristic of English public law is patent in all the facts which we have just noted.   The French mind has a natural taste for simplicity and uniformity.   Its creations bear the impress of these two qualities, and it naïvely ex-

[1] Queen Anne in a letter to the Scotch Parliament in 1703 begged that a little tolerance should be shown to the adherents of the Episcopal Church, she called them " Dissenters," making use of the same name that she would have given to the Presbyterians in addressing the English Parliament.   [See Her Majesty's Letter, Burton, *History of Scotland,* viii., p. 90 (D).]

pects to find the same characteristics in every other human work. Any one who wants to feel at home in the English Constitution, and to understand it thoroughly, must get rid of any such expectation at once, for the English Constitution does not recognize any such ideals as simplicity and uniformity. Indeed, it seems as if its authors had deliberately avoided, as a dangerous extreme, any attempt at unity, or at laying down general principles, or at assimilation and fusion of the different parts of the Constitution. They certainly carefully guarded against all the generalizations and simplifications, which the creators of French public law were always striving for with the greatest faith and ardour, not to say passion.

Strictly speaking, a third Act [1] should come under the head of Treaties, i.e. the statute which was passed in 1858 for the better government of India. In India there existed, in fact, no independent sovereign, but a *quasi*-sovereign whose authority became extinct and has now devolved on the English nation. The East India Company gave up its autonomy by the passing of the Act of 1858. The Crown had alienated part of its regal rights in favour of the Company, which, from the extent of its resources, its military and financial power, and the almost uncontrolled authority it exercised over its conquests, was virtually a state within the state. By means of a compromise which gave to the directors of the Company the power of nominating seven members out of fifteen in the supreme council, the Crown regained possession of this immense Indian Empire

[1] [21 & 22 Vict. c. 106 (D).]

Since that time it has been governed by a special Secretary of State. With regard to her other colonies England has pursued an opposite policy. To the most powerful and most civilized, Canada, the Cape of Good Hope, and the Australian provinces, she first granted a representative and parliamentary constitution with a responsible ministry, then in most cases[1] the right of modifying this constitution themselves with the approval of the Crown. These Acts may be compared to the treaties of union precisely because they are the converse of such treaties. The Treaties of Union absorbed and extinguished old nationalities; these Acts tend to create new nationalities and separate them from the old. These Acts have formed a group of *quasi*-independent States connected with the United Kingdom by three points only : the appointment by the Crown of the governor who is the nominal depositary of the executive power; diplomatic representation for which England holds itself responsible for them; and a superior court of appeal for their especial use. The Parliament of Westminster retains in theory the right of sovereign legislation for all parts of the British Empire, but, in fact, it no longer interferes with the internal government and special legislation of the great colonies. The colonial secretary seems to have given up his right of veto in colonial matters. Australia and

---

[1] [See *e.g.* as to Victoria, 18 & 19 Vict. c. 54, s. 4. Canada, owing to the Federal Constitution of the country, does not apparently possess the power to alter the Canadian Constitution, which is formed by the British North America Act, 1867, 30 Vict. c. 3, by an Act of the Dominion Parliament. Compare 38 & 39 Vict. c. 38 (D).]

Canada perseveringly keep up protective tariffs against the interests of the mother country; nothing can show more clearly than this the complete autonomy they practically enjoy. By degrees England is withdrawing the troops with which she has provided her colonial territories for their defence.[1] She is leaving them to defend themselves. On the other hand, it is clear enough that she can rely on nothing but their good will for efficacious help in case of a war which threatened her alone, or even in case of any enterprise for the common good.[2] The Crown has not even reserved the ownership of free lands, a right which the government of the United States, a purely federal authority, has kept in respect of the territories and new states admitted to the union. And *a fortiori* the Crown has not in the colonies, as it has in England, the right of eminent domain.

At present, or at least in the near future, we must look upon the colonies not even as provinces in possession of self-government, but as almost sovereign states connected with the mother country only by race, language, and common associations.

[1] In 1870 troops were withdrawn from New South Wales.

[2] Not long ago when the Fiji Islands were to be occupied, Lord Carnarvon asked the Australian colonies, who were much interested in this occupation, to contribute an insignificant sum to the expenses of the government of the Islands. England would have taken the larger share. The colonies refused. Again we know that the reclamations of the United States after the War of Secession were founded chiefly on the fact that the authorities of Melbourne had allowed the *Shenandoah* to repair in their harbour. The arbitrators took this view, but it was England and not the Australian colonies which paid the indemnification.

The proposal to unite them in one vast federation governed by the Parliament at Westminster, where their delegates would sit, has not the slightest chance of success;[1] the idea originates with a few isolated publicists who are endeavouring to arrest a separatist movement to which the English Government itself has given the first impulse.

[1] See as to this subject Seeley's interesting volume, *The Expansion of England*, 1883.

Since these lines were written, the partisans of federation have made noisy, but I think vain efforts to overcome the indifference of the mother country, and to persuade the great colonies to favour a federal system. They have lauded up to the skies the spontaneous act of sending reinforcements from Australia to the English army in Egypt. They took advantage of the curiosity and interest excited by the Colonial and Indian Exhibition to found a permanent Institute of that name, which languishes under the presidentship of the Prince of Wales. Besides this, conferences with colonial agents have been set on foot ; they are carried on with a good grace on either side, but both sides have taken good care not to put forward any proposition suggestive of a federative connection. Lord Rosebery, speaking on November 16th, 1887, before a Scotch branch of the Imperial Federation League, declared that any proposition for this end would be considered by the colonies as a return to that same spirit of domination, which in former days caused the mother-country to lose the North American provinces. He added that no plan of union had the slightest chance of being accepted unless the colonial agents themselves took the initiative.

The colonial agents have carefully avoided taking this initiative. They expressed the wish to have the colonies mentioned with India in the Queen's title, but this was a mere act of courtesy, which in no way affected colonial independence. Of the other matter treated of in the conferences, only two are thoroughly and practically political. The Australians and the mother-country have agreed to maintain a fleet for Australasia at their common expense ;

Section iii

THE Treaties[1] and *quasi*-treaties are only addenda to the Constitution, and in a certain way an external portion of it. Customary law, Compacts and Statutes make up the body of English constitutional law.

Customary law, *lex non scripta,* is the mass of precedents and customs known as the Common Law.

The term " unwritten law " must not be taken literally. In reality these precedents and customs are to be found in a number of documents, such as judgments, authoritative reports, and lawyers' opinions, which treat them as

this is really nothing but a defensive alliance such as might be established between two separate States brought together by a common interest. On the other hand, the colonies openly aspire to the right of negotiating on their own behalf, and of concluding treaties through their own agents with foreign powers ; this expectation can scarcely be said to be consistent with the idea of a fusion or a federation with the mother-country. Canada, which is gravitating more and more towards the United States in an economical point of view, had this point much at heart. All the other questions are only matters of business. To sum up, we may say of the union of the colonies with England, that it must exist in form only or not at all. As long as this union remains nothing but a well-sounding word, recalling a common and glorious origin, an incitement to demonstrations of courtesy and cordiality, no one will be in any hurry to withdraw from it. But if the day should come when the mother-country tries to tighten the bond by which her adult sons are attached to her, they will turn to complete separation without a moment's hesitation.

[1] [See p. 8, ante (D).]

C.L.   C

established and in force, but which do not refer them to or deduce them from the terms of any Act of Parliament. In the absence of any enactment they are founded entirely on a more or less ancient usage, or on their having been tolerated or acquiesced in, for a longer or shorter time, by the powers of the State and by public opinion.

The number, and still more, the nature of the matters which are regulated by the customary part of English constitutional law, is most remarkable. These matters are so various and so important that the written constitutional law as a whole may positively be considered as an exceptional law or a kind of complementary legislation. The Compacts deal chiefly with the limitations of the regal power. The Statutes have a wider range; they afford legal securities for the rights roughly sketched out by the Compacts; they embrace the right of religious liberty and the other great political rights, e.g. freedom of the press, right of combination and of public meeting[1] (which the Compacts do not deal with); they also embrace the whole topic of electoral rights.[2]

All the rest, especially the organization, the privileges, the reciprocal relations, and the interaction of the great public powers (the Crown, the Cabinet, the House of

---

[1] [These great political rights, however, in so far as they are recognised at all by English law as separate rights, depend to a great extent on the principles of the Common Law. See Dicey, *Law of the Constitution* (3rd ed.) pp. 190—192; 223—253; 254 —261 (D).]

[2] [Till recent times electoral rights which are now regulated by statute depended wholly upon common law (D).]

Lords and House of Commons) lies outside the domain of written law. All these important matters, which are the very centre and soul of constitutional law, are regulated in England by simple custom; whilst in France a great deal of effort, discussion, and public feeling has been spent upon them by statesmen.

Now let us examine the constitutional texts and see what they say, for example, about the powers of the Cabinet, that pivot of the parliamentary system and centre of political action. According to Blackstone, Hallam and Macaulay, not only the existence, but the very name of a Cabinet is unknown to written law. What of the annual sitting of Parliament?[1] It is not mentioned in any statute. What of the division of Parliament into two Houses? The practice began of itself prior to 1350, and has gone on since that time without being enforced by any law. What of the right of priority of the House of Commons in matters of taxation? This right is entirely founded upon custom. In the French Constitution, and in that of the United States, there are express stipulations about it. What of the other powers and privileges of the House of Lords and House of Commons? They are like disputed territories, always being taken and retaken with no fixed legal frontier. What of the royal prerogative in matters of military organization? No text defines it. The written law is silent on all these and like matters, that is, generally on all that concerns the action of the great public powers. If any dispute arises the answer to it

[1] [See however 4 Ed. III, c. 14 ; 36 Ed. III, Stat. I, Cap. 10 ; Stubbs, *Const. Hist.* iii 380 (D).]

is to be sought, not in the *Statute Book*, but in parliamentary or judicial records; it is given, not according to a general enactment, but in accordance with precedents. This body of precedents will more often than not be found to be uncertain, confused, and contradictory. In fact the most important part of the political organization is just what is kept out of the written law and given over to the sole guardianship of custom.

What happened with regard to the taxation and electoral rights of the clergy is a most curious example of the way in which custom got established in one of the gaps left by a statute, and then acquired the authority of a law. From time immemorial Parliament did not tax the clergy; they taxed themselves in their own special parliament, *i.e.* Convocation. The Houses of Parliament were satisfied with ratifying their Acts. In 1664 a compact was made behind the scenes between Lord Clarendon, then Prime Minister, and the Archbishop of Canterbury, Primate of England.[1] It was agreed that the clergy should no longer tax themselves, but that Parliament should tax both clergy and laity. And so it was. In 1665, the Act [2] imposing the taxation for the year discharges the clergy from the subsidy imposed by the last ecclesiastical convocation, and orders that they should pay the public taxes like other people. The statute, however, expressly reserves to the clergy in Convocation the right of putting

[1] [See Hallam, *Constitutional History of England* iii. (8th ed.) p. 240, note y (D).]

[2] [16 & 17 Car. II. c. 1., ss. 30, 36. Compare Anson, *Law and Custom of the Constitution*, pp. 44, 45 (D).]

an end to the new practice, and of taxing themselves as
before if it were thought desirable. Since 1664 the
clergy have not on any single occasion made use of this
power; they have continued to bear their part in the
payment of the public taxes imposed by Parliament.
But the right is not abolished by any Act, and so even
nowadays the parliamentary power of taxing a whole
class does not rest on a special statutory enactment. It
rests on the fact that a particular class, though quite
free legally to exercise its power, by tacit consent and
long abstention refrains from reviving this special
power or privilege.[1]

Moreover, from this modification, thus casually introduced and unsanctioned by written law, another of the
same kind resulted which seriously altered the composition of the electoral body. When the clergy voted
their own taxes they naturally took no part in electing
the members of the House of Commons. But when
once they were liable to general taxation, it was but just
that they should be represented in the House which
voted the taxes, and that clergymen, who for a long time
had not been in fact eligible [2] as members, should at
least become electors. In fact, a few years later the
clergy came forward at elections and voted for members of Parliament. We look for an Act which has

---

[1] " Gibson, Bishop of London, told me," writes Speaker Onslow,
" that this measure (taxation of the clergy otherwise than by
Convocation) was the greatest alteration that had been made in
the Constitution without a special Act." (*Cf.* Onslow, *Note on
Burnet*, Oxf. ed. iv, 508.) [See Hallam, *Const. Hist.* iii (8th ed.)
p. 240, note y (D).]

[2] Their ineligibility was settled by the Act, 41 Geo. III. ch. 63.

replaced [1] them in the electoral body. It does not exist. The thing was done silently, without its being thought necessary to sanction it by a statute. The first time that any trace of such an Act is found is in a statute of Queen Anne's reign, in 1712 (10 Anne, c. 23) ; but the terms of the Act are not explicit, and take for granted that the custom was already established. Thus the right of the clergy to vote at elections though contrary to the practice of several centuries, and opposed to a long line of precedents was ultimately established simply in virtue of a custom in its favour, which custom itself rested on the mere fact that taxation of the clergy by themselves had fallen into disuse. This is enough to make a Frenchman shudder, possessed as he is with a spirit of love for all that is precise, exact, and explicit, so passionate that it is like a French legislative instinct.

For what end have the English kept the privileges and the interaction of the great public powers in this undetermined and fluid state ? The object is evident. They have wished for a Constitution in which considerable changes, alterations of power, and unexpected revivals could be made almost without remark. There has been many a modification of the Constitution in England over which not a word was breathed, nor a drop of ink spilt, whilst in France it would have necessitated an alteration in the Articles of the Constitution, followed by long and brilliant discussions and much public excitement.

For instance, the royal veto, so greatly abused by

[1] [See Anson, *Law and Custom of the Constitution*, p. 44 (D).]

William III., and the cause of so much disturbance in
France a hundred years later, has in fact disappeared
since 1707. A parallel case is the presence of the king
at the cabinet councils; there is no precedent for it since
George I. Frenchmen would never have let these two
memorable triumphs of popular power take place without recording them in the statute book; Englishmen trusted to the force of things, to custom and to
opinion to establish them as laws.

A close examination of the chief public powers shows
us that each one is surrounded by a crowd of ancient
but disused privileges which are annulled by the
privileges and active rights of neighbouring powers.
But these privileges have purposely never been abro-
gated—we ask why? In order that at any sign of
public opinion, or call of public interest, they might be
revived and made use of to take up and solve a difficult
question, or to serve as the organ for carrying out of
State policy without disturbing the whole constitutional
system. Here is an example. In 1714 [1] the Privy council, which had been politically inert since Charles II.'s
time, appeared on the scene again, very opportunely
disconcerted the ministers whom the Stuarts had
brought over to their side, and fixed the succession to
the Crown on the Protestant line. Burke, in speaking
of convocation, gives an excellent description of this
state of habitual hibernation of certain parts of the
English Constitution, combined with an indefinite power
of rousing themselves to life again. This assembly, he
says, " is now called for form only. It sits for the

[1] [Mahon's *History of England*, i. (1st ed.) pp. 133—137 (D).]

purpose of making some polite ecclesiastical compliments to the king; and when that grace is said, retires and is heard of no more. It is, however, a *part of the Constitution*, and may be called into act and energy whenever there is occasion." [1]

People are fond of talking about the stability of the English Constitution. The truth is that this constitution is always, so to say, in a state of motion and oscillation, and that it lends itself in an extraordinary manner to the play of its different parts. Its solidity comes from its pliability. It bends but does not break. It stands not by the strength of its affirmations, but by the studied vagueness of its reservations.

On the other hand, are not these reservations and the undetermined state of things which they keep up a patent source of danger? What have you done, a foreign critic might say to Englishmen to prevent such and such privileges which date from the middle ages from being suddenly revived under critical circumstances and checking the operation of modern law? What should you say if one day an energetic king, seeing the nation was getting tired of a loquacious and inactive Parliament, should take it into his head to dismiss his Cabinet and govern under the illusory control of the only counsellors whom common law recognises,—I mean the two hundred and odd members of the Privy Council appointed by the king? What should you say if the king chose, as in former times, to create new electoral boroughs by royal charter, or to change the nature of the hereditary chamber, by only appointing life peers?

[1] [Burke, *Works*, iii (1808 ed.) p. 181 (D).]

All this would be in accordance with the Crown's ancient prerogative. No statute has ever deprived the Crown of these rights and privileges. Nothing can be brought up against them except long habit of disuse. What happened in 1860 ? The House of Lords suddenly attacked the privilege of amending the Taxing Acts, a right which the House of Commons had jealously kept hold of for centuries. In the case in point the House of Lords had the last word, the House of Commons could only assert their rights, and hold to them in principle and for the future.

What happened in 1872 ? The Crown interfered about the question of the purchase[1] of commissions, took the matter out of the hands of the House of Lords, and imposed its own decision with a high hand. But still more alarming would be a revival of those terrible powers of the House of Commons which a century ago endangered the life and liberty of the people, served as an instrument of party hatred, and annulled the protective action of the courts of justice. All these powers are still untouched and ready to hand for the day when a despotic majority might take a fancy to crush its adversaries. To all this no answer can be made except that all political organization in England rests on a *parti pris* of optimism and confidence. The English feel the vigour of their public spirit; they have experienced the vigilance of a free press, and the power of associations and of public meetings. They flatter themselves that their political customs need no

---

[1] [Compare Bagehot, *English Constitution* (1878 ed.) pp. **xxxv.**, **xxxvi** (D).]

safeguards in the form of statutes. No doubt they are quite aware that all the public authorities have been left with rights exclusive of each other, and with rival claims and arms to defend them, as well as arms with which individuals can be oppressed. But they are convinced that, under this rule of opinion and tradition, all these different authorities will use the powers left them only with moderation and for the good of the country, that a compromise will be effected, that they will stop short of any arbitrary act, and that a living and supple equilibrium will be kept up in the very heart of the Constitution : a state of things far superior to the strict division of power resulting from a statute. Up to the present day events have justified their hopes.

Section iv

THE Compacts are three in number—the Great Charter (1215), the Bill of Rights[2] (1689), the Act of Settlement[3] (1700)

[1] [See Stubbs, *Select Charters*, 2nd ed. p. 296. (D).]

[2] [See Stubbs, *Select Charters*, 2nd ed. p. 523. The Declaration of Right was presented by the Convention to William and Mary, 13th February, 1689. The Declaration was embodied in the Bill of Rights (1 Will. & Mar. Sess. 2, c. 2), passed later in the same year. See Macaulay, *History of England*, vol. ii. 3rd ed. pp. 657—661 ; and vol. iii. p. 498. (D).]

[3] [12 & 13 Will. III. c. 2. See Stubbs, *Select Charters*, 2nd ed. p. 528. (D).]

These three instruments are the title-deeds of English political liberty. They are the real basis of the written constitutional law of England.

The Compacts are, like the statutes, the common work of the three branches of Parliament, *i.e.* of the king and the two Houses. But what is peculiar to the Compacts, and what distinguishes them from the statutes, is that in the Compacts the king does not appear as an integral part of one and the same legislative power as the Lords and Commons, but as a real contracting party in opposition to whom the nation seems to stand up as a distinct and independent .power. There is no concerted action of the three constitutional powers in its ordinary and regular form. There is only a reconciliation between two powers. These two powers began by observing and distrusting each other. From time to time struggles took place between them, and at last they entered into a treaty with mutual safeguards. This distinction will be made clearer by a rapid survey of the circumstances which produced these three great Compacts.

The Great Charter comes first. King John had been guilty of exaction and violence for many years. His barons resisted him. In 1215 they coalesced and raised troops. They met at Wallingford and declared themselves free from the oath of allegiance to their sovereign. John, deserted by all his followers except seven, consented to negotiate, and signed the document called the Great Charter. The nature of this act is easy to define. It is not exactly a treaty, because there are not two legitimate sovereigns or two nations opposed to each other;

nor is it a statute; as such it would be invalidated by irregularity or violence: it is a compromise or a compact.

The barons do not behave as subjects, they have absolved themselves from their promise of fidelity to their sovereign; they behave as belligerents. The king stands before them like a conquered enemy, almost like a foreign enemy, and has to submit to the conditions imposed by the conqueror. The analogy goes so deep that the charter mentions penalties such as are found in a treaty with a hostile nation. The barons stipulate that if the king breaks his word they are to seize and confiscate his castles and to molest him in every possible way. All through the Great Charter you see the two armed powers standing face to face and ready to use force. Evidently it would be incorrect to put an instrument like this in the same category as ordinary laws and statutes. If it can be compared to any other document, I should say it bears some likeness to the Treaty of Amboise or to the Peace of St. Germain; to the conventions which during the religious war in France gave pledges to the Protestants, put them in possession of cities of refuge, and almost made them into a separate nation within the nation.

This is not the place to analyze the Great Charter. For us it has an historical interest and nothing more. Its principal articles, over and above those which refer to feudal organization, deal with the protection of individual liberty, lay down rules for the accusation and trial of offenders. These are in fact the matters of most pressing need in a semi-barbarous society.

Further, the Great Charter settles that no aids or scutage shall be raised without the consent of the common council of the kingdom.

The text of the Charter is more precise than could have been expected as to the guarantees for the execution thereof. The manner of summoning the common council is carefully fixed, as well as the conditions necessary for the validity of its deliberations.

A permanent body of twenty-five barons was formed; it was co-optative and superintended the administration of the kingdom. These last clauses however, styled *gravia et dubitabilia*, were not reproduced in the confirmation of the Great Charter given in the following year by Henry III. In the number, the precision, and the practical character of its arrangements, the Great Charter is much more like a Constitution than the other instruments which we shall next have to consider. But its real importance arises less from the actual value of its clauses than from its effect on the minds of the English people. Up to this time the national feeling was but feeble and scattered; the Great Charter gave it a centre of action and supplied a name and a date for popular imagination to cling to. It became the embodiment of the great epic struggle of the middle ages which was then going on. In this contest the feudal nobility became a united aristocratic corporation, and stood forth before the world as a political body conscious of its own strength and guided by its natural leaders defending the liberty of the whole community. The Great Charter was its watchword. The express dispositions of the document are obsolete nowadays; but the spirit of the Great Charter is still living, and it penetrates and animates modern English life.

The second Compact is the Bill of Rights.[1]   In 1688 James II. was suspected of wishing to restore Popery in England.   He was hated on account of his despotic measures.   A faction of the nobility called William of Orange to the throne and James II. fled.   The two Houses of Parliament convened by William at the request of an assembly of notables silenced their scruples and declared the throne vacant.   Who was to occupy it ?   The Prince of Wales ?   He was of course the heir to the throne according to the law of the land.   This law was set aside.   In default of the Prince of Wales, Mary, his eldest sister, Princess of Orange, was the legitimate heir, and in default of Mary, Anne, the second sister.   After some hesitation the House of Lords upset this order of things and proposed to confer the royal dignity on William and Mary conjointly, and the real power of government on William alone.   Even Mary's death was not to give any opening for Anne's claims; her rights were to be suspended, and William was to occupy the throne alone.   It was a complete resettling of the law of succession.   The House of Commons approved the formula and the principle without any hesitation, but refused to pass them just as they stood. A document was drawn up setting forth and claiming all the rights and liberties violated by James II., and the precaution was taken of incorporating this document as a preamble and argument in the Declaration which called William and Mary to the throne.   The

[1] [See Stubbs, *Select Charters*, 2nd ed. p. 523. (D).]

whole thing was solemnly read before the prince and princess in the great hall of Whitehall. Neither of them had to pronounce a separate opinion on this declaration of rights and liberties.

After the reading of this document a single question was put in express words by Halifax to the two august personages : would they accept the Crown and the new settlement of the succession ? If they objected to the Declaration of Right they had only one way of showing it, and that was to decline Halifax's offer. If they declined it the Declaration of Right would not fall to the ground, but the royal dignity would pass away from them; the nation would take back its liberty and its gifts and would retain the power of bestowing them in another quarter. If they accepted the offer, they would have to ratify the preamble and the clauses of the Declaration as a matter of course, and bind themselves implicitly to respect all the rights set forth in it.

Nothing can be further from the French idea of a law than an instrument and a proceeding such as this. A law is an imperative rule on some special matter. The Declaration of Right was in fact a memorial of protests and grievances. The laws are made conjointly by Parliament and the Crown. Neither Crown nor Parliament had anything to do with the Declaration of Right. The king did not exist, and his prerogative could not come into existence until the accomplishment of the very act which it ought to have sanctioned and completed. The two Houses were called the Convention, and a general statute was absolutely necessary to give them the name and the rights of a Parliament. In place of the three factors which ought to co-operate freely and as a sovereign power in making any regular legislative Act, we have here the nation standing alone signifying and imposing its conditions upon a pretender to the Crown.

The Declaration of Right can only be compared to an imperative mandate which the delegates of the nation lay before a candidate for the throne. It is in substance the *sinon non* of the Cortes of Aragon.[1]

The Bill of Rights[2] is made up of thirteen articles. Almost all of them contain limitations of the royal prerogative. The king has no right to suspend laws or dispense with their execution, to set up exceptional tribunals or impose excessive fines, to restrain the right of petition in his subjects, or the liberty of speech in Parliament, or to intervene in Parliamentary elections. The law against raising taxes without the concurrence of both Houses is renewed, and to this is added that no standing army is to be kept up without their sanction. It is significant that under such favourable circumstances no claim was made for liberty of the press (which the Bill of Rights in reality left subject to censorship) nor for religious liberty. That this last demand was omitted need not surprise us, because the revolution of 1688 was made in hatred of Popery and against the measures of tolerance granted on his own authority by

---

[1] The formula of the Cortes of Aragon is well known—"We who are equal to thee make thee king on condition that thou upholdest our liberties—*Sinon non.*"

[2] [Which embodies the Declaration of Right. See note 2, p. 26 *ante.* (D).]

James II. The persecution of the Catholics, or at all
events the laws passed against them, were never more
pitiless than under William III. At that time the importance of freedom of discussion and religious liberty
was not felt. A whole century was to elapse—and that
century the eighteenth century—before these liberties
became embodied in the spirit and the habits of the
age. What were the guarantees for the liberties thus
acquired? There was only one. A requisition that
Parliament should meet frequently, that is all.

We have noticed before that royalty paid but little
attention to an express law like that of 1664[1] which
required that there should be a· session every three
years ; when Charles II. died there had not been one
for four years. What then was the use of this simple
requisition, without any precise stipulation or sanction?
The real guarantee was to be found, it must be admitted,
in another clause, that which gave the right to all
Protestants to carry arms, and it is clear that force was
to be resorted to in case of any oppression. This
absence of all scientific mechanism or studied arrangement to ensure respect for the liberties it proclaims is
very characteristic of the Bill of Rights. It simply
does proclaim them ; and to back them up it also gives
the right of, and provides the means for, armed in-
surrection, which right the French asserted with such
éclat ·in 1793, and which England herself, in the year
1710, publicly sanctioned in the Sacheverell Case,[2]
under the milder name of right of resistance.

The Act of Settlement, 1700, presents rather different

[1] [16 Car. II. c. i., s. 2 (D).]   [2] [15 St. Tr. p. i. (D).]

characteristics. William III. had no children. The Princess Anne, presumptive heir to the throne, had just lost her son and did not expect to have any other heir. As all the Protestant heirs descended from James II. had disappeared there was no other alternative but to fall back upon the Catholic heirs, the Pretender and the Duchess of Savoy. According to the Act then in force these latter could not ascend the throne except by renouncing their religion. But there was nothing to prove that when the moment came this condition would not be fulfilled. Parliament took no notice of the dynastic order of succession, not even giving the Pretender time and opportunity to make himself eligible for the throne by a change of religion,[1] and decided that the succession should pass over to a foreign family, that of Brunswick Hanover, descended through a long-forgotten line from King James I. Further, following the example of the Parliament of 1688, eight articles were incorporated in the Act of Settlement which are binding on " *whosoever* (these are the very words) *shall hereafter come to the possession of* [*the*] *Crown*." [2] If this person intends that the Act of Settlement should be carried out in his favour he would naturally have to submit to all the conditions contained in the text.

In contradistinction to the transactions of 1215 and 1689, the Act of Settlement originated as a statute as regards both its form and its mode of enactment. But

---

[1] A motion to this effect proposed by Godolphin was rejected by a large majority.

[2] [See Act of Settlement, s. 3 (D).]

it differs from an ordinary statute and is more than a statute as regards its aim and bearing. It was carried entirely according to legislative rules: it was passed by the two Houses of Parliament and freely sanctioned by King William. But neither he nor Anne after him were bound by this Act. It was only to come into force *after* their death, and with the new dynasty whose representatives had not been consulted and were obliged to accommodate themselves to a situation, planned for them, or in spite of them, without their co-operation. As regards the new dynasty, therefore, there is no statute, but an imperative mandate as in 1689. The new king could not in any way oppose the enforcement of the article which prohibits him from appointing strangers to civil or military functions, or from giving them grants of land; because this article is bound up with the statute which summons the new dynasty to the throne. There is plain proof that Parliament wished to tie the hands of the king in the fact that one of the stipulations in the Act of Settlement is that judges are not to be removable. William III. on one occasion in 1692 had vetoed a Bill passed by both Houses in favour of this irremovability of the judges. Parliament did not choose to run the risk of seeing this essential reform fall to the ground under the next dynasty. It was therefore made inseparable from the title to the Crown of George I. and his descendants.

The Act of Settlement consists in substance of eight articles. The first article, which is a fundamental one, exacts that the King of England be in communion with the Established Church. Three other articles are

required by the circumstances of the time ; they are intended to meet the abuses and dangers resulting from
the arrival of a foreign king, having foreign possessions
and bringing foreign favourites into England. These
precautions were only too necessary in the case of the two
first Georges, but are nowadays without practical interest.

The importance of the Act of Settlement as regards
constitutional law lies in the four remaining articles.
Two of these are an attempt of the same sort, to destroy
the power of the cabinet by excluding members of
Parliament from it, and, as it were, drowning them in a
large privy council. It was the revival of a plan which
had already failed under Charles II. It failed again
and finally.

These two articles were repealed under Queen Anne,[1]
and the government of a cabinet resting on the Parliamentary majority has existed ever since as the basis of
the English political system. Another clause forbids the
pleading of a royal pardon [2] in bar of an impeachment.
Finally, the last article proclaims the important principle
of the irremovability of the judges. This article was
virtually completed by a law passed in the first year of
George III.'s [3] reign, which made the length of the judges'
commissions indefinite and dispensed with the need of
having them renewed at the beginning of a new reign.

[1] [See 4 and 5 Anne, c. 20. (D).] With regard to the Act of
Settlement Oldfield wrote, in 1816, that the instrument partook
of the nature of the Great Charter and was irrepealable.

[2] [The clause is that "no pardon under the Great Seal of
England be pleadable to an impeachment by the Commons of
England." (D).]

[3] [See I George III, ch. 23. (D).]

Here then we have the history, the characteristics, and the contents, of each of the three Compacts. Clearly they occupy a place of their own in English constitutional law. They represent an extra-legal and revolutionary element. During the last 150 years a prejudice in favour of the English has grown up among the French, and is increased, I believe, by a humble-minded retrospect of their own character and history. Whenever a Frenchman discusses the political system of England the words which occur to him are respect for traditions, moderation, wisdom, regular exercise of political power, and legal resistance. These excellent political customs are actual realities, they have developed and strengthened English liberty, but they did not create it. In England, as elsewhere, liberty was the fruit of a struggle, it was conquered not acquired. The history of the era during which the Compacts came into existence shows us royalty humbled, put to flight, excluded from the deliberations of the legislature, giving way to force, or closed in by a dilemma. The nation stands face to face with the royal power and sovereign-like decides matters by regular or irregular organs, fixes the limits of its own rights, and goes to the length of changing the immemorial customs of the kingdom.[1]

[1] In 1884, in consequence of riots provoked by the opposition of the House of Lords to the question of electoral reform, Mr. Chamberlain, then President of the Board of Trade, had hinted that a hundred thousand men might well march from Birmingham to London, and Lord Salisbury had treated this remark as incitement to violence. Mr. Gladstone, in taking up the defence of his colleague in the sitting of October 30, 1884, gave as his opinion

Section v

IN these three Compacts, but especially in the Bill of Rights which is the most important, we cannot but be struck by a turn of mind quite foreign to French ideas. Let us pause a moment, and define it by contrasting it with the spirit which pervades French documents of the same nature. The Declaration of Right of 1689, in reality a revolutionary document, has none of the philosophical and humanitarian character which its title leads us to expect, and which a Frenchman would at once expect to be the outcome of a revolution.[1]

that it was very well to say to the people, "Love order and hate violence," but that it would not do to say that and nothing more. "But while I eschew violence," he adds, "I cannot—I will not—adopt that effeminate method of speech which is to hide from the people of this country the cheering fact that they may derive some encouragement from the recollection of former struggles, from the recollection of the great qualities of their forefathers, and from the consciousness that they possess them still. Sir, I am sorry to say that if no instructions had ever been addressed in political crises to the people of this country except to remember to hate violence, and love order, and exercise patience, the liberties of this country would never have been obtained."—[Hansard, *Parl. Debates*, vol. 293, p. 643 (D).]

[1] This must, no doubt, be put down to the genius of the English nation, and also to the epoch in which the last and most important crisis took place in England. In 1688, and during the whole of the seventeenth century, in France as well as in England, there is one point which characterizes all speculation in theology, science, or politics. It is, that the highest intellectual effort is devoted solely to the recognition of authority, the registration of prece-

In the debates to which it gave rise, in the preamble and the enactment itself, there is no question of principles and axioms, but only of traditions and sources. The Lords indeed speak of an original contract, but in this case it is an immemorial contract between king and people, not an abstract contract between society and its members; there is nothing in it like the theories of Rousseau. The rights claimed are definite ones; the true, ancient, and undoubted rights of the subjects of this kingdom. A little later the Act of Settlement called them birthrights. Birthright is the right of the elder as well as of birth. During this great epoch the nation is full of the pride of a chosen race to whom

dents, and the consecration of documents, whence the truths are deduced which form the creed of the nation. Quite a different spirit springs up in the eighteenth century : authorities are contested, their titles examined, documents are criticized and objected to, if they go against common sense. England had the advantage of passing through her political crisis at a time when the rationalism of Voltaire's age had not run riot and more or less taken possession of all Europe. Things consecrated by time were still honoured. England had another advantage in the fact that her past, to which she turned instinctively, could show a picture of liberties upheld with difficulty, but still always upheld, sometimes violated, but always reclaimed, and which she always meant to reclaim. How different it was in France ! In 1789 the *ancien régime* had kept nothing but the appearance of institutions. Many were quite useless or cancelled by royal order ; others, as, for instance, the States-General, had been suspended for so long that their procedure had been quite forgotten, and long and intricate researches were needed to make out how things were done in 1614 and before that date. It is not surprising that with this dearth of examples, and the absence of traditions, the minds of Frenchmen should have been thrown upon speculative research, towards which the current of the eighteenth century already drew them.

liberty is a privilege of birth rather than a natural law common to all men, and the demands of the nation are made in this spirit. The nation reminds us not of a theorist discussing his reasons, but of a proprietor with an old title going into court with his title-deeds.

What passed in the English Convention of 1688 is most significant with regard to this state of things. The king had fled, a foreign army was in the country, Scotland was wavering, and Ireland ready for revolt. The Lords and Commons chose this very moment for a long and patient examination of the precedents relating to the vacancy of the throne and to abdication.

Somers produced a parliamentary record of the year 1399, which expressly stated that the throne had remained vacant during the interval between the resignation of Richard II. and the accession of Henry IV. The Lords replied by producing the record of the first year of Edward IV.'s reign, which showed that the precedent of 1399 had been formally overruled. Treby came to the rescue of Somers and produced a record of the first year of Henry VII.'s reign, which repealed the Act of Edward IV. and restored the authority of the precedent of 1399. Before this they had gone back as far as William Rufus and Richard of Normandy.

Shortly after this the state of things became more critical, and the danger more pressing, when the question of settling the title-deeds of the Convention which called William III. to the throne was raised. Long and serious, Macaulay tells us,[1] were the discussions on all the circumstances of the deposition of Richard II.;

---

[1] [Macaulay, *Hist. of England*, ii. 3rd ed., p. 651 (D).]

the whole history of royal ordinances was gone through, the etymology of the word " parliament" was discussed. Antiquarian lore ran riot. At last old Maynard (whose name suggests to me a French origin)[1] brought the question back to its true issue, *i.e.* to a revolutionary one. " We are," he said, " at this moment out of the beaten track. If we have made up our minds to proceed only by the beaten track we shall not advance at all. A man in the midst of a revolution, who is set upon doing nothing that is not in conformity with the established rules, is like a man in a desert who stops and says : Where is the high road ? I must and will go by the high road. In a desert a man must take the road which is most likely to lead him home."[2] Maynard's suggestion was followed unwillingly enough, and only because every one was sick of wrangling.

The exact counterpart of this scene took place in the Corps Législatif of 1815, when Blücher was marching on Paris after the battle of Waterloo. In this case too the sovereign had fled, the foreigner was victorious, the choice of a dynasty was in debate. On July 4th, the *Moniteur* tells the people that Paris had surrendered to the Allies. On the 5th, the Chamber of Deputies meets at the usual hour. Instead of making use of the time to discuss the danger which threatens the country, they begin a lively debate on a Declaration of Rights presented by Garat :—

" I. All rights emanate from the people; the

---

[1] [Maynard, the son of a gentleman at Tavistock, was born 1602, and died 1690. See Foss, *Judges of England*, vii., p. 325 (D).]

[2] [Comp. Cobbett, *Parliamentary History*, v., p. 127 (D).]

sovereignty of the people is made up of the rights
of the individuals.

" VIII. The liberty of each individual is limited only
by the liberty of other individuals.

" XI. The elements of all the sciences, of all the ·
talents, of taste and imagination shall be taught in a
university."

The debate goes on. For several hours all manner of
theories are brought forward, every possible definition,
whether traditional or given by authorities, is discussed.
The debaters are full of animation and earnestness.
" It is not a Declaration of Rights, it is a declaration of
violence," cries one. " But the English are coming ! "
interrupts another. " Even if they were here I should
demand the right to state my opinion." The sitting
breaks up at five o'clock and is adjourned till seven.
During the day the Chamber had adopted a Declaration
of Rights. In the evening it is busy over a declaration
of principles. When the president gives out the result
of the voting the enthusiasm is indescribable, all the
deputies rise to their feet, stretching out their hands,
crowding together, embracing each other and bursting
into tears. " Let the enemy come, now we can die."
The next day, while the Allies are taking possession of
the gates of the town, the Chamber is still discussing
and voting on fifty-two articles of the Constitution with
unflagging interest. The debate on the second section of
Chapter IV. is adjourned to the next day. The next
day Blücher enters Paris. Here we see plainly enough
the two opposite currents of opinion, one historical and
the other philosopical. Nothing shows their power over

the minds of men more markedly than the extraordinary ease with which in both countries these futile debates stood in the way of practical measures which seemed imperative.

We are reminded of the Greeks refusing to put off their Olympic games, even at the call to Thermopylæ. In 1689 the ideal which the English were striving after was to see their rights growing up by slow degrees and emerging, as it were, from a distant point in the horizon, and from the background of their natural history. They did not care to see these rights born before their very eyes. The French, with their eminently rationalistic minds, can scarcely conceive of an ideal so different from their own. The ideas which naturally and immediately carry weight in France must be founded on the feeling of sympathy with humanity in general, while the ideas which impress the English must be based on the feeling of sympathy with past generations. The French delight in the notion of a widespread area, into which all nations can enter and join with them in bowing down before the enactments of universal legislation. The English like the idea of a narrow path reaching far back into antiquity, in which they see the centuries of their national life ranged in a long vista one behind the other. The English Constitution is strongly marked by this turn of mind. Historical descent is the very soul of it, just as an ideal fraternity has always been the soul of the French Constitution.

This striking peculiarity explains why there is neither order nor plan in the English Declaration of Right. The order of its thirteen articles seems to be quite a matter of chance. This is quite contrary to the idea that a Frenchman has of an Act born of a revolution. In France an Act of this kind generally has something large and comprehensive about it. In these crises the nation has nothing to impede its action. What an opportunity for elaborating a complete system with all its parts in harmonious connection with each other ! The French achieved this feat in 1789. But in the Bill of Rights the English are striving after something very different. It is, and it is meant to be, purely the work of circumstances. Every one of the thirteen articles in the document of 1689 is framed on purpose to guard against some inconvenience brought to light by recent practices. Not one article springs from a general conception of the matter in question. If James II. had not suspended the effect of the penal laws against the Catholics in the case of Sir Edward Hales, probably the condemnation of the dispensing power would not have appeared in the Bill of Rights.[1]

The consideration of these details really leads us to a deeper view of the subject. If the whole constitutional edifice had been reconstructed from top to bottom it would have stood on its own basis; it would have been like a speculative creation born complete and at a given moment, asserting itself not by its antecedents in the national life, but by its internal logic and its own value. The tie which bound it to the past would have been

---

[1] In like manner, if William III. had not showered benefits upon Bentinck and his other foreign favourites, probably the prohibition of pensions to aliens would not have been found in the Act of Settlement.

loosened, or lost, and at the same time that traditional prestige would have entirely vanished which so impresses the minds of Englishmen. Touching only on points which recent abuses had obscured, the Bill of Rights left the bulk of the Constitution still floating about without any fixed date, and with its background of custom, until it got (to use an expression of Tacitus) impregnated with antiquity. The Bill of Rights itself seemed to be a detached portion of this immemorial Constitution, brought to light by accidental causes. A scientific and systematic creation would not have been so manifestly a restitution and a revival of the common law, it would not have had the supreme authority of this much respected source.

These, then, are the reasons why in the Bill of Rights we find neither a general plan nor any complete series of enactments, neither careful definitions, nor cleverly adapted sanctions. Precisely because it has remained incomplete, incoherent, and incongruous, and because it drily answered questions raised by chance events, has it been impossible not to recognize that it is simply a fragment of a vast whole, nothing but a confirmation, and a partial declaration, of a more ancient law. Therefore Englishmen have always been able to perceive that customary law, the real basis of the Constitution, still existed in all its majesty, unchanged by this important document.

Section vi

STATUTES are the third source of written constitutional law in England. They are Acts passed by the two Houses of Parliament and sanctioned by the Crown. The peculiarity of English law is, that it does not recognize constitutional laws as opposed to and superior to ordinary laws. The most important and serious questions, as well as the most trivial ones, come within the province of the law.[1]

The English do not recognize constituent assemblies as distinct from legislative assemblies. Every Parliament considers itself qualified to act in either capacity. No precaution was ever taken to make the deliberation on important points specially slow and mature. There was no rule to prevent important matters being ever treated as urgent. The revision of the statutes which regulate constitutional matters is not, as in other countries, submitted to a special procedure. The statutes are made and unmade with no more difficulty or hesitation than there is in making ordinary laws. A noteworthy example of this way of mixing up constitutional and ordinary law is found in the compact of 1689. This document was the work of a national Con-

---

[1] The statute 6 Anne, cap. 7, sanctions the right of Parliament to change the succession to the throne by a law. Any one calling this law in question in writings or publications is guilty of treason ; we have noted two occasions on which Parliament made use of this statute, and these are not the only ones.

vention duly elected, except that the decree convoking
the electors did not bear the royal signature. Had the
French been dealing with this great Declaration of
Right they would have tried to preserve its peculiar
and exceptional character, to keep it as a *motu proprio*
of the nation standing outside any rule, because it was
above all rules. This would have shown that the
sovereignty inherent in the nation had reappeared
on the scene. But in England there was no peace
until the Act had been remade, sanctioned, and confirmed under the form of an ordinary law, and by a
regular Parliament. Thus remodelled and disguised, it
takes its place and its date in the peaceful history of
legal progress, and at first sight nothing recalls its
peculiar nature and the exceptional circumstances of
its birth. The same remark holds good of the Treaties
of Union. An Act passed by the joint and free action
of the three powers is the only form of written law
known and recognized by the law of England. There is no
code to which an Act of Parliament need conform. No
Act of Parliament, says Paley, can be unconstitutional.[1]

Does it not look like the height of imprudence to
deliver up the very formation of political institutions to
the summary proceedings of the ordinary legislature ?
How can we expect anything to remain fixed or durable
if the Constitution partakes of the mutability of
statutory law, and if there is nothing to tie the hands
of Parliament, which is so liable to be rash, enthusiastic,
or revolutionary ? The power of the Convention of

---

[1] [Paley, *Principles of Moral and Political Philosophy*, Book vi.
c. vii., p. 464 (2nd ed.) (D).]

1792 was more dangerous because it was in the hands of a single Assembly, but it was not really wider or more arbitrary than that of the English Parliament. The English cannot have been blind to these dangers, but they were not alarmed at them. As usual they have trusted that the hand of the legislator would be restrained by the public spirit of the nation and by the prestige of custom, these trusty guardians of their Constitution. The plan in which they have confided is the very opposite of the French system. They did not intend their Constitution to be a compact whole, because a solid body by its very nature is vulnerable. For this reason it is only partly written, and, when it is written, we find the constitutional articles, instead of being marked out and easily distinguished, are purposely mixed up with ordinary laws, and allowed to fall out of view. A comparison will help to explain this point: if the Constitution had been made to appear on parade in full dress before the battalions of statutes, even if the dress had been a suit of armour, this would have been the surest means of calling attention to it and of courting attacks. The safest course was to keep it out of sight with the reserve force, or, if necessary, to clothe it in the plain uniform of the law and leave it in the ranks without any distinctive mark.

The French have sought for securities against change in giving prominence, splendour, and dignity to their constitutional documents. The English have found this security in the vagueness of custom, in the retiring and commonplace character of ordinary law, and in leaving their Constitution without a name in the midst of a crowd of statutes.   Each system has its theoretical advantages and disadvantages.   When the balance is struck between the two, experience seems to pronounce in favour of the English system.[1]

[1] The want of stability which the statutory form gives to the articles of the Constitution is clearly brought to light by the history of the Declaration of Right and the Act of Settlement. The Declaration of Right, when later in the same year it becomes the Bill of Rights, repeats the condemnation of the dispensing power, *i.e.* the power which the kings have arrogated of dispensing certain individuals from observing the laws.   This condemnation was in the Declaration of Right absolute and unrestricted ; in the Bill of Rights the condemnation is limited and enfeebled by the addition of the words, "in the manner in which the power has been exercised of late."   This was really recognizing that the power still existed and was legitimate in principle.   The violations of the Act of Settlement were still more serious.   Two of the articles were repealed or modified before the accession of the Hanoverian dynasty under Queen Anne.   A third was sacrificed to George the First's restlessness and longing for his native country.   But yet, what a gulf there is between these small changes and the constant revolutions which have given France thirteen constitutions in three quarters of a century !   All these constitutions were apparently fortified and intrenched in a marvellous manner against sudden changes, yet everyone was carried by storm at the first assault, outworks and all !

[See Act of Settlement, (12 & 13 Will. III. c. 2) s. 3, Sub. ss. 3, 4, 6 and 4 & 5 Anne, c. 20 ; 1 Geo. I. Stat. 2, c. 51. (D).]

Section vii

NATIONS compelled to break with their past necessarily fall back on rationalism, and try to invest its
principles with the authority which they can no
longer find in the prestige of history. It requires a
considerable effort on the part of the French to acknowledge that this incongruous compilation which I have
been describing is a constitution. I must compare the
formation of the English Constitution to a slowly
formed and uncertain deposit at the bottom of a dull
and cloudy liquid, as unlike as possible to the rapidly
formed precipitates and brilliant crystallizations to
which I liken the French constitutions. Nevertheless,
this strange English Constitution has its value—which
value has been tested by ages—and it has also its own
peculiar genius.

It has three special characteristics.

First, there once had been revolutionary elements in
this as in other constitutions, but here the revolutionary
spirit has been turned out of its course and absorbed
into the current of tradition. A fiction of old hereditary
liberties is substituted for a fiction of abstract rights,
elaborated by reason and conquered by force.

Secondly, the Constitution is not codified, hardly even
written, and thus it escapes, so to say, all translation
into common language : its language is reticent and
veiled, the whole thing differs little from ordinary
laws, so that amendments brought on by time easily find

their place in it, and enormous changes in the balance of powers are worked out without ever challenging the perils of a revision.

Thirdly, and this gives the Constitution its high moral and educational power, the people are called upon to watch over this ark of national institutions, which has purposely been deprived of all means of defence but the strength of custom and the wisdom of public spirit.

PART II

THE SOURCES AND SPIRIT OF THE
CONSTITUTION OF THE UNITED STATES

PART II

THE SOURCES AND SPIRIT OF THE CONSTITUTION OF THE UNITED STATES

Section i

THE state of things in France has been very un-favourable to the study of constitutional law. The instability of French political institutions was the first thing which brought this study into discredit. Govern-ments which have sprung from a revolution are not anxious to encourage teaching which would recall the circumstances of their origin and raise the question of their legitimacy. Even friendly appreciation has its dangers; it provokes contradiction and suggests inquiry; perfect silence is safest. Only once, and for a very short time, did constitutional law figure on the programme of one of the Faculties of Law in France. A chair in this branch of law was created for the illustrious Rossi, at Paris, in 1835. It lapsed shortly after the *coup d'état* of December 1851, and the Republic did not revive it until 1879. Jurists naturally did not care to pursue a study which led to no openings; they followed up other branches, to which the State gave more encouragement. This explains why the highest branch of public law has no classical literature in France. Problems of this nature may, with a view to some question of the day, have provided matter for important writings on some special point by statesmen, but Rossi's book is almost the only considerable work on constitutional law which can be called a treatise.

If the study of the national constitutions has been neglected in France, that of foreign constitutions has been scarcely attempted, and the French are particularly ill-prepared to understand them. They cannot forget that more than once their own ideas have ruled the world; and they naïvely expect to find them reappearing at every turn. The abstract rationalism, which is the very soul and spirit of their creations, has a tendency to consider itself of universal application. Their classification is so elegant and refined, their plans are arranged with so much skill, that Frenchmen are inclined to invest them with an absolute value, and to think that everything ought to be included within the framework of these plans. Finally, the French language, with its passion for clearness and its fitness for precise formulas, leads Frenchmen to neglect whatever cannot be expressed neatly, or to force a definition on things which can only be described or, at best, indicated. These prejudices and shortcomings are a hindrance to most French authors in the study of foreign constitutions, and especially in the study of the two great Anglo-Saxon polities.

The French have no idea that in the study of other constitutions they are entering another world or a sphere bathed in another light, and that, if they should attempt to take their own atmosphere with them, all that they see will be altered by a faulty refraction.

With regard to the English Constitution, I have already pointed out the mistakes that are likely to be made and how they may be avoided. I wish to show by a few examples that the same care is necessary in studying the American Constitution. For this end also Frenchmen must lay aside their intellectual habits, give up the idea of a ready-made framework, let the facts themselves penetrate their minds by slow degrees, and try to understand the logic of these facts instead of attempting to bend them to a method which never can suit them.

The first thing to be done is to procure the English text of the Federal Constitution, and to be able to read it in the original. This piece of advice is really not superfluous. The knowledge of foreign languages is quite recent in France, and the habit of going to the original text, and of rendering the exact sense of words, is not of much earlier date.[1]

---

[1] An inexact translation may, if not discovered in good time, bring about very serious consequences. Shortly after the year 1830 there were communications between France and the United States on the subject of an indemnity. It will be remembered that the relations between the French Chambers and their own ministry were marked by great bitterness, and those between the two nations were not less so. President Jackson went so far as to propose extreme measures to Congress. At this point a French despatch was received at the White House. It began with these words :—"*Le Gouvernement Français demande,*" which an ignorant secretary translated, quite simply : "The French Government demands." President Jackson did not know French. Hardly had he heard this sentence when he exclaimed, "If the French

We meet with most curious errors of criticism and of interpretation in works which were looked upon as authorities at the beginning of the century, and even in publications which date only fourteen years back.

Two or three examples will enable us to measure the extent of this evil.

In the first edition of their collection of the charters and constitutions of Europe and America, authors as serious as Duvergier, Dufour, and Guadet, give as the Constitution in force in the United States the Articles of the Confederation which had been actually superseded in 1789 by this very Constitution, and the same error is reproduced in their supplement published after 1830. Thus, for at least forty years, and on the eve of Tocqueville's journey, it was believed even among lawyers that in the United States there was neither Senate, House of Representatives, President, nor Supreme Court, and that the great Republic was still under the *régime* of that suspicious and feeble Federalism which had been so gloriously put an end to by Washington, Jefferson, Franklin, and Hamilton, before the beginning of the nineteenth century.[1]

Government dares to *demand* anything in the world of the United States it will never get it." It was only after a better-informed person had explained to the President that the French word "*demander*" answers not to the English word "demand," which means to require or exact, but to the word "request," that the irritated General consented to listen to the representations of France.

[1] A curious fact :—At the end of the list of the constitutions of the States, the authors give the rules of the Senate and of the House of Representatives of the United States. What Senate and what House ? These words do not occur in the original text,

M. Conseil does remark on this fact in a book of considerable merit on Jefferson, and he takes the trouble to translate the original text. But in the translation of the first article he lets a piece of nonsense pass which renders it quite unintelligible.

This piece of nonsense met with such a curious fate that I cannot refrain from telling the story here. The article says that : "All legislative powers herein granted shall be vested in a Congress of the United States, which shall consist of a Senate and a House of Representatives." Instead of "herein granted," M. Conseil puts "granted by the Representatives." Thus the Representatives themselves would determine not only their own powers but those of the Senate and of the whole Congress. How can this absurdity have arisen? Probably the expression "herein granted" was in the translator's version rendered *par les présentes*, the printer's reader by mistake substituted *par les Représentants* for those words, and M. Conseil gave the order for press without re-reading the manuscript. However it happened, Tocqueville in 1834 wanted a translation of the American Constitution and took M. Conseil's ; he did not read it through, and so this bit of nonsense was simply repeated. But this is not the end of it. The two eminent authors of the classical collection of the Constitutions of Europe and of the New World, edited in 1869, thought they could not do better than take Tocqueville's version, naturally trusting to its exactness

but that does not seem to give the learned authors any uneasiness, and they have not the vaguest feeling of the error they are committing.

Like him they did not compare the translation with the original Constitution, and this prodigious blunder was copied mechanically. Thus it happened that a nonsensical reading has obtained a sort of prescriptive authority by being allowed to stand for three-quarters of a century.[1]

In the same translation of the Constitution, in the article [2] which treats of the joint nomination of high functionaries by the President and the Senate the word *nominate*, which means like the Latin *nominare* to " present," " propose," " submit names," is invariably translated by *nommer* (appoint), and the word *appoint* which means " to appoint to a place," " to commission," is invariably translated by *désigner* (designate). Thus the single operation of nominating expressed by a piece of vulgar pleonasm, is erroneously substituted for the ingenious proceeding consisting of two stages (viz. nomination and appointment) which the American legislator has defined in the original text with the greatest precision.

[1] The excellent work by MM. Dareste contains an exact translation of the sentence, for the authors went back to the original.

[2] [" He [the President] shall nominate, and, by and with the advice and consent of the Senate, shall appoint ambassadors, other public ministers, and consuls, judges of the Supreme Court, and all other officers of the United States whose appointments are not herein otherwise provided for, and which shall be established by law : but the Congress may by law vest the appointment of such inferior officers, as they think proper, in the President alone, in the courts of law, or in the heads of departments." Constitution of United States." Art. II., s. 2, 2. See Story, *Commentaries on the Constitution*, s. 1524—1554 (4th ed.). See Bryce, *American Commonwealth*, i. (1st ed.), p. 77 (D).]

This is what has happened in one single document and no doubt I have passed over other like mistakes. Such enormities will fortunately become more and more rare, thanks to the educational improvements lately introduced in France, which I am about to mention. Much greater attention than formerly is now given to the teaching of modern languages in secondary schools, the Society of Comparative Legislation has opened a wider field for law studies, and the committee attached to the Law Department of State issues careful translations made by learned jurists. But I think I have said enough to convince persons who wish to study foreign constitutions that it is not safe to trust to any translation, even should it bear the name of a Tocqueville. Nothing is safe but reading the original. No one can be sure of any step taken without reading a correct and authentic version in the original language, and carefully studying and weighing every expression contained in it.

Section ii

A SMALL amount of attention and study will enable any one to get a general idea of a Federal Constitution. But for persons whose ideas are formed by the observation of French institutions, this will not suffice. Frenchmen need to make a constant effort to fix their minds on this type of constitution so new to them, and to keep up a strong, precise, and continuous impression of it. As surely as this impression is allowed to become feeble or slight, so certainly will the idea of a centralised or unitarian constitution, which Frenchmen have always before their minds, creep at every turn into their studies. This idea will cause them to take up any analogies to it which they may discover in a Federal State, and twist these analogies into conformity with it. This conception will lead them, in places where an imperfect knowledge of American institutions has left a gap, to fill up the sketch in accordance with this idea of an unitarian state, and thus produce a very false picture of the whole Federal system.

The tendency of French lawyers to treat the Constitution of the United States as if it could be compared to the French Constitution, and were amenable to the same kind of analysis, is like an instinct repressed a hundred times, but reviving again and again when it seems to be crushed. The only peculiarity which these critics seem to grasp is that local administration is far more decentralized in America than in France. They are led into a fatal misconception of the Federal Constitution with its two Houses, its President, its Supreme Court, and its Declaration of Rights. The superficial analogy which exists between the two Constitutions, leads to comparisons which give rise to mistaken interpretations.

I take this very Declaration of Rights to which I have just referred as an example.

The six first amendments voted, on Jefferson's motion,

after the whole Constitution was passed, make a separate chapter in the Constitution, an addendum which in a manner recalls all the classical English liberties ; such as the freedom of the press, the right of association, the right of public meeting, religious liberty, trial by jury, the inviolability of a man's house, the sacredness of private property, and the like. Story, and most other American authors, call these amendments, in my opinion quite rightly, a " Declaration of Rights." But the Americans understand what they mean by this expression, and the French misunderstand them. The magic sound of these words " Declaration of Rights " is so French, and appeals so strongly to French pride, that it makes a Frenchman imagine he is still in his own country, and has to deal with such absolute rights of the Man and the Citizen, as French constitutions consecrate in the name of natural liberty and equality. But the bearing as well as the true spirit of these articles of the Federal Constitution is utterly different.

The stipulations which form the substance of the eight first amendments are essentially guarantees taken by the States against the encroachments of a foreign sovereignty of which the President and the Congress are the organs.

At the time when these amendments were proposed, what the States wished to prevent was the possibility that any federal law or the action of any federal official should in any matter concerning religious freedom, the liberty of the press, the right of public meeting, &c., be enforced in any State in contravention of the principles of the State Constitution, or to the detriment of the State's own legislative authority. They were stipulating for their State rights, not for abstract rights. With regard to the bearing of the first article, Story explains very clearly that, at this epoch, the Episcopalians preponderated in one State, the Presbyterians in another, the Congregationalists in a third. There would have been no safety for any of these sects if the Federal Government had been left at liberty to grant the favour and support of the State to any one of them to the exclusion of the others. " The whole power over the subject of religion," adds the learned author, " is left exclusively to the State Governments, to be acted upon according to their own sense of justice and the State Constitutions." [1]

Jefferson is no less explicit. " I hope," said he, " that a Declaration of Rights will be drawn up to protect the people *against the Federal Government,* as they are *already protected* in most cases, against State government."

In a judgment of the Supreme Court, delivered in 1872, Judge Miller expressed himself thus :—" The adoption of the first eleven amendments to the Constitution so soon after the original instrument was accepted, shows a prevailing sense of danger at that time from the Federal power." [2]

The 10th and last Amendment really gives a rule of interpretation applicable to the whole series. It rules that the powers which the Constitution does not delegate to the United States, or which it does not

[1] [Story, *Commentaries on the Constitution of the U.S.,* s. 1879 (4th ed.) (D).]

[2] *Louisiana Slaughter-house Cases,* [16 Wallace, 82 (D).]

refuse to the separate States, are reserved respectively for the States or for the people.[1] " It is to be observed," says Cooley, " as a settled rule of construction of the National Constitution, that the limitations it imposes upon the powers of government are in all cases to be understood as limitations upon the government of the Union only, except where the States are expressly mentioned." [2]

These examples and quotations clearly mark in what sense, and for what reason, several States had demanded a Declaration of Rights, and made it a condition of their adhesion to the Federal Union. Their purpose was that Congress should not be able to perform any sovereign act in any State, and force their citizens in matters in which they intended either to leave them free, or to reserve to the State the right of legislation. This is the point that never entered the minds, or at least never took root in the minds of French critics.

For instance, they see that the sixth and seventh Amendments guarantee trial by jury; from this they naturally infer that trial by jury is the right of every American citizen, and that no law can interfere with this right. Certainly, no law of Congress can take it away; but a State legislature could very well sanction some judiciary organization, in which there should be no jury, either in civil or criminal cases.[3]

[1] ["The powers not delegated to the United States by the Constitution, nor prohibited by it to the States, are reserved to the States respectively or to the people." Amendments to the Constitution, Art. XI. (D.)]

[2] Cooley, *Constitutional Limitations*, [(1st ed.) p. 19 (D).]

[3] See Cooley, *Treatise on the Constitutional Limitations.* Pro-

C.L.   F

With regard to the Amendments, II. to VIII., a mistake is excusable. These Amendments are drawn up in the form "shall not" or "no person shall," and do not indicate the authorities to which their prohibitions are addressed. In order to determine their bearing, we must note that the separate States are supposed, in theory, to keep all rights which are not expressly denied them. It is more curious that a similar mistake could have arisen with regard to the first Amendment, of which the terms are clearly limitative. "Congress," runs the Amendment, "shall make no law, respecting an establishment of religion, or prohibiting the free exercise thereof, or abridging the freedom of speech or of the press, &c."

Here, Congress alone is referred to, not the States, but certain French critics do not seem to understand this. Apparently they think that what binds the central authority, should as in France, *a fortiori*, bind the local and provincial authorities. They are accustomed to see the rights in question conceived of by the legislator, as inherent attributes of the person of a citizen, and pleadable against all authorities of whatever nature and degree. This habit of mind is so strong that it gets the upper hand, even after the truth of a contrary view has been demonstrated. Even Laboulaye after having with his usual clearness pointed out

fessor Baldwin in a memorandum read on September 11, 1879, at the American Association of Social Science at Saratoga, notices what he calls "inroads upon the jury system" in a large number of States. In fact it is chiefly the jury in civil cases which is attacked.

the restricted bearing of the Amendments, in spite of himself comes back to the French point of view, and gets so imbued with it, that he does not see that in his examples he contradicts the principles which he laid down to begin with. He puts as a hypothesis, that the law of a State might establish a censorship of the press, and require editors of papers to give security; and he says that the Supreme Court of the United States, as a guardian of the Federal Constitution, ought to declare such a law unconstitutional. The truth is that in such a case the Supreme Court ought simply to declare that it has no jurisdiction. Such a law would be unconstitutional, only if it proceeded from Congress. It is, if passed by a State legislature, unimpeachable on the ground of unconstitutionality before the Federal Court.

No doubt, even if it is misunderstood, this distinction has no very marked practical effect, first, because in all the States the English Common Law without any statutory enactment, sanctioned most of the liberties specified by the eight first Amendments; secondly, because the States, for reasons which I shall explain hereafter, had from excessive caution in most instances, introduced the liberties guaranteed by the eight first Amendments into their own constitutions. Nevertheless, several events in the history of the United States would be incomprehensible if we lost sight of the fact that the Amendments do not confer absolute rights on the people, but simply give them guarantees against the Federal power.

Among other things it would be especially difficult

to explain the way in which the Southern States were formerly able to restrict the circulation of Abolitionist publications, or the continuance of penalties or legal disabilities, which attached to the omission of all religious practices in some New England States, or the pecuniary grants given by certain States to one or other of the religious sects. The Republican Convention of 1880, after having protested against these subventions, voted that a constitutional Amendment should put an end to such abuses; a clear proof that the first Amendment was in principle aimed at Congress, and did not touch the liberty of the States in any religious matters.[1]

Section iii

THERE is another peculiarity of the Federal Constitution which has been no better understood than the peculiarities I have just commented upon ; namely, that it is a fragment, and is not intelligible when taken alone. It is like a body, of which you see nothing but the head, feet, and hands, in fact, all the parts that

[1] Religious liberty was finally established in all the States except Massachussetts and Connecticut before the adoption of the constitution of the United States. It was at last established in Connecticut by the first Constitution (1818), and in Massachussetts by an amendment to the Constitution (1834). (Ezra Seaman.)

are useful in social life, while the trunk containing the vital organs is hidden from view. This essential part which is hidden, represents the constitutions of the separate States.

They are really the indispensable complement of the Federal Constitution, not merely an example of its working, and a useful addition. The most thorough of the French critics were pre-occupied in finding examples in America in support of their favourite theories, and in looking for a constitution to hold up as an ideal for imitation, and thus they were quite forgetful of this very important peculiarity They could not in fact deduce anything from it, unless indeed it were reasons for showing how rash they themselves had been in proposing to apply certain parts of the Federal Constitution to a country thoroughly imbued with the idea of unity in its institutions. Tocqueville truly remarks that the study of the States is the thing to begin with; but in this study makes it his main object to find an apology for decentralization and self-government. He analyses enthusiastically, and gives a living picture of the township, and the county. He suggests them as models for France. Who does not remember the striking way in which he enlarges on this theme, and is so full of the idea that moral forces are the only permanent value? From this he passes on to the Federal Constitution, and only gives one short chapter—just five pages and a half in three volumes—to the constitutions of the States.

On the other hand, Laboulaye interests himself solely in the mechanism of the national government. Natur-

ally after the publication of Tocqueville's work, he does
not write another monograph on the township, but he
says no more than his illustrious predecessor about the
State constitutions.   In his masterly book he just
makes a few allusions to them, and throws in a few
hasty details.

Yet after all, how many important matters are not
even mentioned in the Federal constitution ? How many
great problems are left quite untouched ?   For instance
to quote one or two facts—it is left to State legislation to decide by whom the presidential electors are
—to be chosen, whether by the legislatures or by the
people, whether the body of these presidential electors
should be chosen in a mass by each State, or individually
by each division, whether the representatives of each
State in Congress should be chosen by universal suffrage
or limited suffrage, by direct or indirect suffrage,
whether the American citizens alone should be admitted to vote, or whether the non-naturalized emigrants should enjoy the same privilege, &c. Is it not
evident from this that the Federal Constitution is not
a complete whole, but requires to be supplemented by
other enactments which settle these important questions ?

We must even go a step further and say not that
the constitutions of the States are the complement
of the Federal Constitution, but that the Federal
Constitution is the complement of the State constitutions. These latter are the foundation of the edifice,
or rather the edifice itself, of which the other is
only the pinnacle and the crown. Doubtless French
publicists know that the authority of Congress and of

the President is restricted to a small number of important matters; they are aware of what there is of relative truth in Jefferson's maxim: " The federal government is only our department of foreign affairs." They would not dispute the fact (though no one remarks on it), that an American citizen can according to Williams,[1] pass all his life without once having recourse to the Federal laws, or putting the powers of the Union in motion. But nevertheless French publicists are not firmly impressed with a permanent sense of these admitted facts. They think about it for a moment, and the next minute the idea is set aside and they rush into unjustifiable comparisons between the organization of this central authority, so restricted in its province, and so rarely called into action—this system of government reduced to a minimum—and that of the French government with its unlimited scope and universal power of action.

I believe most French commentators would be astonished at first (though on reflection they might deny their surprise) if they heard it said that the real analogies in essence and in kind with French constitutions are to be found in the constitutions of the separate States. They are the only constitutions in the Union which are created with general powers of government, and from which emanate as a whole, civil law, criminal law, industrial legislation, together with the officials and judges who put these laws in force. It is the constitution of his State alone of which the citizen feels the protective and repressive action at every turn. In the

[1] *Rise and Fall of the Model Republic.*

State constitutions we find the real groundwork of the political institutions of America; the key to the functions of the Federal Constitution, the explanation of its mysteries and the solution of its destiny.[1]

I add one more remark which proves my point.

Between the beginning of the Union and 1860, the basis of power in America underwent a complete change; from being republican it became democratic, from democratic it became almost ochlocratic. But the unchangeable Federal Constitution shows no sign of this slow and gradual evolution which has lasted nearly a century. If we considered the Federal Constitution alone, it would seem as if nothing had changed since 1789, and that there was no political difference to be

[1] See Jameson's *Study of the Constitutional and Political History of the States*, 4th series of Hopkins' University Studies.

"Let us look for a moment at the constitutional history of England. The most important constitutional measures of the last sixty years have been, we may say, the Parliamentary Reform Acts of 1832, 1867, 1884, the Municipal Corporations Reform Act, the New Poor Law, the removal of Catholic disabilities, the abolition of Church rates, the acts for the organization of elementary education, the reform of the universities, the succession of changes effected in the tenure of land, the Ballot Act, and the Disestablishment of the Irish Church. Now imagine all this legislation transferred to America. A moment's reflection will convince that, with the exception of some minor provisions (such, for instance, as those for redistribution), absolutely every one of these enactments would in this country have been made by State legislation, or possibly State conventions, and not by the National legislature."

There is only one word which a Frenchman would wish to alter in this paragraph—the word "constitutional" applied to the measures quoted. It ought to be, "The great legislative measures, either organic or constitutional, of the last sixty years."

drawn between the America of Washington, of Jackson, or of Buchanan. I leave America of to-day entirely alone. This one startling fact ought to be enough to make future French critics suspicious of the method which their forerunners have followed, and to incite them to give more fundamental study to the State constitutions, and ought, further, to prevent them from taking the exception for the rule, and the smaller part for the whole.

Section iv

I HAVE dwelt upon the fact that the Federal Constitution must never be taken as standing alone, without looking to the State constitutions as its necessary adjuncts. But before we realize the system as a complete whole, we must draw from other sources beside the State constitutions, less important no doubt, but still worthy of notice and more ignored than the State constitutions. If you wish to study a machine which has long been at work, it is no use to look at it only in the inventor's drawing-book, or in the plates in which all the different parts are carefully reproduced. For these plates cannot be quite complete, or perfectly faithful. By constant use the wheels have more or less changed their shape; some have adapted themselves, others have become disjointed and do not work at all, so that new wheels have had to be supplied.

These changes have not always been added to the original working plan; we must look about for them in different places : sometimes in books of sketches, or at the corner of a page ; often they have not been put on paper at all ; they can only be seen by watching the machine itself in motion.

Something of this kind happened with regard to the American Constitution. By the side of the ancient and consecrated law, by degrees a complementary law has sprung up, formed by new interpretations which got established, accidental practices which were repeated, encroachments which were approved, whilst other practices fell into disuse.

These innovations were rarely incorporated in the constitutional and statutory law; they became fixed according to circumstances in one or another collateral and secondary document, so unimportant sometimes that no one would expect it to contain such serious matter. Sometimes they have not taken any written form, and have remained purely customary law. From the fact that on a given point the tenor of the Constitution and the organic laws have not changed since the beginning, we must not conclude that on this point things have not changed at all; this conclusion would lead to serious error. Underneath this deceptive appearance of unchangeableness in the Constitution, a work of disintegration and reformation has been going on, which the American jurists themselves have not always been able to explain and recognize in the extra-constitutional literature, or the unwritten customs in which its traces are to be found.

A fortiori Frenchmen would have no chance of noticing this process of change unless they were thoroughly on the look out for it. There has never been any evolution like this in France. Not one of the French constitutions ever lasted long enough to lose its form or to work out its completion slowly through custom. Every one of these constitutions appears, like a smart new bit of machinery, straight from the workshop, and made in every point like the patented model. There have been frequent changes in the constitutional order of things in France ; but then the whole machine was entirely altered, and all the details of the change could be and were duly entered in authentic documents.

Thus it is that Frenchmen have to overcome a very strong pre-conceived idea, in order to make themselves believe that the American Constitution does not contain everything, and that many important facts are hidden away unnamed in documents which do not form part of the Constitution, or in practices known only to statesmen.

The mode of electing the President furnishes one of the best examples of these gradual changes in the Constitution, and it has been cited more than once. I shall not refer to it again. Some less generally known fact will bring out more strongly how impossible it is to look to the articles of the Constitution alone.

I speak of the change which took place quite quietly in the character and privileges of the highest branch of Congress.

French authors have always considered the Federal

Senate as a moderating chamber, which has the peculiarity of representing the municipal interest of the different States, and which besides has a right of preventive control over the most important acts of the government, *e.g.*, the conclusion of treaties and the nomination of high functionaries. Nowadays, this view is tolerably correct, and will become more so ; but for a long time it did not represent the true state of things. The Senate began by being essentially a diet of plenipotentiaries, an imitation and a sort of prolongation of the Continental Congress, and was, besides this, an executive council like the assemblies, which, under the name of a Council originally assisted the governor in most of the colonies of New England.

To begin with, the Senate itself did not take its functions as a legislative chamber very seriously. Everything which has been collected of the correspondence of the senators with the local assemblies proves that in the early times they considered themselves simply as agents in constant relation with their principals, whose will was their law. The expressions used in the communications of many of the States with their delegates in Congress are—*requested* for the representatives and *instructed* for the senators. In Jackson's time Senator Tyler resigned his seat because his conscience would not allow him, in accordance with the instructions received from the government of his State, to vote for the rescinding of the famous resolution relating to the affair of the National Bank. A scrupulous ambassador could not act otherwise. In 1828 the Senate was discussing a bill, the object of which was to establish protective rights for the sale of hemp. The proposal was very favourable to Kentucky, and the legislature of that State was following the discussion from a distance with great interest.[1] Mr. Rowan, a senator of Kentucky, strongly opposed this protectionist measure. At the end of his speech he added : " It might be supposed after all I have said that I should vote against the bill, but I have no right to substitute my own opinion for that of my State." We find cases of the same kind down to our own time, but they become rarer. Diplomatic dependence is gradually giving way to a kind of parliamentary independence ; and the characteristics of a second chamber, at first very much in the shade, become stronger every year, and gain ground over the type of an international conference which was at first strongly marked.

By means of a similar evolution, the same characteristics end by gaining the upper hand over those which the Senate derives from its functions as an executive council. In 1789 the Senate conceives of itself much less as a branch of the legislature, than as a sort of State Council associated with the exercise of the presidential power.[2] It then consisted of twenty-six members only; it was therefore less fitted than nowadays to give ample deliberation to laws, and more fitted to direct business itself. Its chief occupation was to collaborate with the head of the State in the appointment of ministers, the choice of ambassadors, and the drawing up of treaties.

[1] See Benton, *Thirty Years in Congress.*
[2] Welling, quoted by Francis Lieber (on Civil Liberty).

A document which has been neglected, indeed one might almost say forgotten, the ancient standing orders of the Senate, gives an undeniable proof of the Senate's voluntary avoidance of publicity. We see from these standing orders that for five years the Senate abstained from meeting in public. When it met to deliberate in its executive or diplomatic capacity, *i.e.*, when personal questions were discussed, or the text of a treaty, secrecy was a matter of obvious propriety. Even to-day, debates of this kind are not held in public, and the reason is easily understood. Debates on the other hand, of a legislative or financial nature, are not suited for being carried on behind closed doors. They lose half their value if they are not heard by the outside public. If, nevertheless, as was the case, debates on legislative and financial matters were carried on by the Senate in private, the reason was that they were considered as a merely incidental duty of the Senate, and it was not thought worth while to make an exception in their case to the general rule of privacy.

It was not till February 20, 1794, that the Senate consented to open its doors to the public, and there was even some hesitation about this. More than one member of the assembly considered that the chamber was by this move giving up its somewhat mysterious part of counsel and confidant of the executive power.

Even after this first step the Senate remained more than twenty-five years without providing itself with what in America may be truly called the organs of the legislative function : I mean permanent committees. Since 1799 the House of Representatives had felt the necessity of these organs, and had appointed a certain number of committees: five, I think, quickly increased to nine, and then to forty or fifty. Thus for every important bill there was a commission ready formed, and competent to examine, discuss, and report on it in the chamber. Besides, as we shall see shortly, it is through these committees that the legislative power communicates well or ill with the executive, and that a more or less regular action is brought to bear by the one power on the other.

Later than the beginning of the century (*i.e.* up to 1816), the Senate had no permanent committees; it was only during the second session of the fourteenth Congress, that at last awakening to the importance of its legislative function, it determined to imitate the House of Representatives on this point. From that time the discussions of the Senate became more ample and interesting; it had forty members, nowadays it has more than double the number.[1] The process of evolution by which the Senate was transformed into a legislative Chamber was of necessity followed out until it reached its complete development.

We see, therefore, how very necessary it is to pay great attention to dates in these matters, and how liable the observer, who consults nothing but the official documents, is to obtain incorrect information.

During the early years of the Union, everyone was ready to prophesy for the House of Representatives a destiny as brilliant as that of the English House of Commons. But people were guided by a merely

[1] [The Senate consists now (1891) of eighty-eight members. (D).]

external analogy. If they had looked closer they would have perceived that according to the spirit of the Constitution, as well as according to the letter, the preponderating power must belong to the Senate. But the Senate itself gave way to the same mistaken idea. The standing orders which I have quoted bear the traces of the hesitations and scruples which long kept the power of the Senate far below what it possessed according to the Constitution.

We also see how by degrees the Senate regained the ground which the House of Representatives at first occupied, because it was deserted by the Senate. In fact, a profound transformation, a distinct displacement of authority and influence, a decisive change in the balance of power took place, and this without leaving any mark on the Constitution. On the other hand, this increase in the power of the Senate did not, as one might naturally suppose, accrue to it in its character of a Chamber which represented the States, and the municipal spirit incorporated in such a Chamber. During the period of this change, the Senate had come nearer and nearer to the type of a second legislative Chamber, and had become very markedly imbued with a national spirit. All this complex and varied evolution would be quite concealed from anyone who only referred to the Articles of the Constitution or to Statutes to determine its course, and who did not seek for light in the collateral documents of which I have noticed the importance.

The right of priority in the House of Representatives in financial matters gives rise to remarks of the same nature.

The Constitutional Article, originally proposed in the Convention of Philadelphia, settled that Bills for *raising or appropriating* money should originate in the House of Representatives, but the Article as finally adopted,[1] left this privilege of initiation to the House of Representatives only in the case of Bills for raising revenue. In spite of this the practice, as old as the Constitution itself, is to originate in the House of Representatives, not only for Bills for raising revenue but also general Appropriation Bills. Custom, therefore, has restored to the House of Representatives to the full that right of originating money Bills which a special provision of the Constitution, passed for that very purpose, gave to the House only in part.

But on the other hand, this right which the legislator meant to be advantageous to the popular branch of the Congress became, incredible as it may seem, a cause of inferiority and of diminished influence in financial matters. This was the effect of the standing order which the House of Representatives made for itself.

This is what takes place.

The money Bills passed by the representatives are sent to the Senate, which has power to amend them. The Senate makes great use of this right of amendment, sometimes even abuses it. When a money Bill modified by the Senate comes back to the House of

---

[1] [" All Bills for raising revenue shall originate in the House of Representatives ; but the Senate may propose or concur with amendments as on other Bills." *Constitution of United States,* art. 1, s. 7. Compare Story, *On the Constitution* (4th ed.), ss. 874 —880 (D).]

Representatives it is usually late in the Session. Now
it is the rule that the House of Representatives should
not even take notice of the amendments of the Senate ;
the House without giving them a hearing refuses to
adopt them. The Senate sticks to the amendments,
and by common consent the Bill is sent to a committee
consisting of three representatives and three senators.
This committee examines and discusses, works out a
compromise, and sends it with a report to the two
branches of Congress. One might suppose that at this
stage the clauses of the Bill would be discussed in the
House of Representatives. Quite the contrary. According to the standing orders of each House, no motion
tending to amend the conclusions of the report can be
received and put to the vote by the Chairman. The
House of Representatives, like the Senate, is obliged
to accept or reject the report as a whole exactly as
it comes from the commission. If, as occasionally
happens, the House rejects the report, a new commission meets, makes a new report, and this time it
is difficult for the House, from want of time, not to
give in, and especially in the year when its existence
comes to an end on March 4.

It is easy to see the great advantage which this procedure gives to the Senate.[1] All the clauses which are
originated in the House of Representatives are amply,
seriously, and effectively discussed in the Senate, but
the amendments which originate with the Senate are
hardly ever discussed in the House of Representatives ;

[1] See on this subject an article by Senator Hoar, *North
America Review*, Feb., 1879, vol. 138, p. 113.

in fact, the House does not take cognizance of them. The House knows of nothing but the conclusions of a mixed commission in which it is represented by only three of its members, and which deliberates out of its presence; it pronounces on these conclusions as a whole, and not on each amendment. If only the three senators, members of the commission, show a little firmness, the greater number of the amendments recommended by the Senate are kept in the terms of the compromise recommended by the commission, and the representatives are obliged to ratify it from want of time to do otherwise. The Senate and its commission, to do them justice, never press privileges to the extreme.

The condition in which the House of Representatives of the United States usually finds itself in reference to the budget amended by the Senate resembles the position of the French Senate, when at the end of the year it has submitted to it the budget voted by the Chamber, and the Senate is obliged to pass it in haste, lest it should be compelled to resort to the inevitable expedient of provisional votes for a few months.

An eminent statesman of the United States might well say in 1880 that all the efforts made by the House of Representatives in 1832, 1856, and 1870, to defend its right of priority against the inroads of the Senate had been detrimental to its legislative equality. The House would have gained by dropping a privilege of which the real gain has fallen to the Senate. Of all this no one would have any idea who read nothing but the Articles of the Constitution.

Section v

WE have seen what care must be taken in order to become *thoroughly acquainted* with every part of the American Constitution and its exact meaning. No less care is necessary *to understand* the fitting of all its wheels, the mechanism in its regular working, and to form a judgment of it in accordance with the results of its working.

The first impression which an impartial study of the subject leaves on the mind is that serious faults of construction exist in the Federal Constitution, and that it is a very imperfect machine which must break at the first turn of the wheels. One would imagine that the prime object of any constitution must be to establish concert between the executive and legislative powers to prevent violent conflicts between them, or at all events to prevent such conflicts from perpetuating themselves, and for this end to contrive prompt means of peaceful arrangement; but the Federal Constitution seems almost to have made it an object to raise conflicts, to organize and to embitter them; it multiplies the opportunities for disagreements and lets them last as long as possible.

In all times and in all countries every effort has been made to create and keep up a good understanding between the legislative and the executive power. This is of course an all-important point. In England especially, the first care of statesmen has been to bring the two powers into harmony as much as possible, and to find points of contact between them; they have, so to say, grafted the one power upon the other, and, foreseeing that the harmony between the two might occasionally be troubled, they have made provisions for speedily re-establishing it in accordance with the will of the people. The Convention of Philadelphia, clinging superstitiously to Montesquieu's doctrine of the separation of powers,[1] spent all its efforts in keeping the legislative and executive powers separate. The paths laid out for them are invariably parallel; they do not cross at any point. The powers can see one another threaten each other by a look or by a word from afar, but there are no cross-roads where they can meet and engage in a hand-to-hand struggle, which might give the victory and the last word to the one or to the other.

In England the ministers are members of the Houses, and direct all the legislative work. Nothing can be more rational than this plan. Of course the ministers are those who best know the necessities and difficulties of the government; they see more clearly than others what laws it will be expedient to make. Since they are responsible for the measures passed, they are forced to take good care not to let ill-considered and vexatious schemes be proposed. In America the ministers are not admitted to Congress. The President and his constitutional advisers communicate with the Houses by messages and written statements only. The President, says the Second Article [2] of the Constitution, shall from

---

[1] [See *De l'Esprit des Lois*, livre xi. ch. iv., v (D).]

[2] ["He shall from time to time give to Congress information of

time to time give information to the Congress of the
United States, and recommend to its consideration such
measures as he shall judge necessary or expedient.   But
neither the President nor the ministers can follow up
these propositions, or rather motions, within the precincts of Congress. They may not turn them into formal
Bills and support them with the authority which belongs
to a responsible government; they may not dissipate
misunderstandings and turn aside amendments which
go against the object of the law, or modify the wording
of the Bill in the course of debate according to the
feeling shown by the assembly.   All these conditions of
a matured, wise, and consistent legislative action are
denied to the President and the ministers.   They can
only make themselves heard behind the scenes.

When ministers can be members of the legislature it
very soon becomes the rule that they always must be
members, and better still, that they must also be the
leaders of the parliamentary majority.   This is what
happens in England.   In form it is always the sovereign
who appoints the ministers; but in fact they are chosen
by the most eminent of their number, the Prime
Minister, who is himself more or less directly chosen
by the majority of the House of Commons.   It is a
matter of course that the ministers put into office by
the majority do not remain in office when the majority
is no longer on their side.   The least sign of want of
confidence is enough to make them retire.   They may

the state of the Union, and recommend to their consideration such
measures as he shall judge necessary and expedient."—*Constitution
of United States*, Art. II. sec. 3 (D).]

be eminent personages, adored leaders, or admired orators; one and all make it a point of honour not to be told twice over that they are out of favour. In the case of a disagreement of opinion between the Cabinet and the House the conflict is ended at once. The ministers, struck by an adverse vote, resign; they give way to others whose opinions agree with those of the majority; harmony is re-established between the legislative and the executive.

This mechanism, which makes the Government so sensitive to being placed in a minority, is unknown in the United States. Neither of the two Houses has the power of overturning the ministry. The fact is, that their ministerial Cabinet is not a council of politicians; it is simply a committee of chief officials who are at the head of the Civil Service and are liable to removal. These administrators have nothing to do with the Houses; they are dependent not on the House but on the President. A vote of want of confidence does not affect them as long as they have the confidence of their chief. It is their acknowledged duty to rally round him when Congress is hostile to him; besides, none of the measures brought before Congress bear their names; they do not take part personally in any debate. A parliamentary demonstration does not touch either their vanity as orators or their responsibility as statesmen. Congress has, however, one course of action against them : that is, an impeachment followed by a condemnation by a majority of two-thirds of the Senate.[1]

---

[1] [See *Constitution of United States*, Art. I., sec. 3, and Story *On the Constitution* (4th ed.), ss. 742—813 (D).]

But this is a clumsy and unwieldy weapon which, except in case of open treason, is only fit to be shelved in a museum of constitutional antiquities. The ministry can therefore remain in office against the wish of Congress and lead the country into a course of action which they disapprove, provided the President agrees with them, and this agreement could be prolonged through the whole of a Presidential term, *i.e.* four years. This state of things strikes one as giving rise to a permanent state of conflict established by the Constitution itself.

A legislature systematically hostile, which cannot overturn the Government, can yet prevent it from governing by refusing to pass laws or to grant necessary supplies. For this case the English Constitution provides another way of re-establishing harmony, that is the dissolution of Parliament, followed by fresh elections. Either the old majority remains, or it gives way to a new majority favourable to the ministers; according to the result they remain in office or retire from it. In six weeks harmony is restored between the House of Commons and the Cabinet. In America the ministry has not this resource of appealing to the country and asking to know the wishes of the people. It is obliged to wait till the powers of the House of Representatives (named for two years) have run out, and till the Senate itself (renewed by thirds in the course of six years) has gone through one or two elections. All this time the ministers are tied to hostile Assemblies, subjected to see all their acts taken in bad part, and obliged to do without laws which they think most necessary. They make up their minds to attempt very little; they calculate all their measures so as not to raise a storm; they give up all plans for the carrying out of which a government has to ask for confidence and time. Their policy becomes colourless, hesitating, and aims only at immediate results.

Never was more art brought to bear in keeping up and prolonging the existence of a government which, weak and divided against itself, without policy and without credit, will not or cannot carry out the will of the nation.

There are, however, some exceptions to the theory of separation of the powers in America. I will only mention two which are so singular and in such flagrant contradiction both to the principles of American institutions and to the most evident practical needs that their permanent preservation seems at first sight almost inexplicable.

The American Constitution of 1789 intended the executive power to be master in its own domain; one would therefore have expected the Constitution to have secured to this power the free choice of its own agents and especially of its ministers. By no means; these ministers who, when once appointed, are beyond the control of both Houses, can only be chosen with the assent of one of them, that is of the Senate, and it is not even upon the composition of the ministry as a body that the Senate pronounces a decision. Individual names for each office are submitted to it. It can take one and reject another, and upset all the combinations of the power—*i.e.*, the President—responsible for the appointment. The authority exercised by the Senate

is not a political control in a wide sense, but comes
down to all the pettiness of a personal question. This
authority is not enough to exercise a large and salutary
influence, but is a kind of control which does nothing
but hinder, worry, and weaken. As to the other House,
the popular House, it has no influence on the selection
of ministers either before or after their appointment.
It is not permitted to penetrate the sphere in which the
Government is constituted. Why, if the Senate interferes, is the House of Representatives set aside ? This
can be explained by certain causes which we shall have
to define later on in treating of the spirit of the
Constitution. But why, if the intervention of the
Senate is of value, can it not be renewed and, if
necessary, correct an error in the first choice of
ministers ?

The second exception of which I have spoken is
still more surprising. The President prepares treaties ;
he discusses the conditions with foreign governments,
and signs the treaty. But while in England, for
example, the treaty is rendered complete and perfect
by the signature of the sovereign, the Constitution of
the United States requires over and above this a
sitting of the Senate to discuss and approve the treaty,
and no less than a majority of two-thirds in order to
ratify it.[1] Thus one-third plus one member of the
Senate can hold in check two other thirds of the Senate,
the executive, *i.e.* the President and ministers, in fact all
the other powers of the state. This one-third alone

---

[1] The treaty of 1795 with England was only passed by the
strict constitutional majority (two-thirds).

can set at naught the work of a decided majority, and disturb the friendly relations of the state with a foreign power disposed to be conciliatory. The *liberum veto* of Poland was not a more extraordinary institution.

Finally, that nothing may be wanting to the strangeness of this constitutional mechanism, if this same treaty is passed, it will not be submitted to or referred to the House of Representatives, which has no more right to be informed about it than ordinary citizens. The President and the Senate may, for example, cede or annex territories, and yet nothing of the fact will appear in the discussions of the House of Representatives unless the cession involves expenditure or receipt of money. Besides, I must add that even if the treaty contains clauses imposing a charge on the public revenue, it is the rule, since Washington's time, that the House of Representatives should not discuss the terms of the treaty adopted by the Senate, but accept it in silence as an accomplished fact, and simply vote the necessary funds.[1]

Frenchmen are accustomed to conceive of a constitution as a philosophical work in which everything is deduced from a principle, as a work of art of which the order and symmetry must be perfect, as a scientific machine of which the plan is so exact, the steel so fine and firm, that the very smallest hitch is impossible. They are therefore overcome with astonishment at this rough sketch, full of incongruities and mistakes, this coarse machinery fashioned with a rough implement; and they ask themselves by what mysterious operation

[1] See de Chambrun, *Le Pouvoir Exécutif aux États-Unis.*

everything which ought to produce perpetual accidents, stoppages, and dislocations, yet results in a regular, inoffensive, and even satisfactory movement.

The working of the machines is less mysterious than it seems to be at first sight. Suppose an engine given in charge to machinists with whom dexterity and presence of mind are inherited qualities. Suppose, further, that the engine is something special and peculiar, and that the greater number of machines in the factory are moved by secondary and independent motive powers. Suppose, finally, that the factory is placed in a bare country, far from other factories and human crowds. Many precautions which would be necessary elsewhere will be superfluous here. Many a prohibition, many a preventive measure may be spared, and it will even be expedient to let certain causes of irregularity, or slackening of power, exist if at this price advantages of another kind are secured; for one need not fear that the general action will thereby be disturbed.

I have just quoted an example of what the wisdom of politicians can do to lesson the effect of a vicious constitutional arrangement. We have seen that in Washington's time the House of Representatives was obliged to give up discussing the terms of a treaty concluded by the President with the approval of the Senate. Since that time the House has been wise enough not to raise any sharp conflict in such matters, and to accept the interpretation of the Constitution which so seriously diminished its power. In this there is an amount of self-denial of which few popular assemblies on the Continent would have been capable.

In like manner the Senate, invested by the Constitution with a right of veto in the choice of the Secretaries of State, made a permanent rule for itself to ratify the propositions of the President purely and simply, even when the President is not in agreement with the majority of the Assembly, and from this rule it hardly ever deviated except during a time of crisis or of irreconcilable struggle.[1] A majority which does not abuse its privileges against an adversary, a representative body which keeps discreetly within the rights assigned to it by the Constitution, a legislative body which understands and respects even to its own disadvantage the conditions of a government's existence—these are three

[1] During the conflict with President Johnson, the "Tenure of Office Act" extended the control exercised by the Senate to the case of the *dismissal* of Secretaries of State. The law enjoined the President, whenever he took so extreme a step, to refer the matter to the Senate, and the Senate could, at its pleasure, keep the dismissed minister in office, or reinstate him. This was virtually doing away with the responsibility of the executive. A President, served by subordinates whom he does not wish for, and who are forced upon him after he has mortally offended them, ceases to be the unfettered author of the acts of his Government, and can no longer be held responsible for them. This Act was passed to meet the immediate circumstances of the day ; it was a real measure of war, and was not put in force after the acute stages of the conflict had come to an end. After being modified in 1869, it had become a dead letter, when recently (March 3, 1887) the Americans decided to repeal it. This was a meritorious return to the true principles and evident spirit of their Constitution.

miracles which presuppose more wisdom than one would expect to find in an out and out democracy.

I will quote a final example of this practical American spirit which though always vigorous and clear, has been in this case wanting in breadth of view and foresight. It is a further illustration of how practice silently modifies the text of the law.

Bagehot has given a formula for the paradox which is the basis of the parliamentary *régime*. A representative assembly such as the House of Commons is in substance a meeting. Now the qualities which are most certain to be wanting, or to be nullified, in a meeting are those of self-control, experience, calmness and reflection, prescience and continuity, without which there can be no good laws or good government. A representative assembly is therefore specially unfit to legis-late, and yet this is the special function of such an assembly.

We know how the English have got round the difficulty and have turned the House of Commons into a fairly working legislative body. The members of the two parties which divide the House begin by giving up their initiative into the hands of their chiefs. These chiefs are the ministers or their acknowledged successors. They are prudent and enlightened men, marked out in the country and the House by a slow process of selection and formed by the exercise of power. Their party respects and obeys them. In fact, all the elaboration and preparation of the laws is taken away from the House, or meeting, and delegated to this small number of men who understand the work and agree among themselves. Thus the conditions of good legislative work are re-established.

This ingenious device was not a resource open to the Americans. In the United States the ministers are by the Constitution excluded from Congress; they do not depend on Congress and have no authority in it. No one else, however, takes up the directing power which the ministers do not exercise in Congress. There are, it is true, in America as in England, two great parties. These parties are fairly compact and under discipline throughout the country, because there they need to act together in order to carry by assault the Presidency or a majority in Congress. They are not so much bound together in Congress, because there they have no attacks to lead, the ministerial power being beyond their reach. In the very precincts of Congress the party bond is relaxed; the great political unities tend to become disunited for want of an important end, which cannot be attained without co-ordinated and concerted action, and for want of a supreme chief to whom all submit in order the more surely to attain this end. Every member is left to himself to follow his fancy and consult nothing but his own interests, and is tempted to follow his own course without measure or scruple. This parliamentary individualism can hardly fail to produce legislation which is at once redundant and futile, incoherent and contradictory, which is almost always narrow and partial, lacking any marked character, without connection, and immature.

The Americans felt the danger, and this is how the

House of Representatives went to work to obviate it.
At the beginning of the session the Speaker names
forty-eight committees corresponding to the principal
ministerial departments.   There are distinct committees
for the appropriations, ways and means, elections, foreign
affairs, public lands, railways and canals, commerce,
judiciary, &c.[1] The Bills, thousands of which are presented during the sitting of Congress, are as a matter
of course sent to the committees within whose com-
petence they are held to fall.   It is needless to say
that the immense majority of these Bills has no
chance of being read or reported; there is no time for
it.   The House does not sit (reckoning all deduc-
tions) for more than a hundred days in two years.
This only gives an average of two hours for considering the report of each committee.   Over and
above this, the two financial committees and two or
three others have the privilege of being heard by per-
ference at any time—they displace the committee which
has the floor of the House and present their own reports,
which often give rise to long debates.   The time
allotted to the other committees is thus cut down.   The
consequence is, that an enormous number of Bills are
simply stopped.   Those only reach the House which
have the good luck to interest the chairman or the chief
members of the particular committee.   In a sitting—a
strange rule indeed—the reporter alone has the right of
speaking and that for an hour.   He may give up a few
minutes of this short time to the members who wish to
give their views on the subject, and he generally does

[1] [See Bryce, *American Commonwealth*, i., p. 218 (1st ed.) (D).]

so with a good grace. In every case, before his hour has expired, he always asks for the previous question, and the House hardly ever refuses to vote it. The previous question is a sort of closure after a fixed time ; the effect is to give the reporter an hour longer, after which the matter is dismissed. But, during the first hour, no amendment can have been proposed without the consent of the reporter, nor can it be done in the second hour, after the vote of the previous question therefore it is a most difficult matter to modify in any way whatever the terms of a Bill reported by the committee. They must needs be accepted as they are or rejected entirely. Note, further, that the committee which has the floor in the person of one of its members has always more Bills to report on than there is time for ; it hurries them on, and cuts short discussion in order to introduce its other Bills which are waiting to follow. Note, lastly, that the other committees i.e. in reality all the members of the House, are interested in not letting the discussion be prolonged in order that they may not have to wait too long for their turn. Therefore the members only make a few short remarks before voting. In short, everything contributes, on the one hand, to shorten debates, on the other, to weaken them by hindering the right of proposing amendments. Even with these relative facilities for getting on with business, too few bills, out of the enormous number brought in, would reach the stage of a final vote, unless there were some further resource. For this reason, every Monday at a certain hour, but especially during the last ten days of the session, every member is allowed to demand the suspension of the

standing orders; and if two-thirds of the members
agree to the demand (which is decided simply by
putting it to the vote without discussion), the Bill
before the House is passed or rejected without debate
and without amendment. Thus, at the last moment
and when about to adjourn, the House avoids the
discredit of having done no work at all, by throwing
the doors wide open and letting Bills pass through *pêle-
mêle* without any serious examination; and this care-
lessness is after all as discreditable as the charge of
idleness.

The result of all this is clear. The danger of
excessive legislation has been avoided; but this is
achieved at a great price. In substance, the House
has deprived its members of their initiative, and has
given up its own deliberative function. This state of
things reminds one in more than one respect of the
French Imperial *Corps Législatif* of 1852, which
voted without free power of amendment, on Bills prepared outside its walls by the *Conseil d'État*. In America
the part of the *Conseil d'État* is performed by the forty-
eight small permanent committees. It is they who have
the initiative, the direction, and supreme control of all
the legislative work. In appearance, and in the opinion
of the masses, the House has kept the liberty of speech
and discussion which the first American Constitutions
consider as "essential to the rights of the nation." In
fact, and without any trace in the Articles of the Constitution of such a great change, the House has ceased to be
a debating assembly; it is only an instrument for hasty
voting on the proposals which fifty small committees

have prepared behind closed doors. The Americans are strangers to, or have now lost sight of, that breadth of parliamentary debate which, in the English House of Commons, opens a wide field for talent, for enlightened views, and for new ideas. In England this publicity of debate helps to form public opinion, and gives the whole nation a share in resolutions which are considered at great length, and abundantly attacked and defended before its eyes. By this means the higher political life, after being condensed and purified in Parliament is, in a sense, diffused among the masses. By the dryness, brevity and unseemly haste of its procedure, the House of Representatives has lost touch with the country; it has ceased to awaken any echoes outside its walls. At the present time it is very much farther from representing the people than if, instead of going as far as universal suffrage, it had kept to an infinitely narrower franchise, but had preserved at the same time the freedom, fulness, and majesty of its debates. Threatened with want of moderation and " confusion of tongues " in their legislation, and deprived of the flexible checks afforded by the presence of the ministers in Parliament, the Americans have been obliged to adopt rules so rigid and stringent that they stifle, or as Americans say " gag," all debate in the House. Like causes produce like results, and the House of Representatives is thus brought down to the humiliating condition and *rôle* of the French *Corps Législatifs* under the first and second Empires.

The internal organization of these same Parliamentary committees, both in the House of Representatives and the Senate, is no less important in its political influence.

I have recalled the fact that the American ministers
have no right of entry into Congress, and it is astonish-
ing that such a complete separation of the executive
and legislative power has not been more injurious than
it has been to the management of public affairs.
Among other reasons this is caused by a practice which
has become established between the Senate and the
House of Representatives and which is not even to be
found in the standing orders. It is purely customary,
and not written. It will be understood that among the
permanent committees, of which I have spoken above,
there must be one which corresponds to each ministerial
department. A Secretary of State who wishes to get a
bill introduced first comes to an understanding with the
chairman of the proper committees in the House of
Representatives and in the Senate. Every one of these
chairmen is like an outside head of each of the corresponding ministerial departments, or a counsel whose
advice must be taken for every step; sometimes if one
of these heads is of superior capacity, he becomes the
real minister of the department. This was the case
with Sumner, the illustrious chairman of the committee for foreign affairs in the Senate; for the whole
of a long period he directed the foreign policy of the
Union.

In spite of all this the organization remains a very
faulty one. First of all, these chairmen are two in
number and it may happen that they disagree; or
that they are both opposed to the administration
and will not accept any of its proposals. Apparently
one of these disagreements would be sufficient to

bring affairs to an absolute dead lock. At a very early date Congress in its wisdom took steps to diminish the frequency of these vexatious disagreements. I find in 1841 the following practice established in both Houses : first that the special committees, as well as the permanent committees corresponding to the ministerial departments, should be composed of a majority of members of the government party, plus a considerable minority belonging to the opposition ; secondly that the author of a proposed law should always be chairman of the special committee charged with examining and reporting thereon. In that very year the President *pro tem.* of the Senate had appointed a committee of an entirely party character and consisting of members of the opposition. He was sternly called to order by Mr. King, a man of weight, who bore witness to the fact that the contrary and almost immemorial practice has been always followed by the Senate.[1]

Thus it is no longer impossible to bridge over this gulf which separated the government and Congress. First a ford, so to say, was made over the river, by means of the standing committees ; then, on the other side of the ford, a good landing place was provided, so that the ministers could bring their measure to shore without any difficulty. Now when some friend to the ministers presents the bill it is well received, examined favourably by a competent and friendly committee, and on the report of this committee it is submitted to the final judgment of the Chamber.

A practice which supposes such an extraordinary

[1] *Thirty Years in Congress*, Benton, ii., 235.

degree of moderation and wisdom has not, so far as I can judge, been able to resist party spirit. I have before my eyes the composition of all the committees of the Senate in 1877. The Senate was then democratic, the administration republican. The majority in all the permanent senatorial committees had been given to the democratic party. So much of the ancient practice remained that the governmental minority in these committees was as large as it could be without ceasing to be a minority; it was invariably half the number minus one, and the members called to sit in this minority were necessarily the oldest, the most experienced and consequently the most moderate, and those most free from the passions which rouse systematic opposition.[1] Even without exaggerating the importance of these curious modifications and without denying the uncertainty of the customary law which sanctions them, I think it is impossible to have a true idea of the effects produced in America by the incompatibility between the character of a minister and of a member of Congress, if you content yourself on this point with the rough and categorical assertions contained in the constitutional articles, and if you do not take into account the gifts of prudence, moderation, and political wisdom which a long parliamentary habit, acquired on the soil of Great Britain, had implanted in the instincts, and, so to speak, in the very blood of the emigrants whose descendants now people the United States.

[1] The same observation may be made on the committees of the Senate and of the House of Representatives, organized between 1878 and 1888.

I must remark besides that even if these exceptional qualities had not existed, no irremediable harm would have been done. The results of all the faults of construction which I have noticed may be summed up in one : weakness not only of the executive, as Bagehot says, but also of the executive and the legislative power, *i.e.*, of all the organs of the central government. But there is hardly any occasion when the Americans really suffer from this weakness; all the ordinary routine of the internal policy is carried on by the State governments, and they are competent for the task. Besides, the Americans would be afraid of making the central government more homogeneous, more coherent—more *one* in its action. Who knows ? The central government might perhaps be tempted to make use of its independence and the autonomy of the States would be menaced. The Americans would rather put up with certain weaknesses in the central powers, than run the risk of any interference with this State sovereignty, which in their eyes is the first of blessings.

If however in spite of the defects we have noticed, this mechanism does work well and quietly, it is evident that we must not consider this as a mark of general and theoretic excellence, we must not persuade ourselves that because the Americans acquiesce in this state of things it is possible to carry out the separation of the powers to the same extent in a unified state.

The arrangements which I have criticized have not any sort of absolute excellence, even locally. In the eyes of Americans themselves their value is quite relative and even negative. They recommend themselves not by the good they do, but by the dangers they ward off.

To sum up, they are the least of evils in a federal government; they would be the greatest of evils in a centralized government.

Section vi

HERE let me point out another circumstance which has had a very important effect on the American Constitution. It has not been the habit in France to open the study of French constitutions by remarks on French geography, though if this were done it would certainly throw light on the subject. To lawyers and statesmen the fact I am about to mention is a weighty one, and affording matter for reflection, viz. that the two countries in which political liberty has flourished spontaneously are both beyond the reach of the great military powers of the Continent—one, thanks to its insular position, the other, thanks to its still more protected situation beyond the Atlantic. All the executive organization of the United States shows signs of this security.

In every country which has representative government, even when the sovereign has power to conclude a treaty without the authority of Parliament, the cabinet which directs foreign policy is always subject to be questioned in Parliament. In the course of a negotiation the questions multiply. The ministers are aware that, whenever a treaty is signed and made public, if Parliament thinks they have been mistaken and have misunderstood the interest of the .country, power will be taken out of their hands. It is well understood that nothing less than this would induce ministers to exercise the care and circumspection in public affairs, which is such an essential and vital matter.

The great distance which separates the United States from the great powers of Europe, renders many an imprudence in negotiations of no great account. This fact has really made Americans much less anxious than they would otherwise have been as to the circumspection and prudence of their statesmen. This is the reason why they could dispense with the custom of calling up their ministers at any moment to give an account of their proceedings, and leave them free from parliamentary intervention in the course of a negotiation. On the other hand, this is also the reason why Americans see no drawbacks in obliging their foreign ministers to submit to certain very harassing conditions. A final and secret control over treaties is exercised by an Assembly, viz., the Senate, in which these ministers do not sit, and in which they have neither the credit, nor the influence, nor the authority on which parliamentary ministers can always depend in their diplomatic work. In the United States the Foreign Secretary is less under control in his daily action, and less guarded from his own rashness, than in England, and at the same time he is under special disadvantages for negotiating effectively with foreign powers. He is under the necessity of asking the government with which he is treating to bind itself absolutely while the other contracting power is not bound in the same manner, and has the resource of setting itself free by a vote in a Chamber debating with closed doors.

Mr. Gladstone, in a debate raised by a motion of Mr. Rylands[1] for submitting all treaties to the Houses of Parliament before ratification, pointed out all the faults of this plan, and showed that if these faults could be tolerated in the United States it was on account of the geographical isolation of that country, and that such a plan of action would be fatal in States placed in such close proximity as European countries. Bagehot shows still more clearly that the system is most unfavourable to the good management of foreign affairs and to the development of statesmanlike qualities; that the possibility of its existence is due to the enormous distance which separates America and our continent.[2]

---

[1] Debate in the House of Commons, Feb. 14, 1873. *Hansard*, vol. ccxiv., pp. 476-478.

[2] "They suffer from want of atmospheric pressure, and of some moral coercion to compel them to consider more carefully what they are doing and saying, and of some interest in the remote consequences of their actions. They seem to think a stern rebuke to a friendly state, followed by armed preparations, a mere detail, with which no one has any concern, which needs no explanation, and which can be smoothed away by a brief denial that a particular despatch was ever sent to the foreign court."—Bagehot, *Economist*. Everything is relative. What Bagehot says of the United States, protected by the Atlantic Ocean, is said by the Duc de Broglie, in 1835, of England, defended by the Channel and sheltered by its peculiar position at one of the extremities of

In like manner, almost every nation with warlike and dangerous neighbours considers that for safety's sake it must submit to certain inevitable evils. The chief of the state is obliged to be entrusted with considerable power and effective means of action; the obedience to his commands must be mechanical and prompt, in order that at a given moment he may concentrate in his own hands all the strength of the country and use it to repel external dangers. In a country with an extended frontier open to invasion, centralization and standing armies are to a certain degree a necessity; despotism is always on the point of coming into existence, and whilst the force of the constitution is wasted in efforts to prevent tyranny from gaining ground, the futility of such efforts becomes only too apparent unless the country is greatly favoured by the wisdom and the good luck of its leaders.

Fortune has favoured the United States in this respect. They are the only great power of their Continent. In their case the dispersion of their forces and the difficulty of concentrating them, are inconveniences but not dangers. The Constitution has slightly diminished these inconveniences, but has not exerted itself to get rid of them. This is why the sphere of action allotted to the States is so wide and the sphere of the Federal

Europe. "It is this position of England's," he writes, " which spares her all serious consequences in a hazardous policy and saves her from the immediate effects of any course of action lightly undertaken. It explains why her policy is so often whimsical and inconsequent. She is like a spoilt child, scarcely struggling against its first impulse, and giving way to the fancies of a day or even of an hour." (See Thureau-Dangin.)

power, especially of the Executive, is so narrow. This is also the reason why the division of power between the States and the Union has not greatly varied since the Union began. If Canada had been more rapidly peopled, if the Spanish Republics had been more firmly established, and had been more capable of coalition, the Constitution would rapidly have lent itself to some more or less centralized system, such as Hamilton proposed in the Convention of Philadelphia: *e.g.* a presidency for life, and to some more effectual means than now exist for constraining the States.

The same reasons explain why it has been possible to preserve the election [1] of the President by the people without danger to the Constitution, whilst in other countries this system of election has almost infallibly ended in the downfall of republican government. In America, military glory has not got confused in the minds of the masses with the safety of the frontier, and integrity of the national territory. Military success has been a valued luxury, not a vital necessity, it has been a gratification to national vanity, but has not been considered essential to the safety of the State. On the continent of Europe, the constant menace of foreign aggression keeps alive feelings which explain the eagerness of the people to place power in the hands of an energetic dynasty or a skilful general. Naturally these feelings do not exist in America, and

---

[1] Everybody knows that the Presidential election, as organized by the Constitution, is an indirect election ; but custom has imperatively established direct popular election, ordered by the conventions of the two great parties.

prætorian insolence could hardly develop itself in a hand-
ful of soldiers, more like a body of police than an army.
In reality Americans have shown as much and more
liking than other nations for military show and fame,
and it has been said, with perfect truth, that there has
been no single war in the United States which did not
create a President. In twenty-four presidential elections the army supplied ten successful candidates and
nearly as many who came near being elected. Had this
happened in a country like France what would have
been the result? A unanimous vote of the civil population repeated ten times over and the enthusiasm of a
standing army full of the recollections of a late victory,
would have exposed the persons elected to temptations
too strong for human weakness and would certainly
have produced two or three Cæsars. But in the United
States these military Presidents were looked upon by
the civil population as nothing more than honest
public servants, not one of them except the first has
had anything of the halo of a saviour of his country. These fine energetic figures looked well in the
electoral show, and that was one reason why they were
approved of as candidates. The Anglo-Saxon love of
sport and open air exercise gave rise on these occasions
to lively demonstrations and violent declamation. But
behind all this noise there has been no deep feeling nor
any dangerous prestige. Besides the Presidents have
known very well how the matter stood. When the war
was over there was no army to support them, it was
disbanded at once. Like their soldiers they went back
to civil life; they were only scabbards without swords.

We must say then, that the fact of the presidential
election by popular vote having produced no evil
results, is a fact quite peculiar to America, and moreover a fact, the import and bearing of which depends
entirely on the exceptional geographical position of the
United States. It would be rash to appeal to their experience as a precedent in favour of the same system in
countries existing under perfectly different conditions
—conditions which condemn them to keep up large
military establishments, and which render them liable
alternately to be lost by the incapacity, or saved by the
genius of a general. In a country where a Scipio may
any day arise and go to the Capitol to swear that he is
the saviour of his country, the choice of the executive
government ought not to be confided to the vote of the
multitude (*comitia plebis*), but to some body less liable
to be affected by the reflex action of fear, hope, and
gratitude.

Section vii

I MUST again repeat that just as much careful
attention is required to appreciate the *spirit* of a foreign
constitution as to explain its mechanism. The mistake
most to be guarded against is that of taking the
American Constitution for a democracy of the French
type. A democracy it is, but it is one which took its rise

and was organized under such extraordinary circumstances, which is composed of such exceptional elements, governed by forces so peculiar to itself that we hardly recognize in it the thing we expect to see under the name of a democracy. Many of its characteristics are in complete contradiction to a Frenchman's idea—founded on his own national experience—of a democracy. Above all let us distinguish between the federal institutions and the institutions of the separate States.

The articles of the Federal Constitution, which are the first thing to consider, have one remarkable peculiarity: they are the work of persons who were half-hearted partizans or resigned opponents of the form of government about to be established. The Convention of Philadelphia presents us with a curious paradoxical picture. On the one side we have a party of autonomists, zealots for State sovereignty, who against their will work out a federal constitution; on the other side we have believers in the English Constitution and democrats more or less shaken in their principles, who against their will work out a republican constitution.

Judging simply by the first impression, the Federal Constitution might be described as the least democratic of democracies. We must however remember that it was drawn up in the midst of a state of disorder and violence which imperilled the advantages gained by the War of Independence.

Many an adherent of democratic institutions had given way to pessimism, and one may say that the members of the American Convention chose to adopt as little as possible of the democratic system. They

submitted to the necessity of establishing a popular
government because it was forced upon them by the
condition of a nation which lacked all the historical,
social, and economical elements which make up the
substance of an aristocracy or a monarchy.   In this case
democracy was more or less a *pis aller.*   Democracy is
the basis of the Constitution, because there was no
other foundation on which to raise up a constitutional
edifice; but all the superstructure, if I may say so,
bears the mark of the most strangely anti-democratic
tendency which   ever   influenced   a   constitutional
convention.

The direct or indirect source of all the federal powers
is the national will expressed by elections.   I purposely
say national will and not popular will.   In the Constitution of the United States no pains is taken to
insure   the   democratic   character   of   the   system   of
election for members of Congress.   It is left to each
separate State to determine its own electoral system.
Most of the States had at the time when the constitution was formed a restricted franchise for the
election of their own Assemblies, and in several of them
it was the State legislatures, and not the people, who
had the right of choosing the presidential electors.
Besides, universal suffrage at that time in America would
not have been the institution which has been known under
that name in France since 1848.   In 1789 almost all
the colonists were country landowners, or could become
such if they wished it.   There were no great masses
of urban or industrial population.   Universal suffrage
exercised by a population of landowners living a quiet

country life would have been free from all the perils of demagogy. All the more reason was there for not fearing the restricted suffrage which existed as a rule in almost all the States.

The Convention of Philadelphia had made a marked concession to the principles of democracy in assigning relatively short terms of power to the President and the two branches of Congress. The leading members acquiesced unwillingly in this short tenure of office. To make up for this they showed great determination and ingenuity in preventing any interference on the part of the people in a presidential election except at certain fixed times and seasons.

For instance, if the candidates for the Presidency or the Vice-Presidency did not get an absolute majority, do not suppose that there was a fresh election by the same electoral bodies; the question which of the candidates was to be elected was referred to Congress and was there decided. If the President died during his term of office the people were not called upon to meet and provide for the serious and unforeseen requirements of such a crisis. The successor was already there, an officer whom the people had elected at the same time as the President, possibly two or three years before, at a time when the need of another presidential election could not be foreseen, and the possibility of such an event itself was only a vague contingency which could not be seriously considered in the choice of Vice-President. This appointment beforehand has but one object—that of saving an appeal to the people. And this is so true that the

Constitution, looking to the future, and contemplating
the possibility of the Vice-President himself dying, does
not lay on the nation the duty of re-electing a Vice-
President, but lays on Congress the duty of designating
by an Act the official who, whether elected or not
elected, shall take by succession the highest office in
the State.

The Vice-President is avowedly a difficulty.   Chosen
by the suffrage of the whole Union he can hardly have
any political influence without having too much, and
without becoming irksome to the President.   There are
therefore a hundred reasons for not choosing to be
burdened with this parasitical dignitary.   But all this
seemed a smaller disadvantage than bringing the
electoral machine into action again.   The Vice-President, to use Bonaparte's celebrated expression, was a kind
of " fatted pig," an occupation had to be found for him,
and his political nonentity was masked by giving him
the Presidency of the Senate with nothing but a casting
vote.[1]

Contrast with this state of things the constitutions
formed by Girondins and Jacobins a few years later in
France.   Under their rule purposely multiplied elections
and almost daily *plébiscites* became the main characteristics of democracy.   Evidently the fathers of American
independence do not resemble the French members of

---

[1] [" The Vice-President's office is ill-conceived. His only ordinary
function is to act as Chairman of the Senate ; but as he does not
appoint the committees of that House, and has not even a vote
(except a casting vote) in it, this function is of little moment."
Bryce, *American Commonwealth*, i., p. 399, (1st ed.) (D).]

the Constituent Assembly of 1789, nor those of the Convention of 1793; they look like republicans in spite of themselves, revolutionists filled with a reactionary spirit, or, to express it more clearly, anti-democratic democrats.

However this may be the three great powers which are the result of an election in America are appointed for unequal and fixed terms, the House of Representatives for two years, the President for four years, the Senate for six years, and one-third of its members are subject to biennial re-election. As mentioned above, these terms cannot in any case be shortened. The three powers are often the seat of diverging interests and of fluctuating passions, it is impossible but that conflicts between them should be frequent. If any one of these powers should cling obstinately to its own opinion and be in opposition to the others there is no legal way out of the difficulty. Time only puts an end to their authority; and in spite of everything the nation does exist, knows its own mind, and makes its wishes known in extra constitutional ways through the press and by meetings. But all this avails nothing; the power which defies the nation is out of the reach of attack. So the people have to be patient; they have to wait two, three, and even four years for the expiration of the authority by which they have tied their own hands, in face of which their sovereignty is utterly powerless.

Is not this a strangely accommodating democracy?

Here is a still more striking feature connected with the division of authority between the President, the

Senate, and the House of Representatives. The less a power depends on popular suffrage the more liberally the Constitution endows it with authority. The House of Representatives is chosen by direct election in accordance with the most popular system of voting which exists in each State;[1] and, as we have seen, it is this House which has the least influence; the choice of ministers and making of treaties are beyond its sphere. The Senate is about on an equality with it as regards rights of taxation. The President is chosen by indirect election, which is distinctly less democratic than direct election; but the President has far more power than the House of Representatives. In fact, however, the President is chosen in the second election by persons appointed *ad hoc*, which implies imperative instructions on the part of the primary electors, and is virtually a return to direct election. The Senate, on the contrary, is made up of members chosen by the State legislatures, which are bodies chosen for a fixed time and for various objects; therefore these legislatures have not their hands forced as regards the choice of the federal senators, and hence the election remains an indirect election in fact as well as in form. This is the least democratic mode possible of popular election. Now the balance of political power inclines decidedly to the side of the Senate ; a sort of tax has

[1] ["The House of Representatives shall be composed of members chosen every second year by the people of the several States, and the electors in each State shall have the qualifications requisite for electors of the most numerous branch of the State legislature." *Constitution of the United States*, art. 1, s. 2, sub-s. 1 (D).]

been levied on the authority of all the other powers in favour of the Senate.

Observe, therefore, that the gradation of authority is exactly the inverse of what the strict logic of democratic principles would require.

I have spoken of the President, the House of Representatives, and the Senate, but I have not spoken of the federal judiciary. The Supreme Court is nominated by the executive power and not by the people, and, besides, its members are appointed for life and are irremovable. An unexpected consequence of this state of things is, that this power has the last word in the numberless questions which come under its jurisdiction. The sovereign people after a time conquers the other powers, but this Supreme Court almost always remains beyond its reach. For more than twenty or even thirty years twice the *grande mortalis œvi spatium*, it may misuse its authority with impunity, may practically invalidate a law voted by all the other powers, or a policy unanimously accepted by popular opinion. It may nullify a regular diplomatic treaty (as we have seen lately) by refusing to enforce it by judicial sanction, or may lay hands on matters belonging to the sovereignty of the States and federalize them without one's being able to make any effective opposition, for this Court itself determines its own jurisdiction as against the State tribunals. It is one of Blackstone's maxims that in every constitution a power exists which controls without being controlled, and whose decisions are supreme. This power is represented in the United States by a small oligarchy of nine irremovable judges. I do not know of any more

striking political paradox than this supremacy of a non-
elected power in a democracy reputed to be of the
extreme type.   It is a power which is only renewed
from generation to generation in the midst of a
peculiarly unstable and constantly changing state of
things—a power which in strictness could, by virtue of
an authority now out of date, perpetuate the prejudices
of a past age, and actually defy the changed spirit of
the nation even in political matters.[1]

It is well known that Chief Justice Marshall, the
fourth head of the Supreme Court, remained in office
for thirty-five years !

Section viii

LET me not be misunderstood as to the spirit which
pervades the Constitution of the United States and
marks its character so strongly. I do not consider that
it arises from the anti-democratic prejudices of which
we have traced the existence amongst the makers of
the Constitution : it has its chief source elsewhere.
The members of the Convention of Philadelphia, as
conservatives, were certainly somewhat alarmed when-

---

[1] [For a somewhat different estimate of the power exercised by
the Supreme Court see Bryce, *American Commonwealth*, i.,
cap. 24, pp. 348—368 (1st ed.) (D).]

ever, in the course of their work, the question of popular government was raised, and it may have been rather against their will that they introduced the democratic principle into their Constitution. But for the work in which they were engaged the question of upholding this principle, or rejecting it, was not a vital one ; it was not in their eyes a fundamental principle nor a governing or dominant idea. The idea of forming a strong democracy under wise discipline, which would be rendered innocuous by astute precautionary measures, was only a secondary and passing feature in a plan of which the dominant lines were determined by considerations of another kind.

The members of the Convention had a double and contradictory object in view : they wished to create a common nationality, so that the United States in the eyes of foreign countries should seem to be a solid and united people kept well in hand by its government; and at the same time they wished to maintain almost untouched the independence of the separate States, which were called upon to enter into the federal organization and endow the central government with certain powers deducted from the sovereignty of the States.

The immense majority of the Convention never ceased to conceive of the Union as a nation of *States* and not as a nation of *individuals*. The individual citizen was, so to speak, put aside. The rights of the man and the citizen, which are the bases of a democracy, were no factor in the formula of the equation which the Convention intended to solve. The only two unknown quantities which they tried to find were : the share of power to be given to the municipal authorities of the States, and the share of power to be given to the federal authority. If any question came up at all analogous to inquiries about the rights of the man and the citizen, it arose because of the absolute necessity that the central power, in order not to be an empty name, should have the means of exacting direct obedience from the citizens in matters under its own control, without interfering with the general rights of sovereignty, which each State meant to preserve over its own inhabitants. This is how it happened that we find certain rights of individuals defined in the Constitution, otherwise the question would never have been mooted ; it only presented itself indirectly. I have shown above that, in the same way, the amendments which preserve the liberties of individuals, are guarantees given to the States in the persons of their citizens rather than to the citizens themselves. It is important not to lose sight of the tendency and the scope of the ideas by which the members of the Convention were guided, otherwise we should get a false and incomplete notion of the Constitution which they worked out under such very special and peculiar influences.

Everything for instance, that concerns the composition of the Senate, its formation and its attributes, betrays the handiwork not of timid conservatives, but of statesmen anxious to preserve State rights. The smaller States were the chief authors of the organization of the Senate. They saw very well that everything which was given to popular suffrage would really be given to numbers, and would turn to the advantage of the larger States. In an elected Parliament, whether chosen by universal or even by a limited suffrage, in which representation was in proportion to numbers, the States, with large territories and dense population, were sure within the sphere of the federal authority to gain at least as much in credit and in influence as they gave up by the surrender of their own sovereignty. The less populous States had no hope of any such compensation. They therefore showed extraordinary tenacity in enacting that equality of representation between great and small States should be kept up, in one at least of the two Houses of Congress. Each State, whatever its area and its population, had two representatives in the Senate; and this was considered so essential a provision, that it was put not only into the Constitution but outside and above its authority.[1] This provision holds a perfectly unique position; it cannot be modified by the ordinary means of constitutional revision, and to raise any question about the article which enacts it would involve the dissolution of the Federal compact.

As a matter of course the smaller States made every effort to develop the powers of the body in which they were represented, quite out of proportion to their size and population. Their efforts were successful because they were fighting for their very lives with all the strength given by the instinct of self-preservation, while the larger States were fighting only for preponderance and influence. The large share of power and the manifold rights which devolved upon the American

---

[1] ["No State without its consent shall be deprived of its equal suffrage in the Senate." *Constitution of U.S.*, Art. V. (D).]

Senate were not therefore in theory a tribute to the conservative spirit and to the superior cultivation which is supposed to belong to a political assembly elected by a system of indirect election. These powers were above all a guarantee to be exercised for the benefit of the smaller and middle-sized States—by the Assembly in which their opinion had as much weight as that of the larger States. The disproportionate privileges of the Senate were rather a safeguard for the quasi-international equality of the independent sovereignties which formed the federal union than a bulwark against the effects of democratic equality.

I must further remark that the principle of State sovereignty, then so powerful, must have operated in the same direction as the anti-democratic influence. Constituencies in which every man should have the suffrage—down to the poor man whose changing home is wherever he gets the highest wages, and the emigrant who, coming from a distance, has never known any government but the Federal government, who has never had time to share the special life of the State where fate had cast him—such constituencies would have had much less chance of resisting the current towards centralization than those made up of landholders or tax-payers, who were attached to the State in which they lived by their property or by vested interests. These are the causes which kept up a limited suffrage for so long in America; the maintenance of a limited suffrage yielded in the end to causes to the consideration of which I shall shortly return.

Similarly, in choosing the Senators, we find indirect

election by the State legislatures was preferred to indirect election by voters chosen *ad hoc*, and even more to direct election. The reason is that the belief in State rights, whilst exercising an uncertain and feeble influence on the primary electoral bodies of each State, became in the State legislature a corporate, organized, and conscious force, and was therefore certain to impress its influence strongly upon the two Senators elected by the vote of the State legislature.

Section ix

WHERE then is the democratic spirit to be found in this democracy ?   This spirit is much less evident in the Federal Constitution than in the State constitutions. They show its influence more and more from day to day, and in them it must be studied, for these constitutions are an integral part, and, in one sense, the basis of the whole political system of the United States. Here, too, democracy presents characteristics which it does not possess elsewhere.

In the first place these characteristics depend on a difference in previous conditions. Everywhere in Europe democracy was obliged to dispossess or destroy an aristocracy in order to make a place for itself ; in the United States the place was vacant, and could be occupied without a struggle. The elements out of which a hereditary and privileged class is formed never have existed at any time in America. A political aristocracy must necessarily be the outcome either of a military caste, or of a class of large land-holders, or of a middle-class enriched by trade. A military caste may grow up in a nation surrounded by other warlike nations, ready to conquer or subdue it, but has no chance of coming into existence in a country where the superior race meets no rivals except a few savage tribes, easily driven off the territory. A class of large land-holders exercising seigniorial rights may grow up on a limited territory, where the new comers, not being conquerors, are obliged, in order to have a share of the land and its fruits, to accept conditions from the first occupiers. In America, what bait could a landed nobility have held out to emigrants in order to induce them to accept the place of dependants? By what bonds could a nobility have kept them in a state of vassalage? The emigrants had only to go a few miles further off into the region of free lands to escape from these older settlers, and become in their turn free owners of the soil. An industrial and commercial upper middle-class cannot maintain itself in the position of an hereditary and privileged body except in a country where, in consequence of almost all the available sources of wealth being used up or appropriated, the formation of fortunes is necessarily slow, and where the supremacy of old families which have got the start of the newer ones is easily maintained, simply by the careful management, and the regular hereditary transmission, of the family property. This is the very opposite of what took place in America. There a mass of unused wealth offered itself as a prize to individual enterprise. In a given time acquisition of property made many more rich people than the preservation of it, and speculation easily and far outran thrift. How could a plutocracy, swamped by this enormous and perpetual influx of new-born elements, keep itself in the position of a distinct and stable class ?

The natural elements of a patriciate were lacking, and there existed none of the ordinary reasons why legislation should create an artificial patriciate. When a superabundant population which wants to live and enjoy life is imprisoned in a narrow space where all places are occupied, and threatens to upset everything in order to get its share of wealth, naturally something must be done to keep it within bounds. For a time legislators disarm and disconcert revolutionists by maintaining political inequality ; American legislators had no temptation to take this course. In that country order and peace seemed sufficiently provided for by the ease with which the needy classes could, instead of struggling for their share of the land with people already in possession, expand into those vast tracts of land which were without owners.

Democracy in America was therefore the first and original form, and the natural and necessary type, of political society. From the very earliest time, when the nucleus formed by European emigrants was large enough to have nothing to fear from the Indians, and sufficiently provided with implements to undertake the colonization of the Western regions, it was clear that the definite conditions of national development were all present, and the prevalence of a pure democracy in the States became a certainty. It prevailed there without a conflict; it was founded without destroying anything, and has existed without any admixture of non-democratic elements.[1]

What a contrast this is to the French democracy, the last transformation of a society which had existed for centuries under an aristocratic organization! Democracy in France bears the marks of the " struggle for existence " which it underwent; a hard struggle in which it would have succumbed had it not been upheld by a rooted faith in democratic doctrines, and had it not been intoxicated with the wine of metaphysical abstractions. This was a terrible struggle indeed, rousing fearful passions, causing acts of blood, leaving memories of

[1] The only political aristocracy that ever existed in the United States, viz. the picked body of Virginian families, which directed the destinies of the Union for forty years, was an exceptional phenomenon, and did not last long. This picked body acquired a sort of moral title to political power from the following sources:— the hereditary qualities of the English gentry, whence it sprang; the large and easy way of life encouraged by the possession of slaves ; the high rank taken by Virginia (which was the most densely populated and the most powerful of the States up to the beginning of the present century) ; and the preponderant and glorious part which Washington's country had taken in the War of Independence. All this moral supremacy disappeared very quickly when the Northern States, increased by the immigration of large masses, took the upper hand and began to weigh down the scales of the Union by the weight of increasing population, while, at the same time, the recollection of the great struggle at the end of the eighteenth century lost some of its vividness.

unpardonable crimes—a struggle without a decisive conclusion—a struggle in which, in spite of the prestige given by victory, the conquerors were not able to destroy everything they hated; whence many incongrous and inconsistent remains, both good and bad, of the previous *régime*, are still to be found in the new organization of society.

In the United States nothing of this kind happened. Democracy is not there clothed in any of the more ancient political forms, because democracy is the beginning of everything. It came into existence peacefully, in a world without a past. It arose spontaneously, and arose out of a few simple physical and social necessities, which almost from the very first were definite and fixed. It has no history behind it : it never allowed itself the luxury of a philosophical theory. It has remained eminently realistic, strictly practical; and, on this account, it is perhaps farther removed from the French democracy than is any European constitutional monarchy which has been touched by the breath of the heroism and the idealism of the French Revolution.

Let us, if possible, define more closely the leading cause which has fixed the character of American society.

We have only to cast an eye over this immense zone (eighteen times larger than is the area of France) in which there are at least fifty millions of inhabitants, unequally distributed, in order to understand that their one primary and predominant object is to cultivate and populate these prairies, forests, and vast waste lands.

The striking and peculiar characteristic of American society is, that it is not so much a democracy as a huge commercial company for the discovery, cultivation, and capitalization of its enormous territory. Because Frenchmen have not thoroughly grasped this fundamental characteristic, and have not constantly kept it in mind, they are stopped at every turn, they are apt to fall into misunderstandings, they are constantly puzzled, and they draw false and specious conclusions from secondary or contingent causes.

The United States are primarily a commercial society (*société economique*) and only secondarily a nation (*société politique*). This is the formula which gives the key to many an enigma, and which removes many an apparent contradiction. Why, for instance, is custom and law in America so indulgent to bankrupts? What is the meaning of the articles in some State Constitutions enjoining the legislature to make exceptionally liberal provisions in favour of debtors? The meaning is plain enough : it is that in America the spirit of enterprise, pushed to the extent of speculation, is an indispensable agent of progress. Americans are afraid that energetic men would lose their " go " if they had hanging over them a severe penalty for every commercial mistake, and if they had to look forward to bearing the burden of disrepute and discredit for a length of time after the first failure. Again, what is the explanation of this curious institution of the homestead, this little piece of family property which cannot be taken in execution. It is, clearly, to provide the unsuccessful settler, who is a victim of ill luck, with a safe shelter in which he can have peace and quiet and prepare himself for fresh struggles.[1]

It is quite evident that the system best adapted to a society of this kind is a republic in which all the powers of the State are elective; a democracy which gives no legal advantage to classes which have risen from the ranks over those who are still rising. This form of government opens an immense vista of fortune and power to the independent and energetic men who are the first and indispensable workers in the unlimited field of adventure.

The American republic besides was in the peculiar condition of not having sufficient native population to supply the necessary number of labourers; they had to be brought in from outside. This need had a good deal to do with the very liberal[2] and very democratic legislation which the States from all times have repeatedly put forward with lavish ostentation, especially in the Declarations of Rights at the head of their constitutions. What, for example, is the meaning of the almost universal and very emphatic proclamation of religious liberty, for which many of the colonies seemed hardly prepared by their origin and their early practices? It is, I admit, the spirit of the eighteenth century which

---

[1] Not only his farm and his hired cattle, but even his furniture and his library are protected from execution. (Baldwin.)

[2] It is curious that one of the grievances put forward in the Declaration of Independence is, that the King tried to prevent the increase of population of the States by putting obstacles in the way of the laws for the naturalization of foreigners, by refusing to make other laws to encourage emigration, and by making the conditions for acquiring new land more difficult.

showed itself in these professions of toleration. But it is something more besides. Whether by instinct, or with clear consciousness of what they were doing, the Americans bethought themselves that religious intolerance, or even any favour openly given by law to a particular creed, would be as good as closing the door on emigration—this emigration from all quarters of the globe, which was landing promiscuously on the same coast of America, Anglicans, Lutherans, Catholics, Presbyterians, Unitarians, Quakers, all of them equally determined to hold to their faith and to their own form of worship. It was for the sake of these emigrants that the formulas of the ancient British liberties were repeated, solemnly and sonorously in every State, and surrounded with the prestige and authority due to Constitutional Law. At bottom the tacit guarantee of the common law was fully as efficacious as these pompous declarations. What was the good of trying for anything better than "liberty as it is in England"? But it was only the English emigrants who knew this by experience. Something more was needed, more startling promises were necessary, for the races who were less well prepared.

The same influence betrays itself in the way in which most of the States adopted universal suffrage, and gradually applied the system of election to most of the public offices. A curious document shows us in what spirit, and with what expectations, even before the Union, a clear-sighted statesman contemplated the extension of the suffrage to all the citizens. This is what Penn wrote in the instructions which he had distributed over all Europe at the end of the seventeenth century :—

" The emigrants will be considered as real inhabitants. They will have the right of voting, not only for the election of the magistrates of the place in which they live, but also for the members of the Provincial Council and the General Assembly, which two bodies, conjointly with the governor, form the sovereign power. And what is far more important, they may be *elected* to any sort of office if the community of the place where they live considers them suitable for it, and this of whatever nation or religion they may be." [1]

This is exactly the alluring tone of a mercantile prospectus. The legislative changes which everywhere brought in universal suffrage, between 1830 and 1850, come in part from the business-like calculation which inspired Penn in the declarations we have just quoted. Equality before the ballot-box has been a real premium on immigration.

I need hardly say that universal suffrage began in

[1] [See the instructions in French, cited by Laboulaye, *Histoire Politique des États-Unis*, i. p. 356, and compare the following statements in Penn's *Brief Account of the Province of Pennsylvania*, &c., p. 6, published in 1681 :—

"VII. Of the Government.

" 1st. The *Governour* and *Freeholders* have the power of *making* laws, so that no Law can be made, nor money raised, *But by the People's consent.*

" 2ly. That the *Rights* of the People of *England* are in force there.

" 3ly. That making no law against *Allegiance*, they may make all laws requisite for the Prosperity and Security of the *said Province*." (D.)]

the less populous States, those of the West. These
States more than the others felt the urgent necessity of
not discouraging emigrants by the prospect of their
remaining for a long time politically inferior to the
older inhabitants. One State having taken the initiative, all the others were compelled to follow if they did
not wish to see the current of immigration turn aside
to more hospitable countries, and to find that the
equilibrium of influence in the House of Representatives, where representation is in proportion to numbers,
was upset to their disadvantage. It is noteworthy that
the States which tried hardest to resist the current
were chiefly the oldest :[1] Massachusetts, Rhode Island,
Connecticut, Pennsylvania, and Georgia, countries which
even in 1830 were already densely populated, and where
such an enormous amount of capital had been accumulated for years that emigrants were attracted without
having more ordinary baits held out to them.

Many of the legislatures have shown themselves so
anxious not to keep the emigrant waiting, and not to
make him go through an inconvenient stage, that they
have been ready to dispense with naturalization in the
United States, because it would have caused too much
delay. They have admitted him to the electoral body
of the States at a time when the laws of the Union
shut out emigrants for a long time from citizenship of
the United States.[2] Emigrants only just landed have

[1] Pennsylvania, Massachusetts, Georgia, and Connecticut require
every elector to be a taxpayer. Massachusetts excludes those who
cannot write or read ; Connecticut admits those who can read.

[2] There are *fourteen* States in which the foreigner acquires the
right of voting for the members of the State legislature and

been registered and taken straight from the port, where they were wandering about in search of employment, to the ballot-box ; and here these improvised electors, these *strangers*, have voted not only for representatives of the district in the State legislature, but also for the representatives of the State in the Federal Congress. I think there could not be any more convincing proof than this that extension of the suffrage aimed at had another object besides that of establishing democratic equality among the real citizens.

Statistics confirm this view in a remarkable manner. From 1830 to 1840 we begin to hear of universal suffrage, and between 1840 and 1850 it becomes thoroughly established in all the States. Now, the number of emigrants, which was 68,000 in 1839, after having remained nearly stationary during the eight preceding years, rises gradually to 114,000 in 1845, to 154,000 in 1846, to 235,000 and 266,000 in 1847 and 1848, to over 300,000 in 1849, and finally to 428,000 in 1854—and shows by this ascending scale the sufficiency of the attractions and the success of the arrangements for attracting emigrants.[1]

consequently for members of Congress, simply by declaring that he intends to be naturalized, even though he has never made any regular application for naturalization. Two States stand alone. Massachusetts requires in addition to naturalization a residence of two years, California a lapse of ninety days after naturalization, before making the naturalized foreigner eligible for any office and competent to vote. See Justice M. Strong, *North American Review*, May, 1884, pp. 415, 421. [See Bryce, *American Commonwealth*, ii., pp. 11, 12. (D.)]

[1] In fact this increase coincides with the running of the first Transatlantic steamers in 1838.

Section x

THERE is one more circumstance which must not be forgotten—it is the ever-recurring influence, the counter-shock, so to say, of the great events of the public life of the Federation on the public life of the States.

We have observed that from the beginning, and even in the preliminary discussions on the Constitution, the root of all the difficulties was how to effect a division of power between the sovereignty of the States and the authority of the Federal Government.

In the Convention of Philadelphia there were passionate debates on this vital, essential, I may say unique question, and these debates were only the prelude to the great struggles which the same question continued to raise, even after the Constitution was settled. They have filled the whole history of the United States up to our own days. After the Union was established two great parties sprang up, which have several times changed their names without changing their essence, and which have become, as it were, political contingents enrolled in the service of two opposed political principles. Every American has enrolled himself either as a "republican" or a "democrat," no one has the wish or the power to remain neutral. These are the two parties which control the election of the President, and of the members of Congress ; they throw themselves with extraordinary eagerness into the fray, they leave nothing undone to rally all manner of interests round them, and for this purpose they make use of the patronage of all the federal administrative offices : the victorious party distributes these offices in payment to politicians who have served it. But politicians are difficult to satisfy, and the fund for the payment of partizans, afforded by the places in the gift of the Federal Government, soon proved insufficient. Thereupon the parties were led to lay their hands on the offices in the gift of States governments. To make them serve the purpose better they were all made elective, and the tenure of the offices was made as short as possible. By this means appointments were made constantly renewable so as to be like ready cash in the hands of party managers, and the floating capital of each party's electoral budget could be constantly renewed. Republicans and democrats alike inscribe on the party ticket the names of the candidates for public offices, whether local or federal. The whole list of names is dictated by the same omnipotent party spirit. Calmer and more wholesome municipal interests have had to give way completely to the federal interests. This party action, which has made elections universal and has shortened the terms of office, has inaugurated a fierce democratic spirit which possibly would not have developed so rapidly under purely local influences. Here we have an instance of a curious and unexpected way in which federal influences have acted on State politics. Both the great parties have found it necessary to maintain their war supplies and keep up the fund for paying their electoral army, and therefore both, even the one which professed to protect the sovereignty of the States, have been driven to federalize and democratize the recruiting for the State offices.

However that may be, this state of things differs entirely from what happened in France in 1848. France is essentially a democracy, and is so with all the heat of a religious believer and all the precision of a scholastic logician. She deduces the consequences flowing from her principle of democratic equality, step by step. All her history since 1789 shows that she has been constantly engaged in this abstract speculation, this weighty demonstration, this obstinate pursuit of pure justice. This spirit is continually cropping up in the Declarations of Rights of the revolutionary period, and it shows itself quite as distinctly in the course of action, grounded at once on sentiment and reasoning, which gave birth to the universal suffrage of 1848. The politicians established universal suffrage at a single stroke, and did not reflect or speculate on the effects of such a tremendous and sudden change. They professed to despise the middle class and its petty policy; they felt the need of drawing inspiration from fresher springs of popular feeling. I can hardly describe the sort of brotherly, confiding Christian spirit, in the primitive sense of the expression, which at this period filled the minds of men. Lastly, the establishment of universal suffrage flowed, by a process of invincible logic, from the two principles of the sovereignty of the people, and the equality of civil rights. Logic gave the word of command and it was obeyed. Nothing can be less like a democracy of this type than the United States. In this realm of empiricism principles, however loudly they make themselves heard, however free or independent they seem to be, are always in a great measure subordinate to positive and definite interests. Universal suffrage in America was not simply designed to satisfy a speculative spirit or the demands of natural justice. Its object was chiefly to meet the agricultural, industrial, and commercial needs, of a social organization very different from that of France. The very exceptional economic condition of the American Union, as well as its federal character, must never be forgotten. He who does not keep these facts before his eyes will fall into errors as to the nature of the evolution, and the destiny, of this out-and-out democracy, and also as to the lessons and warnings which he may legitimately draw from the American democracy for the benefit of France.

PART III

THE CONCEPTION OF SOVEREIGNTY
IN FRANCE
AND IN ENGLAND AND IN THE UNITED STATES

PART III

THE CONCEPTION OF SOVEREIGNTY
IN FRANCE
AND IN ENGLAND AND IN THE UNITED STATES [1]

Section i

THE Constitutions of England and of the United States, which are the subject of the two preceding essays, do not appear to lend themselves to comparison, unless the object of the comparison be to bring out the contrasts in the two political organizations. They do indeed differ considerably. The English Constitution is in great part unwritten, that of the United States rests upon a written document. The first is the law of a monarchy, the second the law of a republic; the first is

[1] [This heading is rather an account of the contents of Part III. than a translation of the title affixed to it by Monsr. Boutmy. He entitles this Part " *La Nature de l'Acte Constituant en France, en Angleterre et aux États-Unis.*" The expression " *l'acte constituant* " is a term for which there is no exact English equivalent ; it may be described as "the act whereby the sovereign power in a State creates a constitution." The want of any proper English terminology for expressing this idea is itself a marked illustration of the soundness and importance of the contrast drawn by our author between French and English constitutionalism. (D.)]

unified and imperial, the second is federal. In the relation between Ministry and Parliament, the one upholds the principle of ministerial responsibility, the other the principle of ministerial independence; finally, to go to the bottom of the whole matter, the first is entirely aristocratic in its construction, the second democratic to the very core. My readers may wonder that I should bring together by way of comparison two such apparently opposite types, and the more so because I may be thought to have treated as the antithesis and opposite of them both that French public law which resembles either Constitution in detail, and even in general outline, more than the English and American Constitutions resemble each other. The differences and analogies between the three Constitutions must, however, not be pressed too far; besides, in proportion as democracy spreads its uniformity over all three countries, these differences gradually melt away and disappear. I only keep up the comparison for a moment to deduce the following principle from it: viz. that in order to determine the species of a Constitution, to define it, and class it *per genus et differentiam*, there are factors as important as the imperative provisions which it contains, and as distinctive and specific as the particular amount of equilibrium maintained in the Constitution between the several powers. I refer to forces anterior to the Constitution, which were the source of its existence, and which have brought its very elements together and united them. In other words, some important characteristics of the constitutional law of any country can be gathered at least

as well from a study of the history, the origin, and
the nature of the sovereign power (*acte constituant*),
as from an examination into the relations between the
powers constituted by this sovereign authority. I have
touched on this point more than once in the course of
this work. But the thesis is of so much importance
that doubtless there will be some interest in taking it
up as a conclusion, and in putting it before my readers
in a clearer form, with more unity and connection of
ideas.

Section ii

In France, when the Revolution broke out, all the old
authorities—except the highest—which exercised any
kind of public power—*e.g.*, the nobility, clergy, parliament,
the provincial estates, officers, magistrates in towns, and
parishes; had been, by the very action of the *ancien
régime*, humbled and discredited, dispossessed, or made
powerless. They were like branches of a tree nourished
only by the bark; and there was no object in sparing
this half-dead wood which the sap would never
nourish again. The Revolution rather overthrew these
authorities by its shock than cut them down. Royalty,
deprived of its chief branches, which had withered
under the shadow of its own mighty foliage, was like
a bare trunk standing alone defying the wind, but

ready for the hatchet. It too fell in its turn. Everything therefore had to be planted or sown afresh on this
soil, which had been dug and re-dug, and weeded to ex-
cess, until it was well-nigh exhausted. The whole body
of the people was the only social organization which
remained standing. The people had to create new
powers, so to say, out of nothing—to invent and constitute
a whole new political society. These facts are too well
known to require dwelling upon. I only note this
much : in France every power, every established authority, dates from the revolutionary constitutions—from
them it proceeds, from them it derives its title. In the
case of subordinate officers, their title to authority,
originally inserted in the constitution itself, has been in
later times derived from laws made in virtue of powers
given by the constitution. But the primary source is
the same for both ; neither seek to date their investiture
farther back than the constitution. The only exception
was in the case of royalty in 1814, and rather less clearly
so in 1830. Louis XVIII. flattered himself that he
reigned in virtue of an immemorial right: Louis
Philippe was not in his own eyes an elected king who
owed his crown to a contract between the Chambers
and the younger branch of the Bourbons. But these
two exceptions in some sense confirm the rule, as they
both acted in contradiction to, and as a dissolvent of, the
system to which they belonged. The element which
had a different origin from all the rest was, in the end,
eliminated by violence.

We see the consequences. A day came in history
when France was one single homogeneous mass,

composed of an immense number of small human atoms.
The new groups cut out of this mass could be nothing
at first but bodies arbitrarily created for the convenience
of the government : they were not organic wholes made
by the slow action of long common life. They have all,
except the feeble commune, lasted for less than a
century ; they are all hampered by narrow regulations.
Hence they do not, even to-day, possess that individual
life, I might almost say that consciousness of personality,
which local institutions derive, and derive only, from
long years of existence, and from the moderation or the
neglect, much more than from the favour or the gifts, of
their rulers. They possess, as I said, no individual life.
It is the national life which runs through them, it is the
consciousness of the national spirit, which sustains and
directs their officials. That this is so appears from the
law itself, and is shown by this fact—that until 1838 the
Département had no corporate existence, and that even
now such corporate existence is denied to the *arrondisse-*
ments. The highest authorities in the state have not, any
more than the local authorities, a sense of independent
existence, and have not ever become real " persons."
Born yesterday, they are still bound by a close and
visible tie to the constitution which created them ; they
have not had time to create ways of thinking and
feeling for themselves, and to find in these habits a
stable basis outside the law. The strongest reason for
existence and self-reliance in the case of a collective
body, that which proceeds from the fact of length of
days, could not enter into their being and develop the
instinct for personal rights independent of statutes and

laws. Since 1789 we may say that there have been in
France individuals who were kings, but there has been
no royalty, if by that term we mean to describe a perpetual corporation represented at any given moment by
a single individual, who receives from it something
beyond his own value, his own responsibility, and his
own personal credit. There have been assemblies of
representative individuals under the name of peers,
senators, or deputies, coming together in accordance with
the conditions provided by articles of the constitution,
and finding in their meeting place exactly what they
had brought with them from outside. But there has
been no House of Peers, no Senate, no Chamber of
Deputies, if by these words are meant permanent
bodies possessing a character and spirit of their own,
something of which is communicated to each generation
of their members. These superior authorities are of
but recent date, and have been created by statute ; they
therefore constantly look for support to the law which
created them, and to the people who create the law.
The national will—the will of the whole people—is their
very soul. But this national will is the will of a day
only ; it is now strong and powerful, now nerveless and
languid ; enthusiastically active to-day, to-morrow pas-
sive even unto indolence. This is the reason why at
times these high authorities seem gifted with irresistible
energy, coming from the impulse and the faith of a whole
people, and at other times, on account of the indifference
of the public, seem entirely at the mercy of the weakness and egoism of the individuals of whom they are
composed. Public organization in France is wanting in

the lofty *esprit de corps,* and the comprehensive and admirable self-reliance, exhibited by great corporate bodies existing for partial or special objects, by whom moral life is kept at a constant average level. French organization being so completely national in every pore it follows to their extreme length the oscillations of public spirit.

Section iii

In England the Constitution—I mean by that, the whole of the written or unwritten rules which regulate the exercise of the public powers in all their branches —was never the result of an imperative law passed by a sovereign people creating authorities, so to say, out of nothing, and investing them with fixed powers. The English Constitution is made up out of a long list of bilateral or trilateral acts. These acts are many and varied, they are tacit arrangements, agreements which have been fought out in debate, and solemn compacts made between powers already existing, acknowledged and respected, which were in a sense self-constituted, because they were created by the force of circumstances, and because they claim a title grounded on immemorial

possession. Go back in the history of England as
far as the fourteenth century. We find three powers
standing face to face—the Crown, the Lords, and the
Commons; they are constantly engaged either in
friendly negotiations or in violent opposition. From
year to year they have to rearrange their varying
form, their mobile relations, and their undefined and
unstable balance of power. The two documents generally quoted as the sources of the modern English Constitution, the Declaration of Right of 1689, and the Act
of Settlement of 1701, are but treaties somewhat more
weighty than the others. There is no question of
creating powers—they already exist—nor even of carefully enunciating their attributes—these are already
fixed by custom. The whole object of these famous
documents is to define the limits assigned by custom to
these pre-existing powers on certain points actually in
dispute. The Crown does not owe its authority to
these documents, it is the dynasty only which derives
its title from them. The royal prerogative remains the
prerogative of Henry VIII. and Elizabeth, transmitted
without interruption to their successors; and the new
dynasty simply accepts the order of things, under the
general restrictions of the Common Law, partly confirmed by the Acts which changed the order of
succession to the throne.

To sum up: the great political powers in England are
in no way the creations of a constitution (*pouvoir constituant*), for their existence is anterior to any fundamental law whatever. Their title does not result from
a direct expression of national will promulgated in

express terms and distinct form on a given day, but it is a right originating in actual possession, which has not been contested for centuries. Their foundation is outside any law sanctioned by the seal of national sovereignty; it is therefore outside the Constitution in the sense in which this term is taken in France. And if these extra-constitutional powers look like a part of the Constitution, it is not because they have been made and consecrated by the Constitution, but because the Constitution has been created by them. The Constitution is nothing but the bringing to light of the settlement of frontiers fixed from time to time between these immemorial forces. These forces exist side by side; they perpetually expand, or withdraw their claims to authority, they constantly come into collision with and press upon each other, they make compromises, but they are never at rest.[1]

I have as yet spoken only of the superior powers. The state of the subordinate authorities, local or special, is no less peculiar. These subordinate authorities can generally, as in France, trace back their rights to a definite title granted to them by law at a fixed date; but this original title is so incomplete, and the grant so ancient, that both seem trifling in comparison with the prestige belonging to the fact of ancient possession and customary rights, which constant usage has grafted on to this primary legal basis. National

---

[1] "Of the three powers which exist together, each asserts its own rights but hardly knows their extent. The success of each thus depended on the time, the circumstances, and the king who was on the throne. England owes its existing Constitution to chance." —D'Argenson, *Considerations sur le Gouvernement*, p. 38.

unity in England existed at such an early date, and
the feeling for this unity was so active, in those
earliest times, that the state did not frown upon
these secondary institutions, and even found it advantageous to respect their independent growth, and to
recognize them as the complement of or supplement to
its own somewhat imperfect organization. Thus it was
that the consciousness of a distinct life, and a right
independent of all positive grant, in the long run
developed an immense number of great and small local
and special authorities, such as universities, ecclesiastical corporations, boroughs, parish vestries, and chartered
bodies. Created one by one, each body remained more
or less independent of the others ; not one of them was
content to take rank passively in a co-ordinated whole,
nor to feel itself strictly dependent on an organization,
which was itself subject to the general welfare. Their
past history is so ancient, their origin in some cases so
near the date of the formation of the body politic itself,
they have so completely lost the habit of considering
their immemorial social functions as delegated, they
look upon themselves so naturally and simply as part-
ners and not agents of the state, that an English lawyer
has to reflect seriously, and to philosophize more than is
his wont, before he discovers that these institutions are
really the servants of the state, and that their claims
must give way to considerations of the public good.

My reader will now realize how different all this is from
the state of things in France. In France the nation is a
single mass; in England it is an aggregate. In France
the superior powers have all been created by the

Constitution; in England it is they who daily make and complete the Constitution by the very action of their life, and the natural play of the forces working in them. In France the partial or special groups are all artificial; they make up a regular organized hierarchy, and the powers which rule them derive their rights from the law. In England the partial or special groups, and the powers which rule them, date from far back in the past, and each one for itself derives the most undeniable part of its authority from long possession.

Section iv

I HAVE shown in the preceding essays that in the United States the organization of the federal union ought not to be separated from the interior organization of the different States, and that the two organizations have no complete and precise meaning unless placed side by side. It is well to distinguish them at first, and consider them separately in order to see what the whole body derives from each one. The single States, founded on virgin soil by individuals who, having broken their ties with the old world, found themselves thrown back in some sense on the very origin of political society, were obliged, like the French, to re-organize their local and central authorities from top to bottom. I pointed out that in this respect the State constitutions have

strong analogies with French constitutions. The
Federal Constitution, the only one which I wish to consider here, has a mixed character. It resembles French
constitutions in two points: first, it is based upon an
avowed act of national sovereignty; secondly, all the
federal powers receive their existence and investiture
from this act. Nevertheless, on looking closer we see
that this manifestation of a supposed national will was,
at the outset, only formal and apparent. The name
indeed of the American people appears in the Articles
of the Constitution, but the people is introduced not to
dictate to its statesmen but to receive from their
wisdom, an existence which was destined for a long
period [1] to remain fictitious and to be called in question.
Washington, Jefferson, and Hamilton, were rather the
apologists of a common nationality than its representatives. They were also, and above all, the agents of
several sovereign States. A good number of these
States were more than a century old, some were famous,
each and all incorporated the interests of different
bodies accustomed to act together, and each State was
separated from the other by a powerful and distinct
esprit de corps. I must insist on this important fact.
In the United States it is the American people which
was the artificial element, and, so to speak, created from
above. Here it is not the nation which made the
Constitution, but the Constitution which created the
nation. Effective sovereignty was exercised by the
several States which were then the only living force. In

---

[1] [Compare in confirmation of this view Bryce, *American
Commonwealth*, i., p. 16, 1st ed. (D).]

every line of the Constitution, we see the States trying to take back in detail what they had granted wholesale to the national element. They dispute and cavil over every clause, they are supported throughout the course of these debates over small details by an immense force of popular feeling. The Constitution of 1787—89 left the separate States standing side by side with the federal powers which it created. The States have each continued to live their own separate life; they look with suspicion upon one another and group themselves into rival factions. The States, by an act of prudent self-abnegation, created a superior authority, and the rival factions, have each in their turn, either used it as a means for securing their own domination, or look upon it as a rock of offence. The political history of the United States for more than half a century is almost entirely the the story of a struggle, full of incidents, between these great organized powers, which existed before the Constitution and up to a certain point independently of it. Nowadays a long common life has strengthened the feeling of national unity. The War of Secession has raised, emboldened, and exalted the federal power. But up to 1860, we may say that the Constitution, except in appearance, and in the sight of foreign nations, scarcely upheld the unity and sovereignty of the American nation. The States had existed so long before the Constitution that they were not willing to acknowledge its paramount authority, and but too often they used the organs of national authority which they had created as instruments ready at hand for the promotion of their own objects.

Section v

FROM all that I have said in the preceding pages, we can now define the precise sense and substance of the word "constitution" in the three countries. The type of a French constitution is an imperative law promulgated by the nation calling up the hierarchy of political powers out of chaos and organizing them. The English Constitution is essentially a compact between a small number of ancient corporations—legal persons—who are immemorial depositaries of a part of the public power. The Federal Constitution of the United States is in form an imperative law carrying out the organization and fixing the attributes of the central and superior powers; in this point it can be classed with the French constitutions. But this law rests on a treaty between several distinct and sovereign political bodies, uniting to create, and at the same time to limit, the power of the nation.

The consequences of the differences and resemblances brought out by these three definitions are numerous. Several have been noticed in the course of this volume. I shall here recapitulate those only which affect the conception of sovereignty. The foundations of sovereignty, its essence, its limits, its organization, as well as the form and spirit of the documents which proclaim it, are points on which, up to this day, the Anglo-Saxon Constitutions present special characteristics. In these points I may add their likeness to each other is less striking than the contrasts they each offer to the numerous monuments of French public law.

In France, since 1789, the nation considered as an indivisible whole, has been the only existing corporate body animated by a really powerful spirit of life. And within the nation there has been and is nothing solid and stable but individuals. For it was necessary to find a solid foundation on which the state could rest, and to dig deep to clear away the rubbish left by the crumbling edifices of the ancient political bodies. The determination of individual rights is then the first and principal question which came before the French legislator; all French political history gives evidence of its priority and pre-eminence. From this question we have derived a very simple and very precise conception of sovereignty. The nation, for reasons which have been explained, cannot, in France, be anything but the whole body of citizens. Theoretically, sovereignty is the will of all the citizens, and practically it comes to be the will of the numerical majority. In France, since 1789, this majority has been in fact the sole and necessary source of all legitimate authority. The existing powers are all creations of this majority, and all are based on the constitution which is its work. Any power which is suspected of not representing it, or of misrepresenting it, loses in a sense, its justification for existence, and is marked out by this want of harmony for immediate destruction or transformation. There is no fulcrum *outside* the majority, and therefore there is nothing on which, as *against* the majority resistance or lengthened opposition can lean. This is why all French political systems always gravitate automatically and rapidly towards unity and homogeneity of powers. The progress of enlightenment and of wisdom are the only resources against this kind of instinct inherent in French institutions. In fact there is no internal and spontaneous action which could be roused in these institutions to oppose the strong current which carries them on in their accustomed path.

In England, all the foreground of the political scene is occupied by ancient corporate bodies, national or local, which, on account of their greatness and their cohesion, have secured a basis of their own within the body of the nation, halfway between the individual and the state. Almost up to our own times the English nation has never conceived of itself as independent or distinct from these bodies. Sovereignty belonged now to the Crown, now to the Lords, now to the Commons, and because it was attracted by each of these permanent and powerful bodies in turn, it was never ascribed to the whole collective body of individual citizens. In English constitutional law up to a very recent time, the word "people" did not mean the whole body of persons making up the British State, it was an accepted equivalent for the three great sovereign powers taken together, viz., King, Lords, and Commons. Compared to these great and permanent powers, the changing and insignificant body of citizens sinks to nothing. In the eye of the English Constitution the citizens as individuals do not attain to political rights, such rights are vested in the three members of the sovereign body, or in corporations as old and independent. The House of Commons, for instance, at the outset certainly represented some hundreds of corporate bodies (*personnes morales*), counties,[1] towns, boroughs, and later the universities. The original sense of the word "commons," according to a plausible etymology, is communities, corporate bodies, and not, as we might easily suppose, the common people. These corporate bodies have remained, almost up to the present day, the only persons really entitled to the electoral power. A few individuals have been empowered to vote on their behalf. But the law has taken little cognizance of these individual voters, has scarcely cared to know who they are, and still less to decide who they ought to be. In all boroughs it is local custom which has till recent times decided[2] who are to be the voters. The legal idea of the citizen as a man, who as such is entitled to certain political rights, was for the first time partially recognized in 1832. Up to that date this idea was not so much misapprehended by, as actually unknown to, English law. The entrance on the political scene of citizens as such was at first hardly noticed, but certainly was, on account of its present no less than of its future results, the great political event of the century in England. The Ballot Act, and the statutes against bribery, passed in order to keep the citizen free and uncorrupted in the exercise of his public duty, show that his existence is at last recognized, that he has emerged from the ranks of the corporate bodies, and that he has forced himself on public

---

[1] [A county is not in strictness a corporate body, but is a *personne morale* in the sense in which the term is here used. (D).]

[2] [This is now determined by statute. (D).]

attention, and has become a person known to the law.
Before these Acts were passed, corruption and intimida-
tion were considered to be the private concern of the
local body invested with the franchise, and public opinion
encouraged the non-interference of Parliament ;[1] so true
was it that the ultimate elements of the electorate
seemed to be not the individual citizens but the local
bodies or corporations   Even to-day the opposition and
competition between the two ideas shows itself by a
marked distinction between the reform Acts which
define the qualifications of voters, and the redistribution
Acts which carefully distribute the representative power
between the electoral bodies.   In 1832, in 1867, and
even in 1884, the redistribution of seats excited more
passion, and was thought of more consequence, than the
qualification of voters.   This shows how difficult it
was for the English public to recognize and admit the
idea of political rights belonging to all citizens as individuals.   Mr. Gladstone's Acts,[2] affecting as they do
both the extension of the franchise and the distribution of
seats, has for the future put an end to the interest, or at
least the importance, of the distinction between the two.
In these Acts the individual triumphs, and the historical
bodies are dissolved, by means of the introduction of

[1] [Parliament has from a period long preceding the Reform Act
of 1832, treated corrupt practices as offences (see Blackstone's
Commentaries, i., pp. 178, 179).   What Monsr. Boutmy no doubt
refers to, is the recognised existence of (so-called) rotten boroughs.
(D).]

[2] [See the Representation of the People Act, 1884, 48 Vict. c. 3,
and the Redistribution of Seats Act, 1885, 48 & 49 Vict.
c. 23 (D.)]

districts mapped out in proportion to the number of the electors. According to all appearance the English electoral system is rapidly verging towards the French type.

In the United States the idea of political duties and rights inherent in the individual and citizen has long been familiar to the law; the State Constitutions clearly prove this. It was not therefore for want of recognizing the importance of the electoral franchise, but of set purpose, that the Convention of Phila- delphia left it outside the national compact of 1787. I have noticed in the preceding pages the sense and the exact bearing of the Declaration of Rights formed by the first constitutional amendments. I will recapitulate two points only of this analysis : the first, that these amendments are directed against the federal power alone, and do not in themselves bind the separate States ; the second, that the amendments give guarantees and means of protection to the individual, but do not give him the means of asserting political rights. As to active political rights, the Federal Constitution assures their possession only to the ancient sovereign bodies known as States. The only possessors of active political rights, according to the Federal Constitution, are the States. Citizens as individuals have no share in the sovereign authority. To give one proof only, and that a very striking one, I remind my readers that there are in strictness, under the working of the Federal Constitution, no federal electors. The central power does not go down to matters so fundamental as the question of franchise. It distributes a certain share of electoral representation to each State, and then each State decides, according to its own pleasure under a single slight restriction[1], who are to be the persons qualified to choose its representatives in Congress, and its presidential electors.[2]

The principle that political rights are a personal attribute of the individual citizen, leads necessarily to the consequence that the will of the majority of the citizens is sovereign. Now the chief article of the Constitution concerning the composition of the Senate completely contradicts this latter principle. All the States, however unequal the number of their population, are each represented by two members in the Senate. There we have equality among the States but not among the citizens. The presidential election itself, which the convention of 1787 had intended to reserve to the nation and to the majority, was recovered by the States. Nowadays it is the regular rule that in each State the voting for the presidential electors takes place not in separate districts, but in the mass and by "general ticket," and these presidential electors make up the college called upon to choose the President of the Union. The candidate who gets a majority even of a few hundred votes in the hundreds of thousands of voters in any State—as was once the case at New York—gets the whole vote of that

[1] *Constitution of U.S.*, Art. i., s., ii.

[2] Even since the Fifteenth Amendment the States have been left at liberty to create electoral inequalities between citizens of the United States so that they do not depend on race or colour.

State.   Thus at every election it is a majority of States
rather than a majority of voters which decides the
victory.   This is so distinctly the fact, that Presidents
have been actually elected (when there were more than
two candidates) who might not possess anything
approaching to an absolute majority of the popular
vote ; and some were positively elected when it was
clearly proved that they had a minority of the popular
vote, as against their sole and defeated competitor.
Here we find ourselves confronted by a peculiar conception of sovereignty and of political rights.   In the
sphere of the Federal Constitution there are no political rights (*droits politiques actifs*) belonging to the
citizens as such, there is only the right to representation divided among corporate bodies, *i.e.* the States.[1]
This is as it is in England, but for different reasons.
In the same sphere the formula of sovereignty is a
mixed one ; the supreme power does not belong solely
to the numerical majority of individuals, it belongs also,
and in greater part, to the numerical majority of
thirty-eight powerful corporate bodies.   The States,
and not the individual citizens, are the real members
of the state, the integrant parts and organic elements,
as it were, of the body politic.

[1] [The House of Representatives, however, does represent the
people. (D.)]

Section vi

I SHOULD exceed the limits of a mere summary, if I
followed out the chain of reasoning which I have begun
to the very end.   I must allow myself, however, to
call attention to one or two more points in regard
to the Constitutions of each of the three countries—
points which have reference to the scope and objects
of the sovereign power, to the spirit of the constitution,
to its structure, and to its mode of growth.

We have noticed that in France the political
equation, so to speak, consists of two terms only, the
individual and the state, the infinitely small and the
infinitely great.   There is nothing between these two
to attract attention.   No coherent, solid, and well-tried
organization gives consistency to any considerable
interests, whether local or special.   The local or special
groups of yesterday's growth are mere meeting places
used by individuals for certain transactions of public
life : they are lifeless figures, and not persons gifted with
a consciousness and will of their own.   The superior
paramount interest of the nation stands face to face
with the paltry selfishness of each individual citizen.
The prodigious inequality in value between the only
two living elements of political society produces this
result.   The philosopher, gazing down from the dream-
like heights of public power upon the crowd of
human atoms, necessarily feels that he has the right

to dispose of them despotically without much caring to humour their prejudices. French constitutions further appeal to a people brought back to the indefinite state of nature by the fall of their historical institutions, and gifted anew with an extraordinary plasticity by the ruin of the strong old framework which held the citizens together in fixed compact aggregates. Our philosopher must feel that he has more than enough power to stir up these heaps of human atoms according to his fancy, to bind them together, or to divide them in different ways—in fact to mould them into what he happens to think the best form. In his mind, therefore, there exists a virtually perfect combination of absolute might and absolute right. He needs to make a great effort of reason to prevent dreams from appearing to him easily attainable realities, and it is difficult for him to remember that, among the infinite number of combinations which seem to lie at his disposal, he can hardly expect to find that one which is destined to realize the dream of absolute justice combined with universal happiness. Hence profound idealism and unmistakable optimism are fundamental characteristics of the constitutional creations of the French nation. We find in these creations noble, large, and humane inspirations, which seem to disappear at certain periods of reaction, but which reappear with that sudden power of rejuvenescence of which the French have the secret. This was very noticeable in 1848. But this combination of idealism and optimism naturally increases the ambition, and encourages the presumption, of the state. The state is not sufficiently afraid of summary and authoritative proceedings, and readily inclines towards socialism.

Here we come within view of the fundamental paradox which lies concealed in the constitutional law of France. I have shown above what an important place the individual citizen holds in it. When analysed to its very source sovereignty rests on the individual alone ; public power has authority only because the individual gives up a part of his natural liberty, supposed to be unlimited, and of which he can keep as much as seems good to him. Hence no constitutions abound so much as those of France in decided and emphatic assertions as to the rights of individual citizens. The chief leaning of the French constitution-makers is all in this direction. In this lies their merit and their glory. Whatever criticism may be passed on the Declaration of Rights of 1789, the fact will always remain that the resounding fame of these memorable axioms has rendered this great service to the world, viz., that the principles of liberty and equal justice for all, up to that time locked up in maxims of philosophers and aphorisms of society, became thenceforth indispensable articles of all constitutional legislation. Even those who violated these principles have, from that day forward, been compelled to pay them hypocritical respect, as the homage that vice renders to virtue. But this zeal for individual liberty is only the first of two tendencies. After the state has been created by the will of all these human atoms, a second tendency in the opposite direction becomes apparent. This Leviathan —the state (or rather those who act in its name)—

begins to be conscious of the greatness of its strength in comparison to the weakness of everything that surrounds it; of duties in proportion to this power, and of rights co-extensive with the duties. It tries instinctively to have an aim and an object worthy of the enormous means at its disposal; the idea of a "supreme social good" takes hold of the commonwealth and brings along with it the absolute right of the state (*la raison d'État*). The rights of the individual, the first thesis of the constitution, and the recognized source of all legitimate power, too often fade away during the supremacy of this second tendency, and sink to nothing before this despotic ideal. The intemperance of Parliament and of the public powers in making laws and regulations, the existence and the exaggerated activity of the special administrative courts in which the state appears both as judge and party, are two facts which show most clearly this tendency to hold private interests and liberties of slight account, and to set up a conscientious despotism of public interests. England, and, in the federal sphere, the United States, have suffered less than France from the first of these evils; they have escaped the second altogether.

In these two countries the importance and prestige of the great corporate bodies who preceded and created their Constitutions has been the cause of their never having experienced this shock of opposition between the state and the individual, this uninterrupted oscillation which alternately raises and gives predominance, now to the rights of the individual, and now to the high mission of the state. Another problem, that of keeping

up a balance between the pre-existing powers, has kept
the attention of the makers of the Constitution in a
region of compromise and moderation, and has pre-
vented them from gliding down the slope which leads
to one of two extremes, *viz.* individual license or state
despotism.   Definitions and comparisons must not be
pressed too far ; nevertheless, one of those which I have
suggested above elucidates in a rather striking manner
this capital characteristic of the Anglo-Saxon public
law.   I have shown that the two Anglo-Saxon Constitutions, if they are not really treaties, yet contain
treaties which are an essential part of them, and that
from this fact they derive their most important features.
Now, the object of a treaty between living powers is
always to give securities to each other.   It may happen
that they both fall under a predominant power which
absorbs them, but it is never the object of a treaty to
create such a power ; the most in this respect that parties
to a treaty can propose to themselves (and this is what
happened in the United States) is to create an arbitrator
with limited authority, who may preserve harmony
between the parties.   Absolute justice introduced into
a treaty would only be baffled or violated by the rival
interests of the parties : the perfection of a treaty,
therefore, is not to be an embodiment of ideal justice,
but to express with accuracy, and to consolidate an
effectual balance of power between the contracting
parties.   The maintenance of the *status quo*, a nicely
adapted compromise, is the highest aim that a treaty
can have.   The idea of a supreme social good is quite
foreign to it.   Narrow, but lucid realism, calm satis-

faction or aquiescence in the arrangements of daily life, dislike to great schemes, to heroic remedies and actions, are naturally destructive of a somewhat complex equilibrium : these are the characteristics common to both the Anglo-Saxon Constitutions.

In France, constitution makers (*nos constituants*) saw nothing but the human monads which, looked at from afar, lost their differences of kind as well as of degree. Hence they were led to treat them as equal and similar, *i.e.* as abstractions by their very nature amenable to very general principles. Consequently principles hold a very important place in French public law. In the next place, a circumstance connected with the exercise of national sovereignty (*l'acte constituant*), which is peculiar to France is, that no fabric based on history occupies the ground, and that in the midst of the site to be covered there no longer stands any part of the old edifice, which may hamper the arrangement and complicate the plan of the new construction. The authors of the French constitutions, therefore, have been in the position of an architect about to erect a monument in the centre of a public square—they have a free and clear space at their disposal. How could they escape the temptation of erecting perfectly symmetrical constructions of which all the parts are linked together and radiate from a very few centres? Naturally they would expect that such an edifice, simple, elegant, imposing from the harmony of the whole, and the perfection of detail, would carry prestige with it, and last for centuries. These characteristics are in fact guarantees of solidity, though not the most secure ones ;

they appeal only to the reasoning powers.   But after all
it is wise to have recourse to them when one is deprived
of the other guarantees derived from custom.   French
constitution makers, therefore, have done the work of
logicians, engineers, and artists.   Logic is the soul of
their creations.   Finally, as all the ancient powers were
destroyed or hated, it was impossible to fall back upon
their practice or refer to their precedents for anything
which was not provided for by express rule.   It was
thought necessary to *enunciate everything* afresh, and
to fix everything in conformity with principle.   This is
why the Articles of the earlier French Constitutions aim
at being encyclopedic as well as systematic.   And ever
since the public law of France, following this precedent,
has continued to be inordinately explicit and scrupu-
lously literal.   There is a maxim which has remained
true under all the successive *régimes* in France, viz.,
that all rights must be recorded in writing; that no
right can come into existence without a document to
attest it, or be annulled without express abolition.
There is no country where the feeling for customary law
is more blunted than in France, or where the virtue of
leaving things to be understood is less appreciated.
Nor is there any country where there is a greater dislike
to the idea of an equity (*droit prétorien*), which, while
preserving the form, changes the substance of written
law.

It is due to the nature of sovereignty (*actes constituants*)
in England and the United States that these countries
have escaped from the despotism of logic.   We have

shown that the fundamental laws of these countries if not essentially treaties, yet contain treaties between established powers. Now the one aim of a treaty is not to bring down everything to a few simple axioms and to follow them out to their logical consequences. A treaty cannot help bearing more or less the stamp of circumstances, and reflecting the incoherence, diversity, and complexity of the state of things which it aims at settling; the most it can do is to introduce into that state of things some sort of order and arrangement. The spirit of system does not extend over the domain of diplomacy—a sphere of which the limits are ever shifting under the influence of force and of will. The principle that politics are to be treated in the spirit of a treaty is universally and indisputably recognized in England, of this I have already given proofs. The recognition of this principle is less evident in the Constitution of the United States. In appearance, the Federal Constitution aims at being a well-ordered composition; it lays down general principles. But we need only look closer to see that in it no principle is followed out to the end, but that concrete and varied interests settle everything by a compromise. See, for example, the principle of the liberty of the individual, categorically asserted at the head of the Declaration of Independence, and contradicted in a hypocritical form by Section IX. of the first Article of the Constitution. See again the principle of respect for contracts and federal arbitration between the States, which is categorically affirmed in the text of the Constitution but is openly contradicted by that eleventh Amendment of which the Supreme Court has recently made such an extraordinary application.[1]

On every page contradictory clauses show traces of a constant struggle, and of victory alternating between the Northern and Southern States, the industrial and agricultural States, between the populous States and the small States, between the free and the slave States, and lastly, between all the States, and the yet unborn national authority. Logical sequence and systematic order break down and constantly perish amid these struggles for power.

A treaty further aims at settling only the points already in dispute, or likely to become so. All other points are either not settled or settled by protocols and complementary documents. In this also Anglo-Saxon constitutional law resembles a treaty. Both in England and in the United States, side by side with special and definite constitutional documents, a large field is occupied by custom, by supplementary legislation, and by local law; thus changes and adaptations which the course of time renders necessary, are prudently and, so to speak, noiselessly provided for. Hence on each occasion for change, naturally much less is at stake than if it were necessary solemnly to modify the fundamental provisions of the Constitution. Such a Constitution as that of England or of the United States is therefore freer, more supple, and yet at the same time more stable,

---

[1] It is well known that when certain States repudiated their debt, or reduced the interest assured to their creditors by law, the Supreme Court declared itself incompetent and refused to entertain the claims of the plaintiffs.

than can be any French polity. Every educated person is aware that customary law has a place, and fills a considerable *rôle*, in the English Constitution ; it is not so generally known that in the United States customary law has been the origin of more than one powerful and original development of the Federal Constitution. I have tried in the preceding pages to put this fact in a clear light with reference to the powers of the Senate. It is no less apparent in the system of graduated elections which, as regards the presidential election, has gradually grown up, side by side with the plan provided by the letter of the Constitution.

Is it necessary for me to dwell further on the importance and the bearing of the contrast on which I have been insisting ? Slow changes, careful transitions, which follow and reflect the natural progress of events ; half concealed and almost unconscious transformations, which do not run counter to consecrated formulas until innovation has secretly gained over the instincts of the people, and has allied itself with long custom—all these different forms of growth take place more easily in England, and even in the United States, than in France. As much may be said for the partial modifications of the Constitution, which though in appearance arbitrary are in fact the work of a statesmanlike instinct, constantly checked by regard for what is practical and expedient. In France the logical perfection of the Articles of the Constitution causes this danger ; if any any modification be once admitted, the whole Constitution is put in question, and is liable to be re-arranged in accordance with the new principle which is involved

in the change.   A French constitution may be likened
to a town defended by a single wall without any re-
doubts inside it.   A breach once made, the enemy
pours in and occupies the position.   The two Anglo-
Saxon Constitutions on the other hand, are well provided with these internal defences; by their very
nature they could never go through those sudden
transformations, which are so often in advance of the
needs and ideas of the people.   They have never suffered
from these manifestations of noisy triumph by which
progress is exposed to the reaction of exasperated
prejudice, and which, on account of one faulty feature,
bring about a useless and dangerous revision of the
whole constitutional system.   Compared to French
constitutions they exhibit several defects—they are
inferior, regarded as an artistic whole, they are not
inspired by elevated ideas, and there is little in their
construction to satisfy the intellect.   But to make up
they are endowed with an elasticity, and with a capacity
for adaptation, which have up to this day insured to
them a far longer existence than has been granted to
the classic constructions and the " eternal mansions "
of French constitution-makers.

I say advisedly "up to this day."   The transformation which took place in France in the last century
is not confined to that country; it proceeds from
general causes.   It was accomplished in France at one
stroke; in other countries it has taken place by stages,
or by a process of insensible evolution.   In all societies
the increase of personal property, unlimited as it is,
and accessible to all, equalizes the differences caused by

the preponderance of landed property, which by its
nature is limited in amount, and subject to a natural
monopoly.   In all societies the development of science,
a domain open to all gifted men, equalizes the differences based upon the preponderating influence of
experience and tradition, the inheritance of certain corporations and certain families.   In all societies, thanks
to the improved means of communication and the
activity of commerce, distant regions are brought
nearer, their inhabitants mingle together, and tend to
lose the feeling of a separate life and destiny.   Everywhere we see a daily diminution of the differences between localities, persons, ideas, and interests.   In fact
everything which serves as framework or support to
special or partial groups, intermediate between the State
and the individual, has received a shock, and has been
undermined or destroyed.   It is certain then that sooner
or later all nations will go through the conditions out of
which, in 1789, the French political system arose.   By
the slow action of these causes, we see that in England,
as well as in America, democratic equality and national
homogeneity are growing side by side, and are bringing
about the day, which is still distant, but inevitable, when
these two countries will possess a simple political constitution founded on law, *i.e.* on the express will of
the numerical majority.   Law will then be founded
on logic alone, and logic, left mistress of the field by
the gradual retreat of tradition and custom, will express
its will and find its satisfaction in systematic ideas.
Logic will in consequence be forced to rely on its own
resources alone, and from these, combined with a more

complete and minute knowledge than now exists of the objects aimed at by a constitution, will have to provide those checks on sudden change which policy now draws from custom, tradition, and other sentiments which do not originate in the rational part of human nature but are derived from past history.

An acute observer has remarked that the United States are still in the feudal stage of their history, and that they must in their turn pass through the successive phases of centralization. I have already pointed out the circumstances which have retarded, and which will still greatly delay, the progress of this evolution. In England, at any rate, the Constitution is gradually ceasing to be a government of public opinion, and is becoming an organized democracy. Formerly the majority of the people were excluded from the parliamentary franchise. At that time popular aspirations formed a sort of atmosphere, generally in a state of moderate activity, in which independent political powers floated and moved with apparent spontaneity, but in the end yielded to the course of opinion. Sometimes they delayed and resisted this current for a long time till its accumulated force carried everything away before it. To-day, owing to the existence of almost universal suffrage, the will of the people is condensed and embodied in a legal organ, viz., Parliament. Popular will acts upon the law and upon the government like a powerful and regular spring, presses and bears upon the right spot, and thus produces with perfect certainty the desired movement of the political mechanism.

To sum up the whole matter, the distinctions

already dwelt upon between the three countries may, after all, tend to disappear through partial and gradual assimilation. They proceed in part from the fact that, while all three nations are influenced by a common democratic movement, the progress of this movement has, in the case of England and of the United States, been delayed, whilst in France it has been hurried on, so that France has reached a more advanced stage of the movement than the other two countries. This explanation is necessary in order to make the exact bearing of my preceding remarks intelligible, and with this I close this already too lengthy essay.

INDEX

N

INDEX

.THE END

RICHARD CLAY AND SONS, LIMITED,
LONDON AND BUNGAY.

Catalogue of Books

PUBLISHED BY

MACMILLAN AND CO.

BEDFORD STREET, COVENT GARDEN, LONDON

May, 1891.

NOTE.—In the following Catalogue the titles of books belonging to any Series will only be found under the Series heading.

ABBOTT (Rev. E. A.).—A SHAKESPEARIAN GRAMMAR. Extra fcp. 8vo. 6s.

—— CAMBRIDGE SERMONS. 8vo. 6s.

—— OXFORD SERMONS. 8vo. 7s. 6d.

—— FRANCIS BACON: AN ACCOUNT OF HIS LIFE AND WORKS. 8vo. 14s.

—— BIBLE LESSONS. Crown 8vo. 4s. 6d.

—— PHILOMYTHUS. Crown 8vo. 3s. 6d.

ABBOTT (Rev. E. A.) and RUSHBROOKE (W. G.).—THE COMMON TRADITION OF THE SYNOPTIC GOSPELS, IN THE TEXT OF THE REVISED VERSION. Crown 8vo. 3s. 6d.

ABBOT (Francis).—SCIENTIFIC THEISM. Crown 8vo. 7s. 6d.

—— THE WAY OUT OF AGNOSTICISM; or, The Philosophy of Free Religion. Cr. 8vo. 4s.6d.

ADAMS (Sir F. O.) and CUNNINGHAM (C.)—THE SWISS CONFEDERATION. 8vo. 14s.

ÆSCHYLUS. — THE "SEVEN AGAINST THEBES." With Introduction, Commentary, and Translation by A. W. VERRALL, Litt.D. 8vo. 7s. 6d.

—— AGAMEMNON. With Introduction, Commentary, and Translation, by A. W. VERRALL, Litt.D. 8vo. 12s.

—— THE SUPPLICES. Text, Introduction, Notes, Commentary, and Translation, by Prof. T. G. TUCKER. 8vo. 10s. 6d.
See also pp. 31, 32.

ÆSOP—CALDECOTT.—SOME OF ÆSOP'S FABLES, with Modern Instances, shown in Designs by RANDOLPH CALDECOTT. 4to. 5s.

AGASSIZ (LOUIS): HIS LIFE AND CORRESPONDENCE. Edited by ELIZABETH CARY AGASSIZ. 2 vols. Crown 8vo. 18s.

AINGER (Rev. Alfred).—SERMONS PREACHED IN THE TEMPLE CHURCH. Extra fcp. 8vo. 6s.

AIRY (Sir G. B.).—TREATISE ON THE ALGEBRAICAL AND NUMERICAL THEORY OF ERRORS OF OBSERVATION AND THE COMBINATION OF OBSERVATIONS. Crown 8vo. 6s. 6d.

—— POPULAR ASTRONOMY. With Illustrations. Fcp. 8vo. 4s. 6d.

—— AN ELEMENTARY TREATISE ON PARTIAL DIFFERENTIAL EQUATIONS. Cr. 8vo. 5s.6d.

—— ON SOUND AND ATMOSPHERIC VIBRATIONS. With the Mathematical Elements of Music. 2nd Edition. Crown 8vo. 9s.

—— GRAVITATION. An Elementary Explanation of the Principal Perturbations in the Solar System. 2nd Edit. Crn. 8vo. 7s.6d.

AITKEN (Sir W.)—THE GROWTH OF THE RECRUIT AND YOUNG SOLDIER. With a view to the selection of "Growing Lads" for the Army, and a Regulated System of Training for Recruits. Crown 8vo. 8s. 6d.

ALBEMARLE (Earl of).—FIFTY YEARS OF MY LIFE. 3rd Edit., revised. Cr. 8vo. 7s.6d.

ALDIS (Mary Steadman).—THE GREAT GIANT ARITHMOS. A MOST ELEMENTARY ARITHMETIC. Illustrated. Globe 8vo. 2s. 6d.

ALDRICH (T. Bailey). — THE SISTERS' TRAGEDY, WITH OTHER POEMS, LYRICAL AND DRAMATIC. Fcp. 8vo. 3s. 6d. net.

ALEXANDER (T.) and THOMSON (A.). —ELEMENTARY APPLIED MECHANICS. Part II. Transverse Stress; upwards of 150 Diagrams, and 200 Examples carefully worked out. Crown 8vo. 10s. 6d.

ALLBUTT (Dr. T. Clifford).—ON THE USE OF THE OPHTHALMOSCOPE. 8vo. 15s.

AMIEL (Henri Frederic).—THE JOURNAL INTIME. Translated by Mrs. HUMPHRY WARD. 2nd Edition. Crown 8vo. 6s.

AN AUTHOR'S LOVE. Being the Unpublished Letters of PROSPER MÉRIMÉE'S "Inconnue." 2 vols. Ex. cr. 8vo. 12s.

ANDERSON (A.).—BALLADS AND SONNETS. Crown 8vo. 5s.

ANDERSON (L.).—LINEAR PERSPECTIVE AND MODEL DRAWING. Royal 8vo. 2s.

ANDERSON (Dr. McCall).—LECTURES ON CLINICAL MEDICINE. Illustrated. 8vo. 10s. 6d.

ANDREWS (Dr. Thomas): THE SCIENTIFIC PAPERS OF THE LATE. With a Memoir by Profs. TAIT and CRUM BROWN. 8vo. 18s.

ANGLO-SAXON LAW: ESSAYS ON. Med. 8vo. 18s.

APPLETON (T. G.).—A NILE JOURNAL. Illustrated by EUGENE BENSON. Crown 8vo. 6s.

ARATUS.—THE SKIES AND WEATHER FORECASTS OF ARATUS. Translated by E. POSTE, M.A. Crown 8vo. 3s. 6d.

ARIOSTO.—PALADIN AND SARACEN. Stories from Ariosto. By H. C. HOLLWAY-CALTHROP. Illustrated. Crown 8vo. 6s.

ARISTOPHANES.—THE BIRDS. Translated into English Verse, with Introduction, Notes, and Appendices. By Prof. B. H. KENNEDY, D.D. Crown 8vo. 6s.

—— HELP NOTES FOR THE USE OF STUDENTS. Crown 8vo. 1s. 6d.

ARISTOTLE ON FALLACIES; OR, THE SOPHISTICI ELENCHI. With Translation and Notes by E. POSTE, M.A. 8vo. 8s. 6d.

ARISTOTLE.—THE FIRST BOOK OF THE METAPHYSICS OF ARISTOTLE. Translated with marginal Analysis and Summary. By a Cambridge Graduate. 8vo. 5s.

—— THE POLITICS. Translated with an Analysis and Critical Notes by J. E. C. WELLDON, Litt.D. 2nd Edition. 10s. 6d.

—— THE RHETORIC. By the same Translator. Crown 8vo. 7s. 6d.

ARMY PRELIMINARY EXAMINATION, Specimens of Papers set at the, 1882-89. With Answers to the Mathematical Questions. Crown 8vo. 3s. 6d.

ARNAULD, ANGELIQUE. By FRANCES MARTIN. Crown 8vo. 4s. 6d.

ARNOLD (Matthew).—THE COMPLETE POETICAL WORKS. New Edition. 3 vols. Crown 8vo. 7s. 6d. each.—Vol. I. Early Poems, Narrative Poems, and Sonnets. —Vol. II. Lyric and Elegiac Poems.—Vol. III. Dramatic and Later Poems.

—— COMPLETE POETICAL WORKS. 1 vol. With Portrait. Crown 8vo. 7s. 6d.

ARNOLD (M.).—Essays in Criticism. 6th Edition. Crown 8vo. 9s.

—— Essays in Criticism. Second Series. With an Introductory Note by Lord Coleridge. Crown 8vo. 7s. 6d.

—— Isaiah XL.—LXVI. With the Shorter Prophecies Allied to it. With Notes. Crown 8vo. 5s.

—— Isaiah of Jerusalem. In the Authorised English Version, with Introduction, Corrections, and Notes. Crown 8vo. 4s. 6d.

—— A Bible-Reading for Schools. The Great Prophecy of Israel's Restoration (Isaiah xl.-lxvi.) 4th Edition. 18mo. 1s.

—— Higher Schools and Universities in Germany. Crown 8vo. 6s.

—— Discourses in America. Cr. 8vo. 4s. 6d.

—— Johnson's Lives of the Poets, The Six Chief Lives from. With Macaulay's "Life of Johnson." With Preface by Matthew Arnold. Crown 8vo. 4s. 6d.

—— Edmund Burke's Letters, Tracts and Speeches on Irish Affairs. Edited by Matthew Arnold. Crown 8vo. 6s.

—— Reports on Elementary Schools, 1852-82. Edited by the Right Hon. Sir Francis Sandford, K.C.B. Cr. 8vo. 3s. 6d.

ARNOLD (T.)—The Second Punic War. By the late Thomas Arnold, D.D. Edited by William T. Arnold, M.A. With Eight Maps. Crown 8vo. 5s.

ARNOLD (W. T.).—The Roman System of Provincial Administration. Crn. 8vo. 6s.

ART AT HOME SERIES. Edited by W. J. Loftie, B.A.
Music in the House. By John Hullah. Fourth Edition. Crown 8vo. 2s. 6d.
The Dining-Room. By Mrs. Loftie. With Illustrations. 2nd Edition. Crown 8vo. 2s. 6d.
The Bedroom and Boudoir. By Lady Barker. Crown 8vo. 2s. 6d.
Amateur Theatricals. By Walter H. Pollock and Lady Pollock. Illustrated by Kate Greenaway. Crown 8vo. 2s. 6d.
Needlework. By Elizabeth Glaister. Illustrated. Crown 8vo. 2s. 6d.
The Library. By Andrew Lang, with a Chapter on English Illustrated Books, by Austin Dobson. Crown 8vo. 3s. 6d.

ARTEVELDE. James and Philip van Artevelde. By W. J. Ashley. Cr. 8vo. 6s.

ATKINSON (J. B.).—An Art Tour to Northern Capitals of Europe. 8vo. 12s.

ATKINSON (J. C.).—Forty Years in a Moorland Parish. Crn. 8vo. 8s. 6d. net.

AUSTIN (Alfred).—Poetical Works. New Collected Edit. In 6 vols. Cr. 8vo. 5s. each. Monthly Vols. from December, 1890:
Vol. I. The Tower of Babel.
Vol. II. Savonarola, etc.
Vol. III. Prince Lucifer.
Vol. IV. The Human Tragedy.
Vol. V. Narrative Poems.
Vol. VI. Lyrical Poems.

—— Soliloquies in Song. Crown 8vo. 6s.

—— At the Gate of the Convent; and other Poems. Crown 8vo. 6s.

AUSTIN (A.).—Madonna's Child. Crown 4to. 3s. 6d.

—— Rome or Death. Crown 4to. 9s.

—— The Golden Age. Crown 8vo. 5s.

—— The Season. Crown 8vo. 5s.

—— Love's Widowhood: and other Poems. Crown 8vo. 6s.

—— English Lyrics. Crown 8vo. 3s. 6d.

AUTENRIETH (Dr. G.).—An Homeric Dictionary. Translated from the German, by R. P. Keep, Ph.D. Crown 8vo. 6s.

BABRIUS. With Introductory Dissertations, Critical Notes, Commentary, and Lexicon, by W. G. Rutherford, LL.D. 8vo. 12s. 6d.

"BACCHANTE." The Cruise of H.M.S. "Bacchante," 1879-1882. Compiled from the private Journals, Letters and Note-books of Prince Albert Victor and Prince George of Wales. By the Rev. Canon Dalton. 2 vols. Medium 8vo. 52s. 6d.

BACON (Francis): Account of his Life and Works. By E. A. Abbott. 8vo. 14s.

BAINES (Rev. Edward).—Sermons. With a Preface and Memoir, by Alfred Barry, D.D., late Bishop of Sydney. Crn. 8vo. 6s.

BAKER (Sir Samuel White).—Ismailia. A Narrative of the Expedition to Central Africa for the Suppression of the Slave Trade, organised by Ismail, Khedive of Egypt. Crown 8vo. 6s.

—— The Nile Tributaries of Abyssinia, and the Sword Hunters of the Hamran Arabs. Crown 8vo. 6s.

—— The Albert N'yanza Great Basin of the Nile and Exploration of the Nile Sources. Crown 8vo. 6s.

—— Cyprus as I saw it in 1879. 8vo. 12s. 6d.

—— Cast up by the Sea: or, The Adventures of Ned Gray. With Illustrations by Huard. Crown 8vo. 6s.

—— The Egyptian Question. Letters to the Times and the Pall Mall Gazette. 8vo. 2s.

—— True Tales for my Grandsons. Illustrated by W. J. Hennessy. Cr. 8vo. 3s. 6d.

—— Wild Beasts and their Ways: Reminiscences of Europe, Asia, Africa, and America. Illustrated. Ex. cr. 8vo. 12s. 6d.

BALCH (Elizabeth). — Glimpses of Old English Homes. Illustrated. Gl. 4to. 14s.

BALDWIN (Prof. J. M.)—Handbook of Psychology: Senses and Intellect. 2nd Edition. 8vo. 12s. 6d.

BALFOUR (The Right Hon. A. J.)—A Defence of Philosophic Doubt. Being an Essay on the Foundations of Belief. 8vo. 12s.

BALFOUR (Prof. F. M.).—Elasmobranch Fishes. With Plates. 8vo. 21s.

—— Comparative Embryology. With Illustrations. 2 vols. 2nd Edition. 8vo.—Vol. I. 18s.—Vol. II. 21s.

—— The Collected Works. Memorial Edition. Edited by M. Foster, F.R.S., and Adam Sedgwick, M.A. 4 vols. 8vo. 6l. 6d.
Vols. I. and IV. Special Memoirs. May be had separately. Price 73s. 6d. net.

BALL (Sir R. S.).—EXPERIMENTAL ME-CHANICS. Illustrated. New Ed. Cr. 8vo. 6s.

BALL (W. Platt).—ARE THE EFFECTS OF USE AND DISUSE INHERITED? An Examination of the View held by Spencer and Darwin. Crown 8vo. 3s. 6d.

BALL (W. W. R.).—THE STUDENT'S GUIDE TO THE BAR. 5th Edition, revised. Crown 8vo. 2s. 6d.

—— A SHORT ACCOUNT OF THE HISTORY OF MATHEMATICS. Crown 8vo. 10s. 6d.

BALLANCE (C. A.) and EDMUNDS (W.)—LIGATION IN CONTINUITY. 8vo.

BARKER (Lady).—FIRST LESSONS IN THE PRINCIPLES OF COOKING. 3rd Ed. 18mo. 1s.

—— A YEAR'S HOUSEKEEPING IN SOUTH AFRICA. Illustrated. Crown 8vo. 3s. 6d.

—— STATION LIFE IN NEW ZEALAND. Crown 8vo. 3s. 6d.

—— LETTERS TO GUY. Crown 8vo. 5s.

BARNES. LIFE OF WILLIAM BARNES, POET AND PHILOLOGIST. By his Daughter, LUCY BAXTER (" Leader Scott "). Cr. 8vo. 7s. 6d.

BARRY (Bishop).—FIRST WORDS IN AUS-TRALIA : Sermons. Crown 8vo. 5s.

BARTHOLOMEW (J. G.).—LIBRARY RE-FERENCE ATLAS OF THE WORLD. With Index to 100,000 places. Folio. 2l.12s.6d. net. Also issued in Monthly Parts. Part I. March, 1891, 5s. net.

—— PHYSICAL AND POLITICAL SCHOOL ATLAS. With 80 maps. 4to. 7s.6d.; half mor. 10s.6d.

—— ELEMENTARY SCHOOL ATLAS. 4to. 1s.

BARWELL (Richard, F.R.C.S.).—THE CAUSES AND TREATMENT OF LATERAL CURVATURE OF THE SPINE. Crown 8vo. 5s.

—— ON ANEURISM, ESPECIALLY OF THE THORAX AND ROOT OF THE NECK. 3s. 6d.

BASTIAN (H. Charlton).—THE BEGINNINGS OF LIFE. 2 vols. Crown 8vo. 28s.

—— EVOLUTION AND THE ORIGIN OF LIFE. Crown 8vo. 6s. 6d.

—— ON PARALYSIS FROM BRAIN DISEASE IN ITS COMMON FORMS. Crown 8vo. 10s. 6d.

BATHER (Archdeacon).—ON SOME MINIS-TERIAL DUTIES, CATECHIZING, PREACHING, &c. Edited, with a Preface, by C. J. VAUGHAN, D.D. Fcp. 8vo. 4s. 6d.

BEASLEY (R. D.) — AN ELEMENTARY TREATISE ON PLANE TRIGONOMETRY. With numerous Examples. 9th Edition. Crown 8vo. 3s. 6d.

BEAUMARCHAIS. LE BARBIER DE SEVILLE, OU LE PRÉCAUTION INUTILE. Comedie en Quatre Actes. Edited by L. P. BLOUET, B.A., Univ. Gallic. Fcp. 8vo. 3s. 6d.

BEESLY (Mrs.).—STORIES FROM THE HISTORY OF ROME. Fcp. 8vo. 2s. 6d.

BEHAGHEL (Otto).—THE GERMAN LAN-GUAGE. Translated by EMIL TRECHMANN, B.A., Ph.D. Globe 8vo.

BELCHER (Rev. H.).—SHORT EXERCISES IN LATIN PROSE COMPOSITION, AND EXAMINA-TION PAPERS IN LATIN GRAMMAR. 18mo. 1s. 6d.—KEY (for Teachers only). 3s. 6d.

BELCHER (Rev. H.).—SHORT EXERCISES IN LATIN PROSE COMPOSITION. Part II. On the Syntax of Sentences. With an Appendix. 18mo. 2s.

KEY (for Teachers only). 18mo. 3s.

BENHAM (Rev. W.).—A COMPANION TO THE LECTIONARY. Crown 8vo. 4s. 6d.

BERLIOZ (Hector): AUTOBIOGRAPHY OF. Transl. by RACHEL and ELEANOR HOLMES. 2 vols. Crown 8vo. 21s.

BERNARD (M.).—FOUR LECTURES ON SUB-JECTS CONNECTED WITH DIPLOMACY. 8vo. 9s.

BERNARD (St.) THE LIFE AND TIMES OF ST. BERNARD, ABBOT OF CLAIRVAUX. By J. C. MORISON, M.A. Crown 8vo. 6s.

BERNERS (J.)—FIRST LESSONS ON HEALTH. 18mo. 1s.

BETHUNE-BAKER (J. F.).—THE INFLU-ENCE OF CHRISTIANITY ON WAR. 8vo. 5s.

—— THE STERNNESS OF CHRIST'S TEACHING, AND ITS RELATION TO THE LAW OF FOR-GIVENESS. Crown 8vo. 2s. 6d.

BETSY LEE: A FO'C'S'LE YARN. Extra fcp. 8vo. 3s. 6d.

BETTANY (G. T.).—FIRST LESSONS IN PRAC-TICAL BOTANY. 18mo. 1s.

BIGELOW (M. M.).—HISTORY OF PROCE-DURE IN ENGLAND FROM THE NORMAN CONQUEST. The Norman Period, 1066-1204. 8vo. 16s.

BIKÉLAS (D.).—LOUKIS LARAS; OR, THE REMINISCENCES OF A CHIOTE MERCHANT DURING THE GREEK WAR OF INDEPENDENCE. Translated by J. GENNADIUS, Greek Minister in London. Crown 8vo. 7s. 6d.

BINNIE (the late Rev. William).—SERMONS. Crown 8vo. 6s.

BIRKS (Thomas Rawson, M.A.).—FIRST PRINCIPLES OF MORAL SCIENCE ; OR, FIRST COURSE OF LECTURES DELIVERED IN THE UNIVERSITY OF CAMBRIDGE. Cr. 8vo. 8s. 6d.

—— MODERN UTILITARIANISM ; OR, THE SYS-TEMS OF PALEY, BENTHAM, AND MILL EXAMINED AND COMPARED. Crown 8vo. 6s. 6d.

—— THE DIFFICULTIES OF BELIEF IN CON-NECTION WITH THE CREATION AND THE FALL, REDEMPTION AND JUDGMENT. 2nd Edition. Crown 8vo. 5s.

—— COMMENTARY ON THE BOOK OF ISAIAH, CRITICAL, HISTORICAL, AND PROPHETICAL; INCLUDING A REVISED ENGLISH TRANSLA-TION. 2nd Edition. 8vo. 12s. 6d.

—— THE NEW TESTAMENT. Essay on the Right Estimation of MS. Evidence in the Text of the New Testament. Cr. 8vo. 3s. 6d.

—— SUPERNATURAL REVELATION ; OR, FIRST PRINCIPLES OF MORAL THEOLOGY. 8vo. 8s.

—— MODERN PHYSICAL FATALISM, AND THE DOCTRINE OF EVOLUTION. Including an Examination of Mr. Herbert Spencer's " First Principles." Crown 8vo. 6s.

—— JUSTIFICATION AND IMPUTED RIGHTE-OUSNESS. Being a Review of Ten Sermons on the Nature and Effects of Faith by JAMES THOMAS O'BRIEN, D.D., late Bishop of Ossory, Ferns, and Leighlin. Cr. 8vo. 6s.

BJÖRNSON (B.).—SYNNÖVÉ SOLBAKKEN. Translated by JULIE SUTTER. Cr. 8vo. 6s.

BLACK (William). See p. 28.

BLACKBURNE. LIFE OF THE RIGHT HON. FRANCIS BLACKBURNE, late Lord Chancellor of Ireland, by his son, EDWARD BLACKBURNE. With Portrait. 8vo. 12s.

BLACKIE (Prof. John Stuart.).—GREEK AND ENGLISH DIALOGUES FOR USE IN SCHOOLS AND COLLEGES. 3rd Edition. Fcp. 8vo.2s. 6d.

—— GREEK PRIMER, COLLOQUIAL AND CONSTRUCTIVE. Globe 8vo.

—— HORÆ HELLENICÆ. 8vo. 12s.

—— THE WISE MEN OF GREECE : IN A SERIES OF DRAMATIC DIALOGUES. Cr. 8vo. 9s.

—— GOETHE'S FAUST. Translated into English Verse. 2nd Edition. Crown 8vo. 9s.

—— LAY SERMONS. Crown 8vo. 6s.

—— MESSIS VITÆ : Gleanings of Song from a Happy Life. Crown 8vo. 4s. 6d.

—— WHAT DOES HISTORY TEACH? Two Edinburgh Lectures. Globe 8vo. 2s. 6d.

BLAKE (J. F.)—ASTRONOMICAL MYTHS. With Illustrations. Crown 8vo. 9s.

BLAKE. LIFE OF WILLIAM BLAKE. With Selections from his Poems and other Writings. Illustrated from Blake's own Works. By ALEXANDER GILCHRIST. 2nd Edition. 2 vols. cloth gilt. Medium 8vo. 2l. 2s.

BLAKISTON (J. R.).—THE TEACHER: HINTS ON SCHOOL MANAGEMENT. Cr. 8vo. 2s. 6d.

BLANFORD (H. F.).—THE RUDIMENTS OF PHYSICAL GEOGRAPHY FOR THE USE OF INDIAN SCHOOLS. 12th Edition. Illustrated. Globe 8vo. 2s. 6d.

—— A PRACTICAL GUIDE TO THE CLIMATES AND WEATHER OF INDIA, CEYLON AND BURMA, AND THE STORMS OF INDIAN SEAS. 8vo. 12s. 6d.

—— ELEMENTARY GEOGRAPHY OF INDIA, BURMA, AND CEYLON. Illus. Gl. 8vo. 2s. 6d.

BLANFORD (W. T.).—GEOLOGY AND ZOOLOGY OF ABYSSINIA. 8vo. 21s.

BLYTH (A. Wynter).—A MANUAL OF PUBLIC HEALTH. 8vo. 17s. net.

BÖHM-BAWERK (Prof.).—CAPITAL AND INTEREST. Translated by W. SMART, M.A. 8vo. 14s.

—— THE POSITIVE THEORY OF CAPITAL. Translated by W. SMART, M.A. 8vo.

BOISSEVAIN (G. M.).—THE MONETARY PROBLEM. 8vo, sewed. 3s. net.

BOLDREWOOD (Rolf).—A COLONIAL REFORMER. 3 vols. Crn. 8vo. 31s. 6d. See also p. 29.

BOLEYN (ANNE): A Chapter of English History, 1527-1536. By PAUL FRIEDMANN. 2 vols. 8vo. 28s.

BONAR (James).—MALTHUS AND HIS WORK. 8vo. 12s. 6d.

BOOLE (George).—A TREATISE ON THE CALCULUS OF FINITE DIFFERENCES. Edited by J. F. MOULTON. 3rd Edition. Cr. 8vo. 10s. 6d.

—— THE MATHEMATICAL ANALYSIS OF LOGIC. 8vo. Sewed, 5s

BOTTOMLEY (J. T.). — FOUR-FIGURE MATHEMATICAL TABLES. Comprising Logarithmic and Trigonometrical Tables, and Tables of Squares, Square Roots and Reciprocals. 8vo. 2s. 6d.

BOUGHTON (G. H.) and ABBEY (E. A.).— SKETCHING RAMBLES IN HOLLAND. With Illustrations. Fcp. 4to. 21s.

BOUTMY (M.). — STUDIES IN CONSTITUTIONAL LAW. Translated by Mrs. DICEY, with Preface by Prof. A. V. DICEY. Crown 8vo. [In the Press.

—— THE ENGLISH CONSTITUTION. Translated by Mrs. EADEN, with Introduction by Sir F. POLLOCK, Bart. Crown 8vo. 6s.

BOWEN (H. Courthope).—FIRST LESSONS IN FRENCH. 18mo. 1s.

BOWER (Prof. F. O.).—A COURSE OF PRACTICAL INSTRUCTION IN BOTANY. Cr. 8vo. 10s. 6d.

BRADSHAW (J. G.).—A COURSE OF EASY ARITHMETICAL EXAMPLES FOR BEGINNERS. Globe 8vo. 2s. With Answers. 2s. 6d.

BRAIN. A JOURNAL OF NEUROLOGY. Edited for the Neurological Society of London, by A. DE WATTEVILLE. Published Quarterly. 8vo. 3s. 6d. Yearly Vols. I. to XII. 8vo, cloth. 15s. each.

BREYMANN (Prof. H.).—A FRENCH GRAMMAR BASED ON PHILOLOGICAL PRINCIPLES. 3rd Edition. Extra fcp. 8vo. 4s. 6d.

—— FIRST FRENCH EXERCISE BOOK. 2nd Edition. Extra fcp. 8vo. 4s. 6d.

—— SECOND FRENCH EXERCISE BOOK. Extra fcp. 8vo. 2s. 6d.

BRIDGES (John A.).—IDYLLS OF A LOST VILLAGE. Crown 8vo. 7s. 6d.

BRIGHT (John).—SPEECHES ON QUESTIONS OF PUBLIC POLICY. Edited by THOROLD ROGERS. 2nd Edit. 2 vols. 8vo. 25s.— Cheap Edition. Extra fcp. 8vo. 3s. 6d.

—— PUBLIC ADDRESSES. Edited by THOROLD ROGERS. 8vo. 14s.

BRIGHT (H. A.)—THE ENGLISH FLOWER GARDEN. Crown 8vo. 3s. 6d.

—— A YEAR IN A LANCASHIRE GARDEN. New Edition. Crown 8vo. 3s. 6d.

BRIMLEY (George).—ESSAYS. Globe 8vo. 5s.

BRODIE (Sir Benjamin).—IDEAL CHEMISTRY. Crown 8vo. 2s.

BROOKE, Sir JAS., THE RAJA OF SARAWAK (Life of). By GERTRUDE L. JACOB. 2 vols. 8vo. 25s.

BROOKE (Stopford A.).—PRIMER OF ENGLISH LITERATURE. 18mo. 1s.

Large Paper Edition. 8vo. 7s. 6d.

—— EARLY ENGLISH LITERATURE. 2 vols. 8vo. [Vol. I. in the Press.

—— RIQUET OF THE TUFT : A LOVE DRAMA. Extra crown 8vo. 6s.

—— POEMS. Globe 8vo. 6s.

—— MILTON. Fcp. 8vo. 1s. 6d.

Large Paper Edition. 8vo. 21s. net.

—— DOVE COTTAGE, WORDSWORTH'S HOME, FROM 1800—1808. Globe 8vo. 1s.

BROOKS (Rev. Phillips).—The Candle of the Lord, and other Sermons. Cr. 8vo. 6s.

—— Sermons Preached in English Churches. Crown 8vo. 6s.

—— Twenty Sermons. Crown 8vo. 6s.

—— Tolerance. Crown 8vo. 2s. 6d.

—— The Light of the World, and other Sermons. Crown 8vo. 3s. 6d.

BROOKSMITH (J.).——Arithmetic in Theory and Practice. Crown 8vo. 4s. 6d. Key. Crown 8vo. 10s. 6d.

BROOKSMITH (J. and E. J.).—Arithmetic for Beginners. Globe 8vo. 1s. 6d.

BROOKSMITH (E. J.).—Woolwich Mathematical Papers, for Admission in the Royal Military Academy, 1880—1888. Edited by E. J. Brooksmith, B.A. Crown 8vo. 6s.

—— Sandhurst Mathematical Papers, for Admission into the Royal Military College, 1881—89. Edited by E. J. Brooksmith, B.A. Crown 8vo. 3s. 6d.

BROWN (J. Allen).—Palæolithic Man in North-West Middlesex. 8vo. 7s. 6d.

BROWN (T. E.).—The Manx Witch: and other Poems. Crown 8vo. 7s. 6d.

BROWNE (J. H. Balfour).—Water Supply. Crown 8vo. 2s. 6d.

BRUNTON (Dr. T. Lauder).—A Text-Book of Pharmacology, Therapeutics, and Materia Medica. 3rd Edition. Medium 8vo. 21s.

—— Disorders of Digestion: their Consequences and Treatment. 8vo. 10s. 6d.

—— Pharmacology and Therapeutics; or, Medicine Past and Present. Cr. 8vo. 6s.

—— Tables of Materia Medica: A Companion to the Materia Medica Museum. 8vo. 5s.

—— The Bible and Science. With Illustrations. Crown 8vo. 10s. 6d.

—— Croonian Lectures on the Connection between Chemical Constitution and Physiological Action. Being an Introduction to Modern Therapeutics. 8vo.

BRYANS (Clement).—Latin Prose Exercises Based upon Caesar's "Gallic War." With a Classification of Caesar's Phrases, and Grammatical Notes on Caesar's Chief Usages. Pott 8vo. 2s. 6d. Key (for Teachers only). 4s. 6d.

BRYCE (James, M.P., D.C.L.).—The Holy Roman Empire. 8th Edition. Crown 8vo. 7s. 6d.—Library Edition. 8vo. 14s.

—— Transcaucasia and Ararat. 3rd Edition. Crown 8vo. 9s.

—— The American Commonwealth. 2nd Edition. 2 vols. Extra Crown 8vo. 25s.

BUCHHEIM (Dr.).—Deutsche Lyrik. 18mo. 4s. 6d.

—— Deutsche Balladen und Romanzen. 18mo. [In the Press.

BUCKLAND (Anna).—Our National Institutions. 18mo. 1s.

BUCKLEY (Arabella).—History of England for Beginners. With Coloured Maps and Chronological and Genealogical Tables. Globe 8vo. 3s.

BUCKNILL (Dr.).—The Care of the Insane. Crown 8vo. 3s. 6d.

BUCKTON (G. B.).—Monograph of the British Cicadæ, or Tettigidæ. In 8 parts, Quarterly. Part I. January, 1890. 8vo. I.—V. ready. 8s. each net.—Vol. I. 8vo. 33s. 6d. net.

BUMBLEBEE BOGO'S BUDGET. By a Retired Judge. Illustrations by Alice Havers. Crown 8vo. 2s. 6d.

BURGON (Dean).—Poems. Ex. fcp. 8vo. 4s. 6d.

BURKE (Edmund).—Letters, Tracts, and Speeches on Irish Affairs. Edited by Matthew Arnold, with Preface. Cr. 8vo. 6s.

—— Reflections on the French Revolution. Ed. by F. G. Selby. Gl. 6vo. 5s.

BURN (Robert).—Roman Literature in Relation to Roman Art. With Illustrations. Extra Crown 8vo. 14s.

BURNS.—The Poetical Works. With a Biographical Memoir by Alexander Smith. In 2 vols. fcp. 8vo. 10s.

BURY (J. B.).—A History of the Later Roman Empire from Arcadius to Irene, A.D. 390—800. 2 vols. 8vo. 32s.

BUTLER (Archer).—Sermons, Doctrinal and Practical. 11th Edition. 8vo. 8s.

—— Second Series of Sermons. 8vo. 7s.

—— Letters on Romanism. 8vo. 10s. 6d.

BUTLER (George).—Sermons preached in Cheltenham College Chapel. 8vo. 7s. 6d.

BUTLER'S HUDIBRAS. Edited by Alfred Milnes. Fcp. 8vo. Part I. 3s. 6d. Part II. and III. 4s. 6d.

CÆSAR. See pp. 31, 32.

CAIRNES (Prof. J. E.).—Political Essays. 8vo. 10s. 6d.

—— Some Leading Principles of Political Economy newly Expounded. 8vo. 14s.

—— The Slave Power. 8vo. 10s. 6d.

—— The Character and Logical Method of Political Economy. Crown 8vo. 6s.

CALDERON.—Select Plays of Calderon. Edited by Norman MacColl, M.A. Crown 8vo. 14s.

CALDERWOOD (Prof.)—Handbook of Moral Philosophy. Crown 8vo. 6s.

—— The Relations of Mind and Brain. 2nd Edition. 8vo. 12s.

—— The Parables of Our Lord. Crown 8vo. 6s.

—— The Relations of Science and Religion. Crown 8vo. 5s.

—— On Teaching. 4th Edition. Extra fcp. 8vo. 2s. 6d.

CAMBRIDGE. Cooper's Le Keux's Memorials of Cambridge. Illustrated with 90 Woodcuts in the Text, 154 Plates on Steel and Copper by Le Keux, Storer, &c., including 20 Etchings by R. Farren. 3 vols. 4to half levant morocco. 10l. 10s.

CAMBRIDGE SENATE-HOUSE PROBLEMS AND RIDERS, WITH SOLUTIONS: 1848—51. RIDERS. By JAMESON. 8vo. 7s. 6d.

1875. PROBLEMS AND RIDERS. Edited by Prof. A. G. GREENHILL. Crown 8vo. 8s. 6d.

1878. SOLUTIONS BY THE MATHEMATICAL MODERATORS AND EXAMINERS. Edited by J. W. L. GLAISHER, M.A. 8vo. 12s.

CAMEOS FROM ENGLISH HISTORY. See p. 54, under YONGE.

CAMPBELL (Dr. John M'Leod).—THE NATURE OF THE ATONEMENT. 6th Edition. Crown 8vo. 6s.

—— REMINISCENCES AND REFLECTIONS. Ed., with an Introductory Narrative, by his Son, DONALD CAMPBELL, M.A. Crown 8vo. 7s. 6d.

—— RESPONSIBILITY FOR THE GIFT OF ETERNAL LIFE. Compiled from Sermons preached at Row, in the years 1829—31. Crown 8vo. 5s.

—— THOUGHTS ON REVELATION. 2nd Edit. Crown 8vo. 5s.

CAMPBELL (J. F.).—MY CIRCULAR NOTES. Cheaper issue. Crown 8vo. 6s.

CANDLER (H.).—HELP TO ARITHMETIC. 2nd Edition. Globe 8vo. 2s. 6d.

CANTERBURY (His Grace Edward White, Archbishop of).—BOY-LIFE: ITS TRIAL, ITS STRENGTH, ITS FULNESS. Sundays in Wellington College, 1859—73. 4th Edition. Crown 8vo. 6s.

—— THE SEVEN GIFTS. Addressed to the Diocese of Canterbury in his Primary Visitation. 2nd Edition. Crown 8vo. 6s.

—— CHRIST AND HIS TIMES. Addressed to the Diocese of Canterbury in his Second Visitation. Crown 8vo. 6s.

CARLES (W. R.).—LIFE IN COREA. 8vo. 12s. 6d.

CARLYLE (Thomas).—REMINISCENCES. Ed. by CHARLES ELIOT NORTON. 2 vols. Crown 8vo. 12s.

—— EARLY LETTERS OF THOMAS CARLYLE. Edited by C. E. NORTON. 2 vols. 1814—26. Crown 8vo. 18s.

—— LETTERS OF THOMAS CARLYLE. Edited by C. E. NORTON. 2 vols. 1826—36. Crown 8vo. 18s.

—— GOETHE AND CARLYLE, CORRESPONDENCE BETWEEN. Edited by C. E. NORTON. Crown 8vo. 9s.

CARNOT—THURSTON.—REFLECTIONS ON THE MOTIVE POWER OF HEAT, AND ON MACHINES FITTED TO DEVELOP THAT POWER. From the French of N. L. S. CARNOT. Edited by R. H. THURSTON, LL.D. Crown 8vo. 7s. 6d.

CARPENTER (Bishop W. Boyd).—TRUTH IN TALE. Addresses, chiefly to Children. Cr. 8vo. 4s. 6d.

—— THE PERMANENT ELEMENTS OF RELIGION: Bampton Lectures, 1887. Cr. 8vo. 6s.

CARR (J. Comyns).—PAPERS ON ART. Cr. 8vo. 8s. 6d.

CARROLL (Lewis).—ALICE'S ADVENTURES IN WONDERLAND. With 42 Illustrations by TENNIEL. Crown 8vo. 6s. net.

People's Edition. With all the original Illustrations. Crown 8vo. 2s. 6d. net.

A GERMAN TRANSLATION OF THE SAME. Crown 8vo, gilt. 6s. net.

A FRENCH TRANSLATION OF THE SAME. Crown 8vo, gilt. 6s. net.

AN ITALIAN TRANSLATION OF THE SAME. Crown 8vo, gilt. 6s. net.

—— ALICE'S ADVENTURES UNDER-GROUND. Being a Facsimile of the Original MS. Book, afterwards developed into "Alice's Adventures in Wonderland." With 27 Illustrations by the Author. Crown 8vo. 4s. net.

—— THROUGH THE LOOKING-GLASS AND WHAT ALICE FOUND THERE. With 50 Illustrations by TENNIEL. Cr. 8vo, gilt. 6s. net.

People's Edition. With all the original Illustrations. Crown 8vo. 2s. 6d. net.

People's Edition of "Alice's Adventures in Wonderland," and "Through the Looking-Glass." 1 vol. Crown 8vo. 4s. 6d. net.

—— THE GAME OF LOGIC. Cr. 8vo. 3s. net.

—— RHYME? AND REASON? With 65 Illustrations by ARTHUR B. FROST, and 9 by HENRY HOLIDAY. Crown 8vo. 6s. net.

—— A TANGLED TALE. Reprinted from the "Monthly Packet." With 6 Illustrations by ARTHUR B. FROST. Crn. 8vo. 4s. 6d. net.

—— SYLVIE AND BRUNO. With 46 Illustrations by HARRY FURNISS. Cr. 8vo. 7s 6d. net.

—— THE NURSERY "ALICE." Twenty Coloured Enlargements from TENNIEL'S Illustrations to "Alice's Adventures in Wonderland," with Text adapted to Nursery Readers. 4to. 4s. net.

—— THE HUNTING OF THE SNARK, AN AGONY IN EIGHT FITS. With 9 Illustrations by HENRY HOLIDAY. Cr. 8vo. 4s. 6d. net.

CARSTARES (WM.): A Character and Career of the Revolutionary Epoch (1649—1715). By R. H. STORY. 8vo. 12s.

CARTER (R. Brudenell, F.C.S.).—A PRACTICAL TREATISE ON DISEASES OF THE EYE. 8vo. 16s.

—— EYESIGHT, GOOD AND BAD. Cr. 8vo. 6s.

—— MODERN OPERATIONS FOR CATARACT. 8vo. 6s.

CASSEL (Dr. D.).—MANUAL OF JEWISH HISTORY AND LITERATURE. Translated by Mrs. HENRY LUCAS. Fcp. 8vo. 2s. 6d

CAUCASUS: NOTES ON THE. By "Wanderer." 8vo. 9s.

CAUTLEY (G. S.).—A CENTURY OF EMBLEMS. With Illustrations by the Lady MARIAN ALFORD. Small 4to. 10s. 6d.

CAZENOVE (J. Gibson).—CONCERNING THE BEING AND ATTRIBUTES OF GOD. 8vo. 5s.

CHALMERS (J. B.).—GRAPHICAL DETERMINATION OF FORCES IN ENGINEERING STRUCTURES. 8vo. 24s.

CHASSERESSE (D.).—SPORTING SKETCHES. Illustrated. Crown 8vo. 3s. 6d.

CHATTERTON: A BIOGRAPHICAL STUDY. By Sir DANIEL WILSON, LL.D.   Crown 8vo. 6s. 6d.

CHERRY (Prof. R. R.).—LECTURES ON THE GROWTH OF CRIMINAL LAW IN ANCIENT COMMUNITIES.   8vo.   5s. net.

CHEYNE (C. H. H.).—AN ELEMENTARY TREATISE ON THE PLANETARY THEORY. Crown 8vo.   7s. 6d.

CHEYNE (T. K.).—THE BOOK OF ISAIAH CHRONOLOGICALLY ARRANGED.   Crown 8vo. 7s. 6d.

CHOICE NOTES ON THE FOUR GOSPELS, drawn from Old and New Sources. Crown 8vo.   4 vols.   4s. 6d. each.   (St. Matthew and St. Mark in 1 vol.   9s.)

CHRISTIE (J.).—CHOLERA EPIDEMICS IN EAST AFRICA.   8vo.   15s.

CHRISTIE (J. R.).—ELEMENTARY TEST QUESTIONS IN PURE AND MIXED MATHEMATICS.   Crown 8vo.   8s. 6d.

CHRISTMAS CAROL, A.   Printed in Colours, with Illuminated Borders from MSS. of the Fourteenth and Fifteenth Centuries. 4to.   21s.

CHURCH (Very Rev. R. W.).—THE SACRED POETRY OF EARLY RELIGIONS.   2nd Edition. 18mo.   1s.

—— HUMAN LIFE AND ITS CONDITIONS.   Cr. 8vo.   6s.

—— THE GIFTS OF CIVILISATION, and other Sermons.   2nd Edition.   Crown 8vo.   7s. 6d.

—— DISCIPLINE OF THE CHRISTIAN CHARACTER, and other Sermons.   Crown 8vo.   4s. 6d.

—— ADVENT SERMONS.   1885.   Cr. 8vo.   4s. 6d.

—— MISCELLANEOUS WRITINGS.   Collected Edition.   5 vols.   Globe 8vo.   5s. each.
   Vol. I. MISCELLANEOUS ESSAYS.   II DANTE: AND OTHER ESSAYS.   III. ST. ANSELM.   IV. SPENSER.   V. BACON.

—— THE OXFORD MOVEMENT.   1833—45. 8vo.   12s. 6d. net.

CHURCH (Rev. A. J.).—LATIN VERSION OF SELECTIONS FROM TENNYSON.   By Prof. CONINGTON, Prof. SEELEY, Dr. HESSEY, T. E. KEBBEL, &c.   Edited by A. J. CHURCH, M.A.   Extra fcp. 8vo.   6s.

—— STORIES FROM THE BIBLE.   Illustrated. Crown 8vo.   5s.

CICERO.   THE LIFE AND LETTERS OF MARCUS TULLIUS CICERO.   By the Rev. G. E. JEANS, M.A.   2nd Edition.   Crown 8vo.   10s. 6d.

—— THE ACADEMICA.   The Text revised and explained by J. S. REID, M.L.   8vo.   15s.

—— THE ACADEMICS.   Translated by J. S. REID, M.L.   8vo.   5s. 6d.
   See also pp. 31, 32.

CLARK.   MEMORIALS FROM JOURNALS AND LETTERS OF SAMUEL CLARK, M.A.   Edited by his Wife.   Crown 8vo.   7s. 6d.

CLARK (L.) and SADLER (H.).—THE STAR GUIDE.   Royal 8vo.   5s.

CLARKE (C. B.).—A GEOGRAPHICAL READER AND COMPANION TO THE ATLAS.   Cr. 8vo.   2s.

—— A CLASS-BOOK OF GEOGRAPHY.   With 18 Coloured Maps.   Fcp. 8vo.   3s.; swd., 2s. 6d.

—— SPECULATIONS FROM POLITICAL ECONOMY.   Crown 8vo.   3s. 6d.

CLASSICAL WRITERS.   Edited by JOHN RICHARD GREEN.   Fcp. 8vo.   1s. 6d. each.
   EURIPIDES.   By Prof. MAHAFFY.
   MILTON.   By STOPFORD A. BROOKE.
   LIVY.   By the Rev. W. W. CAPES, M.A.
   VERGIL.   By Prof. NETTLESHIP, M.A.
   SOPHOCLES.   By Prof. L. CAMPBELL, M.A.
   DEMOSTHENES.   By Prof. BUTCHER, M.A.
   TACITUS.   By CHURCH and BRODRIBB.

CLAUSIUS (R.).—THE MECHANICAL THEORY OF HEAT.   Translated by WALTER R. BROWNE.   Crown 8vo.   10s. 6d.

CLERGYMAN'S SELF-EXAMINATION CONCERNING THE APOSTLES' CREED.   Extra fcp. 8vo.   1s. 6d.

CLIFFORD (Prof. W. K.).—ELEMENTS OF DYNAMIC.   An Introduction to the Study of Motion and Rest in Solid and Fluid Bodies. Crown 8vo.   Part I. Kinematic.   Books I.—III.   7s. 6d.   Book IV. and Appendix, 6s.

—— LECTURES AND ESSAYS.   Ed. by LESLIE STEPHEN and Sir F. POLLOCK.   Cr. 8vo.   8s. 6d.

—— SEEING AND THINKING.   With Diagrams. Crown 8vo.   3s. 6d.

—— MATHEMATICAL PAPERS.   Edited by R. TUCKER.   With an Introduction by H. J. STEPHEN SMITH, M.A.   8vo.   30s.

CLIFFORD (Mrs. W. K.).—ANYHOW STORIES. With Illustrations by DOROTHY TENNANT. Crown 8vo.   1s. 6d. ; paper covers, 1s.

CLOUGH (A. H.).—POEMS.   New Edition. Crown 8vo.   7s. 6d.

—— PROSE REMAINS.   With a Selection from his Letters, and a Memoir by his Wife. Crown 8vo.   7s. 6d.

COAL: ITS HISTORY AND ITS USES.   By Profs. GREEN, MIALL, THORPE, RÜCKER, and MARSHALL.   8vo.   12s. 6d.

COBDEN (Richard.).—SPEECHES ON QUESTIONS OF PUBLIC POLICY.   Ed. by J. BRIGHT and J. E. THOROLD ROGERS.   Globe 8vo. 3s. 6d.

COCKSHOTT (A.) and WALTERS (F. B.). —A TREATISE ON GEOMETRICAL CONICS. Crown 8vo.   5s.

COHEN (Dr. Julius B.).—THE OWENS COLLEGE COURSE OF PRACTICAL ORGANIC CHEMISTRY.   Fcp. 8vo.   2s. 6d.

COLENSO (Bp.).—THE COMMUNION SERVICE FROM THE BOOK OF COMMON PRAYER, WITH SELECT READINGS FROM THE WRITINGS OF THE REV. F. D. MAURICE.   Edited by BISHOP COLENSO.   6th Edition.   16mo. 2s. 6d.

COLERIDGE.—THE POETICAL AND DRAMATIC WORKS OF SAMUEL TAYLOR COLERIDGE.   4 vols.   Fcp. 8vo.   31s. 6d.
   Also an Edition on Large Paper, 2l. 12s. 6d.

COLLECTS OF THE CHURCH OF ENGLAND. With a Coloured Floral Design to each Collect. Crown 8vo. 12s.

COLLIER (Hon. John).—A PRIMER OF ART. 18mo. 1s.

COLSON (F. H.).—FIRST GREEK READER. Stories and Legends. With Notes, Vocabulary, and Exercises. Globe 8vo. 3s.

COMBE. LIFE OF GEORGE COMBE. By CHARLES GIBBON. 2 vols. 8vo. 32s.

—— EDUCATION: ITS PRINCIPLES AND PRACTICE AS DEVELOPED BY GEORGE COMBE. Edited by WILLIAM JOLLY. 8vo. 15s.

CONGREVE (Rev. John).—HIGH HOPES AND PLEADINGS FOR A REASONABLE FAITH, NOBLER THOUGHTS, LARGER CHARITY. Crown 8vo. 5s.

CONSTABLE (Samuel).—GEOMETRICAL EXERCISES FOR BEGINNERS. Cr. 8vo. 3s. 6d.

COOK (E. T.).—A POPULAR HANDBOOK TO THE NATIONAL GALLERY. Including, by special permission, Notes collected from the Works of Mr. RUSKIN. 3rd Edition. Crown 8vo, half morocco. 14s.

Also an Edition on Large Paper, limited to 250 copies. 2 vols. 8vo.

COOKE (Josiah P., jun.).—PRINCIPLES OF CHEMICAL PHILOSOPHY. New Ed. 8vo. 16s.

—— —RELIGION AND CHEMISTRY. Crown 8vo. 7s. 6d.

—— ELEMENTS OF CHEMICAL PHYSICS. 4th Edition. Royal 8vo. 21s.

COOKERY. MIDDLE CLASS BOOK. Compiled for the Manchester School of Cookery. Fcp. 8vo. 1s. 6d.

CO-OPERATION IN THE UNITED STATES: HISTORY OF. Edited by H. B. ADAMS. 8vo. 15s.

COPE (E. D.).—THE ORIGIN OF THE FITTEST. Essays on Evolution. 8vo. 12s. 6d.

COPE (E. M.).—AN INTRODUCTION TO ARISTOTLE'S RHETORIC. 8vo. 14s.

CORBETT (Julian).—THE FALL OF ASGARD: A Tale of St. Olaf's Day. 2 vols. 12s.

—— FOR GOD AND GOLD. Crown 8vo. 6s.

—— KOPHETUA THE THIRTEENTH. 2 vols. Globe 8vo. 12s.

CORE (T. H.).—QUESTIONS ON BALFOUR STEWART'S "LESSONS IN ELEMENTARY PHYSICS." Fcp. 8vo. 2s.

CORFIELD (Dr. W. H.).—THE TREATMENT AND UTILISATION OF SEWAGE. 3rd Edition, Revised by the Author, and by LOUIS C. PARKES, M.D. 8vo. 16s.

CORNELL UNIVERSITY STUDIES IN CLASSICAL PHILOLOGY. Edited by I. FLAGG, W. G. HALE, and B. I. WHEELER. I. The C UM-Constructions: their History and Functions. Part I. Critical. 1s. 8d. net. Part II. Constructive. By W. G. HALE. 3s. 4d. net. II. Analogy and the Scope of its Application in Language. By B. I. WHEELER. 1s. 3d. net.

COSSA.—GUIDE TO THE STUDY OF POLITICAL ECONOMY. From the Italian of Dr. LUIGI COSSA. Crown 8vo. 4s. 6d.

COTTERILL (Prof. James H.).—APPLIED MECHANICS: An Introduction to the Theory of Structures and Machines. 2nd Edition. Med. 8vo. 18s.

COTTERILL (Prof. J. H.) and SLADE (J. H.). — LESSONS IN APPLIED MECHANICS. Fcp. 8vo. 5s. 6d.

COTTON (Bishop).—SERMONS PREACHED TO ENGLISH CONGREGATIONS IN INDIA. Crown 8vo. 7s. 6d.

COUES (Elliott).—KEY TO NORTH AMERICAN BIRDS. Illustrated. 8vo. 2l. 2s.

—— HANDBOOK OF FIELD AND GENERAL ORNITHOLOGY. Illustrated. 8vo. 10s. net.

COX (G. V.).—RECOLLECTIONS OF OXFORD. 2nd Edition. Crown 8vo. 6s.

CRAIK (Mrs.).—POEMS. New and Enlarged Edition. Extra fcp. 8vo. 6s.

—— CHILDREN'S POETRY. Ex. fcp. 8vo. 4s. 6d.

—— SONGS OF OUR YOUTH. Small 4to. 6s.

—— CONCERNING MEN: AND OTHER PAPERS. Crown 8vo. 4s. 6d.

—— ABOUT MONEY: AND OTHER THINGS. Crown 8vo. 6s.

—— SERMONS OUT OF CHURCH. Cr. 8vo. 6s.

—— AN UNKNOWN COUNTRY. Illustrated by F. NOEL PATON. Royal 8vo. 7s. 6d.

—— ALICE LEARMONT: A FAIRY TALE. With Illustrations. 4s. 6d.

—— AN UNSENTIMENTAL JOURNEY THROUGH CORNWALL. Illustrated. 4to. 12s. 6d.

—— OUR YEAR: A CHILD'S BOOK IN PROSE AND VERSE. Illustrated. 2s. 6d.

—— LITTLE SUNSHINE'S HOLIDAY. Globe 8vo. 2s. 6d.

—— THE ADVENTURES OF A BROWNIE. Illustrated by Mrs. ALLINGHAM. 4s. 6d.

—— THE LITTLE LAME PRINCE AND HIS TRAVELLING CLOAK. A Parable for Old and Young. With 24 Illustrations by J. McL. RALSTON. Crown 8vo. 4s. 6d.

—— THE FAIRY BOOK: THE BEST POPULAR FAIRY STORIES. 18mo. 4s. 6d.
See also p. 29.

CRAIK (Henry).—THE STATE IN ITS RELATION TO EDUCATION. Crown 8vo. 3s. 6d.

CRANE (Lucy).—LECTURES ON ART AND THE FORMATION OF TASTE. Cr. 8vo. 6s.

CRANE (Walter).—THE SIRENS THREE. A Poem. Written and Illustrated by WALTER CRANE. Royal 8vo. 10s. 6d.

CRAVEN (Mrs. Dacre).—A GUIDE TO DISTRICT NURSES. Crown 8vo. 2s. 6d.

CRAWFORD (F. Marion).—A CIGARETTE MAKER'S ROMANCE. Crown 8vo. 6s.

—— KHALED. 2 vols. Globe 8vo.
See also p. 29.

CROSS (Rev. J. A.).—BIBLE READINGS SELECTED FROM THE PENTATEUCH AND THE BOOK OF JOSHUA. 2nd Ed. Globe 8vo. 2s. 6d.

CROSSLEY (E.), GLEDHILL (J.), and WILSON (J. M.).—A HANDBOOK OF DOUBLE STARS. 8vo. 21s.—CORRECTIONS TO THE SAME. 8vo. 1s.

CUMMING (Linnæus).—ELECTRICITY. An Introduction to the Theory of Electricity. With numerous Examples. Cr. 8vo. 8s. 6d.

CUNNINGHAM (Rev. John). — THE GROWTH OF THE CHURCH IN ITS ORGANISATION AND INSTITUTIONS. Being the Croall Lectures for 1886. 8vo. 9s.

CUNNINGHAM (Rev. W.).—THE EPISTLE OF ST. BARNABAS. A Dissertation, including a Discussion of its Date and Authorship. Together with the Greek Text, the Latin Version, and a New English Translation and Commentary. Crown 8vo. 7s. 6d.

—— CHRISTIAN CIVILISATION, WITH SPECIAL REFERENCE TO INDIA. Crown 8vo. 5s.

—— THE CHURCHES OF ASIA: A METHODICAL SKETCH OF THE SECOND CENTURY. Crown 8vo. 6s.

CUNYNGHAME (Gen. Sir A. T.).—MY COMMAND IN SOUTH AFRICA, 1874—78. 8vo. 12s. 6d.

CURTEIS (Rev. G. H.).—DISSENT IN ITS RELATION TO THE CHURCH OF ENGLAND. Bampton Lectures for 1871. Cr. 8vo. 7s. 6d.

—— THE SCIENTIFIC OBSTACLES TO CHRISTIAN BELIEF. The Boyle Lectures, 1884. Cr. 8vo. 6s.

CUTHBERTSON (Francis). — EUCLIDIAN GEOMETRY. Extra fcp. 8vo. 4s. 6d.

DAGONET THE JESTER. Cr. 8vo. 4s. 6d.

DAHN (Felix).--FELICITAS. Translated by M. A. C. E. Crown 8vo. 4s. 6d.

"DAILY NEWS."—CORRESPONDENCE OF THE WAR BETWEEN RUSSIA AND TURKEY, 1877. TO THE FALL OF KARS. Cr. 8vo. 6s.

—— CORRESPONDENCE OF THE RUSSO-TURKISH WAR. FROM THE FALL OF KARS TO THE CONCLUSION OF PEACE. Crown 8vo. 6s.

DALE (A. W. W.).—THE SYNOD OF ELVIRA, AND CHRISTIAN LIFE IN THE FOURTH CENTURY. Crown 8vo. 10s. 6d.

DALTON (Rev. T.).—RULES AND EXAMPLES IN ARITHMETIC. New Edition. 18mo. 2s. 6d.

—— RULES AND EXAMPLES IN ALGEBRA. Part I. New Edit. 18mo. 2s. Part II. 2s.6d. KEY TO ALGEBRA. Part I. Crn. 8vo. 7s.6d.

DAMIEN (Father): A JOURNEY FROM CASHMERE TO HIS HOME IN HAWAII. By EDWARD CLIFFORD. Portrait. Crown 8vo. 2s. 6d.

DANIELL (Alfred).—A TEXT-BOOK OF THE PRINCIPLES OF PHYSICS. With Illustrations. 2nd Edition. Medium 8vo. 21s.

DANTE.—THE PURGATORY OF DANTE ALIGHIERI. Edited, with .Translations and Notes, by A. J. BUTLER. Cr. 8vo. 12s. 6d.

—— THE PARADISO OF DANTE. Edited, with a Prose Translation and Notes, by A. J. BUTLER. 2nd Edit. Crown 8vo. 12s. 6d.

—— DE MONARCHIA. Translated by F. J. CHURCH. 8vo. 4s. 6d.

—— DANTE: AND OTHER ESSAYS. By DEAN CHURCH. Globe 8vo. 5s

—— READINGS ON THE PURGATORIO OF DANTE. Chiefly based on the Commentary of Benvenuto Da Imola. By the Hon. W. W. VERNON, M.A. With an Introduction by DEAN CHURCH. 2 vols. Crn. 8vo. 24s.

DARWIN (CHAS.): MEMORIAL NOTICES, reprinted from Nature. By T. H. HUXLEY, G. J. ROMANES, ARCHIBALD GEIKIE, and W. THISELTON DYER. With a Portrait. Crown 8vo. 2s. 6d.

DAVIES (Rev. J. Llewelyn).—THE GOSPEL AND MODERN LIFE. 2nd Edition, to which is added MORALITY ACCORDING TO THE SACRAMENT OF THE LORD'S SUPPER. Extra fcp. 8vo. 6s.

—— WARNINGS AGAINST SUPERSTITION. Ex. fcp. 8vo. 2s. 6d.

—— THE CHRISTIAN CALLING. Ex.fcp. 8vo. 6s.

—— THE EPISTLES OF ST. PAUL TO THE EPHESIANS, THE COLOSSIANS, AND PHILEMON. With Introductions and Notes. 2nd Edition. 8vo. 7s. 6d.

—— SOCIAL QUESTIONS FROM THE POINT OF VIEW OF CHRISTIAN THEOLOGY. 2nd Ed. Crown 8vo. 6s.

—— ORDER AND GROWTH AS INVOLVED IN THE SPIRITUAL CONSTITUTION OF HUMAN SOCIETY. Crown 8vo.

DAWKINS (Prof. W. Boyd).—EARLY MAN IN BRITAIN AND HIS PLACE IN THE TERTIARY PERIOD. Medium 8vo. 25s.

DAWSON (Sir J. W.).—ACADIAN GEOLOGY, THE GEOLOGICAL STRUCTURE, ORGANIC REMAINS, AND MINERAL RESOURCES OF NOVA SCOTIA, NEW BRUNSWICK, AND PRINCE EDWARD ISLAND. 3rd Ed. 8vo. 21s.

DAWSON (James).—AUSTRALIAN ABORIGINES. Small 4to. 14s.

DAY (H. G.).—PROPERTIES OF CONIC SECTIONS PROVED GEOMETRICALLY. Crown 8vo. 3s. 6d.

DAY (Rev. Lal Behari).—BENGAL PEASANT LIFE. Crown 8vo. 6s.

—— FOLK TALES OF BENGAL. Cr. 8vo. 4s. 6d.

DAY (R. E.).—ELECTRIC LIGHT ARITHMETIC. Pott 8vo. 2s.

DAYS WITH SIR ROGER DE COVERLEY. From the Spectator. With Illustrations by HUGH THOMSON. Fcp. 4to. 6s.

DEÁK (FRANCIS): HUNGARIAN STATESMAN. A Memoir. 8vo. 12s. 6d.

DEAKIN (R.).—RIDER PAPERS ON EUCLID Books I. and II. 18mo. 1s.

DELAMOTTE (Prof. P. H.).—A BEGINNER'S DRAWING-BOOK. Progressively arranged. With Plates. 3rd Edit. Crn. 8vo. 3s. 6d.

DEMOCRACY: AN AMERICAN NOVEL. Crown 8vo. 4s. 6d.

DE MORGAN (Mary).—THE NECKLACE OF PRINCESS FIORIMONDE, AND OTHER STORIES. Illustrated by WALTER CRANE. Extra fcp. 8vo. 3s. 6d. Also a Large Paper Edition, with the Illustrations on India Paper. 100 copies only printed.

DEMOSTHENES.—See p. 32.

DE VERE (Aubrey).—ESSAYS CHIEFLY ON POETRY. 2 vols. Globe 8vo. 12s.

—— ESSAYS, CHIEFLY LITERARY AND ETHICAL. Globe 8vo. 6s.

DICEY (Prof. A. V.).—LECTURES INTRODUCTORY TO THE STUDY OF THE LAW OF THE CONSTITUTION. 3rd Edition. 8vo. 12s. 6d.

DICEY (Prof. A. V.).—LETTERS ON UNIONIST DELUSIONS. Crown 8vo. 2s. 6d.

—— THE PRIVY COUNCIL. Crown 8vo 3s. 6d.

DICKENS (Charles). — THE POSTHUMOUS PAPERS OF THE PICKWICK CLUB. With Notes and numerous Illustrations. Edited by CHARLES DICKENS the younger. 2 vols. Extra crown 8vo. 21s.

DICKSON (R.) and EDMOND (J. P.).— ANNALS OF SCOTTISH PRINTING, FROM THE INTRODUCTION OF THE ART IN 1507 TO THE BEGINNING OF THE SEVENTEENTH CENTURY. Dutch hand-made paper. Demy 4to, buckram, 2l. 2s. net.—Royal 4to, 2 vols. half Japanese vellum, 4l. 4s. net.

DIDEROT AND THE ENCYCLOPÆDISTS. By JOHN MORLEY. 2 vols. Globe 8vo. 10s.

DIGGLE (Rev. J. W.). — GODLINESS AND MANLINESS. A Miscellany of Brief Papers touching the Relation of Religion to Life. Crown 8vo. 6s.

DILETTANTI SOCIETY'S PUBLICATIONS.—ANTIQUITIES OF IONIA. Vols. I. II. and III. 2l. 2s. each, or 5l. 5s. the set, net. Vol. IV., folio, half mor., 3l. 13s. 6d. net.

—— PENROSE (Francis C.). An Investigation of the Principles of Athenian Architecture. Illustrated by numerous engravings. New Edition. Enlarged. Folio. 7l. 7s. net.

—— SPECIMENS OF ANCIENT SCULPTURE: EGYPTIAN, ETRUSCAN, GREEK, AND ROMAN. Selected from different Collections in Great Britain by the Society of Dilettanti. Vol. II. Folio. 5l. 5s. net.

DILKE (Sir C. W.).—GREATER BRITAIN. A RECORD OF TRAVEL IN ENGLISH-SPEAKING COUNTRIES DURING 1866-67. (America, Australia, India.) 9th Edition. Crown 8vo. 6s.

—— PROBLEMS OF GREATER BRITAIN. Maps. 4th Edition. Extra crown 8vo. 12s. 6d.

DILLWYN (E. A.).—JILL. Crown 8vo. 6s.

—— JILL AND JACK. 2 vols. Globe 8vo. 12s.

DODGSON (C. L.).—EUCLID. Books I. and II. With Words substituted for the Algebraical Symbols used in the first edition. 4th Edition. Crown 8vo. 2s.

—— EUCLID AND HIS MODERN RIVALS. 2nd Edition. Cr. 8vo. 6s.

—— SUPPLEMENT TO FIRST EDITION OF "EUCLID AND HIS MODERN RIVALS." Cr. 8vo. Sewed, 1s.

—— CURIOSA MATHEMATICA. Part I. A New Theory of Parallels. 3rd Ed. Cr. 8vo. 2s.

DONALDSON (Prof. James).—THE APOSTOLICAL FATHERS. A CRITICAL ACCOUNT OF THEIR GENUINE WRITINGS, AND OF THEIR DOCTRINES. 2nd Ed. Cr. 8vo. 7s. 6d.

DONISTHORPE (Wordsworth). — INDIVIDUALISM : A SYSTEM OF POLITICS. 8vo. 14s.

DOYLE (Sir F. H.).—THE RETURN OF THE GUARDS: AND OTHER POEMS. Cr. 8vo. 7s. 6d.

DREW (W. H.).—A GEOMETRICAL TREATISE ON CONIC SECTIONS. 8th Ed. Cr. 8vo. 5s.

DRUMMOND (Prof. James). —INTRODUCTION TO THE STUDY OF THEOLOGY. Crown 8vo. 5s.

DRYDEN : ESSAYS OF. Edited by Prof. C. D. YONGE. Fcp. 8vo. 2s. 6d.

DUFF (Right Hon. Sir M. E. Grant).—NOTES OF AN INDIAN JOURNEY. 8vo. 10s. 6d.

—— MISCELLANIES, POLITICAL AND LITERARY. 8vo. 10s. 6d.

DÜNTZER (H.).—LIFE OF GOETHE. Translated by T. W. LYSTER. With Illustrations. 2 vols. Crown 8vo. 21s.

—— LIFE OF SCHILLER. Translated by P. E. PINKERTON. Illustrations. Cr. 8vo. 10s. 6d.

DUPUIS (Prof. N. F.).—ELEMENTARY SYNTHETIC GEOMETRY OF THE POINT, LINE, AND CIRCLE IN THE PLANE. Gl. 8vo. 4s. 6d.

DYER (J. M.).—EXERCISES IN ANALYTICAL GEOMETRY. Crown 8vo. 4s. 6d.

DYER (Louis).—STUDIES OF THE GODS IN GREECE AT CERTAIN SANCTUARIES RECENTLY EXCAVATED. Extra crown 8vo.

DYNAMICS, SYLLABUS OF ELEMENTARY. Part I. LINEAR DYNAMICS. With an Appendix on the Meanings of the Symbols in Physical Equations. Prepared by the Association for the Improvement of Geometrical Teaching. 4to, sewed. 1s.

EADIE (Prof. John).—THE ENGLISH BIBLE : AN EXTERNAL AND CRITICAL HISTORY OF THE VARIOUS ENGLISH TRANSLATIONS OF SCRIPTURE. 2 vols. 8vo. 28s.

—— ST. PAUL'S EPISTLES TO THE THESSALONIANS, COMMENTARY ON THE GREEK TEXT. 8vo. 12s.

—— LIFE OF JOHN EADIE, D.D., LL.D. By JAMES BROWN, D.D. 2nd Ed. Cr. 8vo. 7s. 6d.

EAGLES (T. H.).—CONSTRUCTIVE GEOMETRY OF PLANE CURVES. Crown 8vo. 12s.

EASTLAKE (Lady).—FELLOWSHIP: LETTERS ADDRESSED TO MY SISTER-MOURNERS. Cr. 8vo. 2s. 6d.

EBERS (Dr. George).—THE BURGOMASTER'S WIFE. Translated by CLARA BELL. Crown 8vo. 4s. 6d.

—— ONLY A WORD. Translated by CLARA BELL. Crown 8vo. 4s. 6d.

ECCE HOMO. A SURVEY OF THE LIFE AND WORK OF JESUS CHRIST. 20th Ed. Cr. 8vo. 6s.

ECONOMIC JOURNAL (THE). Edited by F. Y. EDGEWORTH. No. 1, Ap. 1891. 8vo. 5s.

ECONOMICS, THE QUARTERLY JOURNAL OF. Vol. II. Parts II. III. IV. 2s. 6d. each; Vol. III. 4 parts, 2s. 6d. each ; Vol. IV. 4 parts, 2s. 6d. each. Vol. V. Part I. 2s. 6d. net.

EDGAR (J. H.) and PRITCHARD (G. S.).— NOTE-BOOK ON PRACTICAL SOLID OR DESCRIPTIVE GEOMETRY, CONTAINING PROBLEMS WITH HELP FOR SOLUTION. 4th Edition, Enlarged. By ARTHUR G. MEEZE. Globe 8vo. 4s. 6d.

EDWARDS (Joseph). — AN ELEMENTARY TREATISE ON THE DIFFERENTIAL CALCULUS. Crown 8vo. 10s. 6d.

EDWARDS-MOSS (Sir J. E.).—A SEASON IN SUTHERLAND. Crown 8vo. 1s. 6d.

EICKE (K. M.).—FIRST LESSONS IN LATIN. Extra fcp. 8vo. 2s.

EIMER (G. H. T.).—ORGANIC EVOLUTION AS THE RESULT OF THE INHERITANCE OF ACQUIRED CHARACTERS ACCORDING TO THE LAWS OF ORGANIC GROWTH. Translated by J. T. CUNNINGHAM, M.A. 8vo. 12s. 6d.

ELDERTON (W. A.).—MAPS AND MAP DRAWING. Pott 8vo. 1s.

ELLERTON (Rev. John).—THE HOLIEST MANHOOD, AND ITS LESSONS FOR BUSY LIVES. Crown 8vo. 6s.

ELLIOTT. LIFE OF HENRY VENN ELLIOTT, OF BRIGHTON. By JOSIAH BATEMAN, M.A. 3rd Edition. Extra fcp. 8vo. 6s.

ELLIS (A. J.).—PRACTICAL HINTS ON THE QUANTITATIVE PRONUNCIATION OF LATIN. Extra fcp. 8vo. 4s. 6d.

ELLIS (Tristram).—SKETCHING FROM NATURE. Illustr. by H. STACY MARKS, R.A., and the Author. 2nd Edition. Cr.8vo. 3s.6d.

EMERSON. THE LIFE OF RALPH WALDO EMERSON. By J. L. CABOT. 2 vols. Crown 8vo. 18s.

—— THE COLLECTED WORKS OF RALPH WALDO EMERSON. 6 vols. (1) MISCELLANIES. With an Introductory Essay by JOHN MORLEY. (2) ESSAYS. (3) POEMS. (4) ENGLISH TRAITS; AND REPRESENTATIVE MEN. (5) CONDUCT OF LIFE; AND SOCIETY AND SOLITUDE. (6) LETTERS; AND SOCIAL AIMS, &c. Globe 8vo. 5s. each.

ENGLAND (E. B.).—EXERCISES IN LATIN SYNTAX AND IDIOM. Arranged with reference to Roby's School Latin Grammar. Crn. 8vo. 2s. 6d.—KEY. Crn. 8vo. 2s. 6d.

ENGLISH CITIZEN (THE).—A Series of Short Books on his Rights and Responsibilities. Edited by HENRY CRAIK, C.B. Crown 8vo. 3s. 6d. each.

CENTRAL GOVERNMENT. By H. D. TRAILL.

THE ELECTORATE AND THE LEGISLATURE. By SPENCER WALPOLE.

THE POOR LAW. By the Rev. T. W. FOWLE.

THE NATIONAL BUDGET; THE NATIONAL DEBT; TAXES AND RATES. By A. J. WILSON.

THE STATE IN RELATION TO LABOUR. By W. STANLEY JEVONS, LL.D., F.R.S.

THE STATE AND THE CHURCH. By the Hon. ARTHUR ELLIOTT, M.P.

FOREIGN RELATIONS. By SPENCER WALPOLE.

THE STATE IN ITS RELATION TO TRADE. By Sir T. H. FARRER, Bart.

LOCAL GOVERNMENT. By M. D. CHALMERS.

THE STATE IN ITS RELATION TO EDUCATION. By HENRY CRAIK, C.B.

THE LAND LAWS. By Sir F. POLLOCK, Bart. 2nd Edition.

COLONIES AND DEPENDENCIES.
Part I. INDIA. By J. S. COTTON, M.A.
II. THE COLONIES. - By E. J. PAYNE.

JUSTICE AND POLICE. By F. W. MAITLAND.

THE PUNISHMENT AND PREVENTION OF CRIME. By Colonel Sir EDMUND DU CANE.

THE NATIONAL DEFENCES. By Colonel MAURICE, R.A.   [*In the Press.*

ENGLISH CLASSICS. With Introductions and Notes. Globe 8vo.

BACON.—ESSAYS. Edited by F. G. SELBY, M.A. 3s.; sewed, 2s. 6d.

BURKE.—REFLECTIONS ON THE FRENCH REVOLUTION. By the same. 3s.

ENGLISH CLASSICS—*continued.*

GOLDSMITH.—THE TRAVELLER AND THE DESERTED VILLAGE. Edited by ARTHUR BARRETT, B.A. 1s. 9d.; sewed, 1s. 6d.— THE TRAVELLER (separately), sewed, 1s.

HELPS: ESSAYS WRITTEN IN THE INTERVALS OF BUSINESS. Edit. by F. J. ROWE and W. T. WEBB. 1s. 9d.; sewed, 1s. 6d.

MILTON —PARADISE LOST, BOOKS I. and II. Edited by M. MACMILLAN, B.A. 1s. 9d.; sewed, 1s. 6d.—BOOKS I. and II. (separately), 1s. 3d. each; sewed, 1s. each.

— L'ALLEGRO, IL PENSEROSO, LYCIDAS, ARCADES, SONNETS, ETC. Edit. by WM. BELL, M.A. 1s. 9d.; sewed, 1s. 6d.

— COMUS. By the same. 1s. 3d.; swd. 1s.

— SAMSON AGONISTES. Edited by H. M. PERCIVAL, M.A. 2s.; sewed, 1s. 9d.

SCOTT.—THE LAY OF THE LAST MINSTREL. By G. H. STUART, M.A., and E. H. ELLIOT, B.A. Canto I. 9d.; Cantos I.— III. 1s. 3d.; sewed, 1s. Cantos IV.— VI. 1s. 3d.; sewed, 1s.

— MARMION. Edited by MICHAEL MACMILLAN, B.A. 3s.; sewed, 2s. 6d.

— ROKEBY. By the same. 3s.; swd. 2s.6d.

— THE LADY OF THE LAKE. Edited by G. H. STUART, M.A. 2s. 6d.; sewed, 2s.

SHAKESPEARE —THE TEMPEST. Edited by K. DEIGHTON. 1s. 9d.: sewed, 1s. 6d.

— MUCH ADO ABOUT NOTHING. By the same. 2s.; sewed, 1s. 9d.

— A MIDSUMMER NIGHT'S DREAM. By the same. 1s. 9d.; sewed, 1s. 6d.

— THE MERCHANT OF VENICE. By the same. 1s. 9d.; sewed, 1s. 6d.

— AS YOU LIKE IT. By the same.

— TWELFTH NIGHT. By the same. 1s.9d.; sewed, 1s. 6d.

— THE WINTER'S TALE. By the same. 2s.; sewed, 1s. 9d.

— KING JOHN. By the same. 1s. 9d.; sewed, 1s. 6d.

— RICHARD II. By the same. 1s. 9d.; sewed, 1s. 6d.

— HENRY V. By the same. 1s.9d.: swd. 1s.6d.

— RICHARD III. Edited by C. H. TAWNEY, M.A. 2s. 6d.; sewed, 2s.

— CORIOLANUS. Edited by K. DEIGHTON. 2s. 6d.; sewed, 2s.

— JULIUS CÆSAR. By the same. 1s. 9d.; sewed, 1s. 6d.

— MACBETH. By the same. 1s.9d.; swd.1s.6d.

— HAMLET. By the same. 2s.6d.; swd. 2s.

— KING LEAR. By the same.

— OTHELLO. By the same. 2s.; swd. 1s. 9d.

— ANTONY AND CLEOPATRA. By the same.

— CYMBELINE. By the same. 2s.6d.; swd.2s.

SOUTHEY.—LIFE OF NELSON. By MICHAEL MACMILLAN, B.A. 3s.; sewed, 1s. 6d.

TENNYSON.—SELECTIONS. By F. J. ROWE, M.A., and W. T. WEBB, M.A. 3s. 6d.

— THE COMING OF ARTHUR, AND THE PASSING OF ARTHUR. By F. J. ROWE. 2s.

— ENOCH ARDEN. Edit. by W. T. WEBB.

ENGLISH HISTORY, READINGS IN.— Selected and Edited by JOHN RICHARD GREEN. 3 Parts. Fcp. 8vo. 1s. 6d. each.

Part I. Hengist to Cressy. II. Cressy to Cromwell. III. Cromwell to Balaklava.

ENGLISH ILLUSTRATED MAGAZINE (THE). — Profusely Illustrated. Published Monthly. Number I. October, 1883. 6d. net. Vol. I. 1884. 7s. 6d. Vols. II.—VII. Super royal 8vo, extra cloth, coloured edges. 8s. each. [Cloth Covers for binding Volumes, 1s. 6d. each.]

—— Proof Impressions of Engravings originally published in *The English Illustrated Magazine*. 1884. In Portfolio 4to. 21s.

ENGLISH MEN OF ACTION. — Crown 8vo. With Portraits. 2s. 6d. each.

The following Volumes are Ready:

GENERAL GORDON. By Col. Sir W. BUTLER.
HENRY V. By the Rev. A. J. CHURCH.
LIVINGSTONE. By THOMAS HUGHES.
LORD LAWRENCE. By Sir RICHARD TEMPLE.
WELLINGTON. By GEORGE HOOPER.
DAMPIER. By W. CLARK RUSSELL.
MONK. By JULIAN CORBETT.
STRAFFORD. By H. D. TRAILL.
WARREN HASTINGS. By Sir ALFRED LYALL.
PETERBOROUGH. By W. STEBBING.
CAPTAIN COOK. By WALTER BESANT.
SIR HENRY HAVELOCK. By A. FORBES.
CLIVE. By Colonel Sir CHARLES WILSON.
SIR CHARLES NAPIER. By Col. Sir WM. BUTLER.
DRAKE. By JULIAN CORBETT.
WARWICK, THE KING-MAKER. By C. W. OMAN.

The undermentioned are in the Press or in Preparation :

MONTROSE. By MOWBRAY MORRIS.
RODNEY. By DAVID HANNAY.
SIR JOHN MOORE. By Colonel MAURICE.
BRUCE. By Sir SAMUEL BAKER.
SIMON DE MONTFORT. By G. W. PROTHERO.

ENGLISH MEN OF LETTERS.—Edited by JOHN MORLEY. Crown 8vo. 2s. 6d. each. Cheap Edition. 1s. 6d. ; sewed, 1s.

JOHNSON. By LESLIE STEPHEN.
SCOTT. By R. H. HUTTON.
GIBBON. By J. COTTER MORISON.
HUME. By T. H. HUXLEY.
GOLDSMITH. By WILLIAM BLACK.
SHELLEY. By J. A. SYMONDS.
DEFOE. By W. MINTO.
BURNS. By Principal SHAIRP.
SPENSER. By R. W. CHURCH.
THACKERAY. By ANTHONY TROLLOPE.
MILTON. By MARK PATTISON.
BURKE. By JOHN MORLEY.
HAWTHORNE. By HENRY JAMES.
SOUTHEY. By Prof. DOWDEN.
BUNYAN. By J. A. FROUDE.
CHAUCER. By Prof. A. W. WARD.
COWPER. By GOLDWIN SMITH.
POPE. By LESLIE STEPHEN.
BYRON. By Prof. NICHOL.
DRYDEN. By G. SAINTSBURY.
LOCKE. By Prof. FOWLER.
WORDSWORTH. By F. W. H. MYERS.
LANDOR. By SIDNEY COLVIN.
DE QUINCEY. By Prof. MASSON.
CHARLES LAMB. By Rev. ALFRED AINGER.

ENGLISH MEN OF LETTERS—*contd.*

BENTLEY. By Prof. JEBB.
DICKENS. By A. W. WARD.
GRAY. By EDMUND GOSSE.
SWIFT. By LESLIE STEPHEN.
STERNE. By H. D. TRAILL.
MACAULAY. By J. COTTER MORISON.
FIELDING. By AUSTIN DOBSON.
SHERIDAN. By Mrs OLIPHANT.
ADDISON. By W. J. COURTHOPE.
BACON. By R. W. CHURCH.
COLERIDGE. By H. D. TRAILL.
SIR PHILIP SIDNEY. By J. A. SYMONDS.
KEATS. By SIDNEY COLVIN.

ENGLISH POETS. Selections, with Critical Introductions by various Writers, and a General Introduction by MATTHEW ARNOLD. Edited by T. H. WARD, M.A. 2nd Edition. 4 vols. Crown 8vo. 7s. 6d. each.

Vol. I. CHAUCER TO DONNE. II. BEN JONSON TO DRYDEN. III. ADDISON TO BLAKE. IV. WORDSWORTH TO ROSSETTI.

ENGLISH STATESMEN (TWELVE). Crown 8vo. 2s. 6d. each.

WILLIAM THE CONQUEROR. By EDWARD A. FREEMAN, D.C.L., LL.D. [*Ready.*
HENRY II. By Mrs. J. R. GREEN. [*Ready.*
EDWARD I. By F. YORK POWELL.
HENRY VII. By JAMES GAIRDNER. [*Ready.*
CARDINAL WOLSEY. By Bishop CREIGHTON. [*Ready.*
ELIZABETH. By E. S. BEESLY.
OLIVER CROMWELL. By FREDERIC HARRISON. [*Ready.*
WILLIAM III. By H. D. TRAILL. [*Ready.*
WALPOLE. By JOHN MORLEY. [*Ready.*
CHATHAM. By JOHN MORLEY.
PITT. By JOHN MORLEY.
PEEL. By J. R. THURSFIELD. [*Ready*

ESSEX FIELD CLUB MEMOIRS. Vol. I. REPORT ON THE EAST ANGLIAN EARTHQUAKE OF 22ND APRIL, 1884. By RAPHAEL MELDOLA, F.R.S., and WILLIAM WHITE, F.E.S. Maps and Illustrations. 8vo. 3s. 6d.

ETON COLLEGE, HISTORY OF, 1440—1884. By H. C. MAXWELL LYTE, C.B. Illustrations. 2nd Edition. Med. 8vo. 21s.

EURIPIDES.—MEDEA. Edited by A. W. VERRALL, Litt.D. 8vo. 7s. 6d.

—— IPHIGENEIA IN AULIS. Edited, with Introduction, Notes, and Commentary, by E. B. ENGLAND, M.A. 8vo.

—— ION. Translated by Rev. M. A. BAYFIELD, M.A. Crown 8vo. 2s. net. With Music, 4to. 4s. 6d. net.

See also pp. 31, 32.

EUROPEAN HISTORY, NARRATED IN A SERIES OF HISTORICAL SELECTIONS FROM THE BEST AUTHORITIES. Edited and arranged by E. M. SEWELL and C. M. YONGE. 2 vols. 3rd Edition. Crown 8vo. 6s. each.

EVANS (Sebastian). — BROTHER FABIAN'S MANUSCRIPT, AND OTHER POEMS. Fcp. 8vo, cloth. 6s.

—— IN THE STUDIO : A DECADE OF POEMS. Extra fcp. 8vo. 5s.

EVERETT (Prof. J. D.).—UNITS AND PHYSICAL CONSTANTS. 2nd Ed. Globe 8vo. 5s.

FAIRFAX. LIFE OF ROBERT FAIRFAX OF STEETON, Vice-Admiral, Alderman, and Member for York, A.D. 1666—1725. By CLEMENTS R. MARKHAM, C.B. 8vo. 12s. 6d.

FAITH AND CONDUCT: AN ESSAY ON VERIFIABLE RELIGION. Crown 8vo. 7s. 6d.

FARRAR (Archdeacon).—THE FALL OF MAN, AND OTHER SERMONS. 5th Ed. Cr. 8vo. 6s.

—— THE WITNESS OF HISTORY TO CHRIST. Hulsean Lectures for 1870. 7th Ed. Cr. 8vo. 5s.

—— SEEKERS AFTER GOD. THE LIVES OF SENECA, EPICTETUS, AND MARCUS AURELIUS. 12th Edition. Crown 8vo. 6s.

—— THE SILENCE AND VOICES OF GOD. University and other Sermons. 7th Ed. Cr. 8vo. 6s.

—— IN THE DAYS OF THY YOUTH. Sermons on Practical Subjects, preached at Marlborough College. 9th Edition. Cr. 8vo. 9s.

—— ETERNAL HOPE. Five Sermons, preached in Westminster Abbey. 28th Thousand. Crown 8vo. 6s.

—— SAINTLY WORKERS. Five Lenten Lectures. 3rd Edition. Crown 8vo. 6s.

—— EPHPHATHA; OR, THE AMELIORATION OF THE WORLD. Sermons preached at Westminster Abbey. Crown 8vo. 6s.

—— MERCY AND JUDGMENT. A few Last Words on Christian Eschatology. 2nd Ed. Crown 8vo. 10s. 6d.

—— THE MESSAGES OF THE BOOKS. Being Discourses and Notes on the Books of the New Testament. 8vo. 14s.

—— SERMONS AND ADDRESSES DELIVERED IN AMERICA. Crown 8vo. 7s. 6d.

—— THE HISTORY OF INTERPRETATION. Being the Bampton Lectures, 1885. 8vo. 16s.

FASNACHT (G. Eugène).—THE ORGANIC METHOD OF STUDYING LANGUAGES. I. FRENCH. Extra fcp. 8vo. 3s. 6d.

—— A SYNTHETIC FRENCH GRAMMAR FOR SCHOOLS. Crown 8vo. 3s. 6d.

—— FRENCH READINGS FOR CHILDREN. Illustrated. Globe 8vo.

FAWCETT (Rt. Hon. Henry).—MANUAL OF POLITICAL ECONOMY. 7th Edition, revised. Crown 8vo. 12s.

—— AN EXPLANATORY DIGEST OF PROFESSOR FAWCETT'S MANUAL OF POLITICAL ECONOMY. By CYRIL A. WATERS. Cr. 8vo. 2s. 6d.

—— SPEECHES ON SOME CURRENT POLITICAL QUESTIONS. 8vo. 10s. 6d.

—— FREE TRADE AND PROTECTION. 6th Edition. Crown 8vo. 3s. 6d.

FAWCETT (Mrs. H.).—POLITICAL ECONOMY FOR BEGINNERS, WITH QUESTIONS. 7th Edition. 18mo. 2s. 6d.

—— SOME EMINENT WOMEN OF OUR TIMES. Short Biographical Sketches. Cr. 8vo. 2s. 6d.

FAWCETT (Rt. Hon. Henry and Mrs. H.).— ESSAYS AND LECTURES ON POLITICAL AND SOCIAL SUBJECTS. 8vo. 10s. 6d.

FAY (Amy.).—MUSIC-STUDY IN GERMANY. Preface by Sir GEO. GROVE. Cr. 8vo. 4s. 6d.

FEARNLEY (W.).—A MANUAL OF ELEMENTARY PRACTICAL HISTOLOGY. Cr. 8vo. 7s. 6d.

FEARON (D. R.).—SCHOOL INSPECTION. 6th Edition. Crown 8vo. 2s. 6d.

FERREL (Prof. W.).—A POPULAR TREATISE ON THE WINDS. 8vo. 18s.

FERRERS (Rev. N. M.).—A TREATISE ON TRILINEAR CO-ORDINATES, THE METHOD OF RECIPROCAL POLARS, AND THE THEORY OF PROJECTIONS. 4th Ed. Cr. 8vo. 6s. 6d.

—— SPHERICAL HARMONICS AND SUBJECTS CONNECTED WITH THEM. Crown 8vo. 7s. 6d.

FESSENDEN (C.).—ELEMENTS OF PHYSICS FOR PUBLIC SCHOOLS. Globe 8vo.

FINCK (Henry T.).—ROMANTIC LOVE AND PERSONAL BEAUTY. 2 vols. Cr. 8vo. 18s.

FIRST LESSONS IN BUSINESS MATTERS. By A BANKER'S DAUGHTER. 2nd Edition. 18mo. 1s.

FISHER (Rev. Osmond).—PHYSICS OF THE EARTH'S CRUST. 2nd Edition. 8vo. 12s.

FISKE (John).—OUTLINES OF COSMIC PHILOSOPHY, BASED ON THE DOCTRINE OF EVOLUTION. 2 vols. 8vo. 25s.

—— DARWINISM, AND OTHER ESSAYS. Crown 8vo. 7s. 6d.

—— MAN'S DESTINY VIEWED IN THE LIGHT OF HIS ORIGIN. Crown 8vo. 3s. 6d.

—— AMERICAN POLITICAL IDEAS VIEWED FROM THE STAND-POINT OF UNIVERSAL HISTORY. Crown 8vo. 4s.

—— THE CRITICAL PERIOD IN AMERICAN HISTORY, 1783—89. Ex. Cr. 8vo. 10s. 6d.

—— THE BEGINNINGS OF NEW ENGLAND; OR, THE PURITAN THEOCRACY IN ITS RELATIONS TO CIVIL AND RELIGIOUS LIBERTY. Crown 8vo. 7s. 6d.

—— CIVIL GOVERNMENT IN THE UNITED STATES CONSIDERED WITH SOME REFERENCE TO ITS ORIGIN. Crown 8vo. 6s. 6d.

FISON (L.) and HOWITT (A. W.).—KAMILAROI AND KURNAI GROUP. Group-Marriage and Relationship and Marriage by Elopement. 8vo. 15s.

FITCH (J. G.).—NOTES ON AMERICAN SCHOOLS AND TRAINING COLLEGES. Globe 8vo. 2s. 6d.

FITZGERALD (Edward): LETTERS AND LITERARY REMAINS OF. Ed. by W. ALDIS WRIGHT, M.A. 3 vols. Crown 8vo. 31s. 6d.

—— THE RUBÁIYAT OF OMAR KHÁYYÁM. Extra Crown 8vo. 10s. 6d.

FITZ GERALD (Caroline).—VENETIA VICTRIX, AND OTHER POEMS. Ex. fcp. 8vo. 3s. 6d.

FLEAY (Rev. F. G.).—A SHAKESPEARE MANUAL. Extra fcp. 8vo. 4s. 6d.

FLEISCHER (Dr. Emil).—A SYSTEM OF VOLUMETRIC ANALYSIS. Translated by M. M. PATTISON MUIR, F.R.S.E. Cr. 8vo. 7s. 6d.

FLOWER (Prof. W. H.).—AN INTRODUCTION TO THE OSTEOLOGY OF THE MAMMALIA. With numerous Illustrations. 3rd Edition, revised with the assistance of HANS GADOW, Ph.D., M.A. Crown 8vo. 10s. 6d.

FLÜCKIGER (F. A.) and HANBURY (D.). —PHARMACOGRAPHIA. A History of the principal Drugs of Vegetable Origin met with in Great Britain and India. 2nd Edition, revised. 8vo. 21s.

FO'C'SLE YARNS, including "Betsy Lee," and other Poems. Crown 8vo. 7s. 6d.

FORBES (Archibald).—SOUVENIRS OF SOME CONTINENTS. Crown 8vo. 6s.

FORBES (Edward): MEMOIR OF. By GEORGE WILSON, M.D., and ARCHIBALD GEIKIE, F.R.S., &c. Demy 8vo. 14s.

FORSYTH (A. R.).—A TREATISE ON DIFFERENTIAL EQUATIONS. Demy 8vo. 14s.

FOSTER (Prof. Michael).—A TEXT-BOOK OF PHYSIOLOGY. Illustrated. 5th Edition. 8vo. Part I., Book I. Blood—The Tissues of Movement, the Vascular Mechanism. 10s. 6d. - Part II., Book II. The Tissues of Chemical Action, with their Respective Mechanisms—Nutrition. 10s. 6d. Part III., Book III. The Central Nervous System. 7s. 6d.—Book IV. The Tissues and Mechanisms of Reproduction.

—— PRIMER OF PHYSIOLOGY. 18mo. 1s.

FOSTER (Prof. Michael) and BALFOUR (F. M.) (the late).—THE ELEMENTS OF EMBRYOLOGY. Edited by ADAM SEDGWICK, M.A., and WALTER HEAPE. Illustrated. 3rd Ed., revised and enlarged. Cr. 8vo. 10s. 6d.

FOSTER (Michael) and LANGLEY (J. N.).—A COURSE OF ELEMENTARY PRACTICAL PHYSIOLOGY AND HISTOLOGY. 6th Edition, enlarged. Crown 8vo. 7s. 6d.

FOTHERGILL (Dr. J. Milner).—THE PRACTITIONER'S HANDBOOK OF TREATMENT; OR, THE PRINCIPLES OF THERAPEUTICS. 3rd Edition, enlarged. 8vo. 16s.

—— THE ANTAGONISM OF THERAPEUTIC AGENTS, AND WHAT IT TEACHES. Cr. 8vo. 6s.

—— FOOD FOR THE INVALID, THE CONVALESCENT, THE DYSPEPTIC, AND THE GOUTY. 2nd Edition. Crown 8vo. 3s. 6d.

FOWLE (Rev. T. W.).—A NEW ANALOGY BETWEEN REVEALED RELIGION AND THE COURSE AND CONSTITUTION OF NATURE. Crown 8vo. 6s.

FOWLER (Rev. Thomas). — PROGRESSIVE MORALITY: AN ESSAY IN ETHICS. Crown 8vo. 5s.

FOWLER (W. W.).—TALES OF THE BIRDS. Illustrated. Crown 8vo. 3s. 6d.

—— A YEAR WITH THE BIRDS. Illustrated. Crown 8vo. 3s. 6d.

FOX (Dr. Wilson). — ON THE ARTIFICIAL PRODUCTION OF TUBERCLE IN THE LOWER ANIMALS. With Plates. 4to. 5s. 6d.

—— ON THE TREATMENT OF HYPERPYREXIA, AS ILLUSTRATED IN ACUTE ARTICULAR RHEUMATISM BY MEANS OF THE EXTERNAL APPLICATION OF COLD. 8vo. 2s. 6d.

FRAMJI (Dosabhai). — HISTORY OF THE PARSIS: INCLUDING THEIR MANNERS, CUSTOMS, RELIGION, AND PRESENT POSITION. Illustrated. 2 vols. Med. 8vo. 36s.

FRANKLAND (Prof. Percy).—A HANDBOOK OF AGRICULTURAL CHEMICAL ANALYSIS. Crown 8vo. 7s. 6d.

FRASER — HUGHES. — JAMES FRASER, SECOND BISHOP OF MANCHESTER: A Memoir. By T. HUGHES. Crown 8vo. 6s.

FRASER.—SERMONS. By the Right Rev. JAMES FRASER, D.D., Second Bishop of Manchester. Edited by Rev. JOHN W. DIGGLE. 2 vols. Crown 8vo. 6s. each.

FRASER-TYTLER. — SONGS IN MINOR KEYS. By C. C. FRASER-TYTLER (Mrs. EDWARD LIDDELL). 2nd Ed. 18mo. 6s.

FRATERNITY: A Romance. 2 vols. Cr. 8vo. 21s.

FRAZER (J. G.).—THE GOLDEN BOUGH: A Study in Comparative Religion. 2 vols. 8vo. 28s.

FREDERICK (Mrs.).—HINTS TO HOUSEWIVES ON SEVERAL POINTS, PARTICULARLY ON THE PREPARATION OF ECONOMICAL AND TASTEFUL DISHES. Crown 8vo. 1s.

FREEMAN (Prof. E. A.).—HISTORY OF THE CATHEDRAL CHURCH OF WELLS. Crown 8vo. 3s. 6d.

—— OLD ENGLISH HISTORY. With 5 Col. Maps. 9th Edition, revised. Extra fcp. 8vo. 6s.

—— HISTORICAL ESSAYS. First Series. 4th Edition. 8vo. 10s. 6d.

—— HISTORICAL ESSAYS. Second Series. 3rd Edition. With Additional Essays. 8vo. 10s. 6d.

—— HISTORICAL ESSAYS. Third Series. 8vo. 12s.

—— THE GROWTH OF THE ENGLISH CONSTITUTION FROM THE EARLIEST TIMES. 5th Edition. Crown 8vo. 5s.

—— GENERAL SKETCH OF EUROPEAN HISTORY. With Maps, &c. 18mo. 3s. 6d.

—— COMPARATIVE POLITICS. Lectures at the Royal Institution. To which is added "The Unity of History." 8vo. 14s.

—— HISTORICAL AND ARCHITECTURAL SKETCHES: CHIEFLY ITALIAN. Illustrated by the Author. Crown 8vo. 10s. 6d.

—— SUBJECT AND NEIGHBOUR LANDS OF VENICE. Illustrated. Crown 8vo. 10s. 6d.

—— ENGLISH TOWNS AND DISTRICTS. A Series of Addresses and Essays. 8vo. 14s.

—— THE OFFICE OF THE HISTORICAL PROFESSOR. Inaugural Lecture at Oxford. Crown 8vo. 2s.

—— DISESTABLISHMENT AND DISENDOWMENT. WHAT ARE THEY? 4th Edition. Crown 8vo. 1s.

—— GREATER GREECE AND GREATER BRITAIN: GEORGE WASHINGTON THE EXPANDER OF ENGLAND. With an Appendix on IMPERIAL FEDERATION. Cr. 8vo. 3s. 6d.

—— THE METHODS OF HISTORICAL STUDY. Eight Lectures at Oxford. 8vo. 10s. 6d.

—— THE CHIEF PERIODS OF EUROPEAN HISTORY. Six Lectures read in the University of Oxford, with an Essay on GREEK CITIES UNDER ROMAN RULE. 8vo. 10s. 6d.

—— FOUR OXFORD LECTURES, 1887. FIFTY YEARS OF EUROPEAN HISTORY—TEUTONIC CONQUEST IN GAUL AND BRITAIN. 8vo. 5s.

FRENCH COURSE.—See p. 34.

FRIEDMANN (Paul).—ANNE BOLEYN. A Chapter of English History, 1527—36. 2 vols. 8vo. 28s.

FROST (Percival).—AN ELEMENTARY TREA-
TISE ON CURVE TRACING. 8vo. 12s.

—— THE FIRST THREE SECTIONS OF NEW-
TON'S PRINCIPIA. 4th Edition. 8vo. 12s.

—— SOLID GEOMETRY. 3rd Edition. 8vo. 16s.

—— HINTS FOR THE SOLUTION OF PROBLEMS
IN THE THIRD EDITION OF SOLID GEOME-
TRY. 8vo. 8s. 6d.

FURNIVALL (F. J.).—LE MORTE ARTHUR.
Edited from the Harleian MS. 2252, in the
British Museum. Fcp. 8vo. 7s. 6d.

GAIRDNER (Jas.).—HENRY VII. Crown
8vo. 2s. 6d.

GALTON (Francis).— METEOROGRAPHICA ;
OR, METHODS OF MAPPING THE WEATHER.
4to. 9s.

—— ENGLISH MEN OF SCIENCE: THEIR NA-
TURE AND NURTURE. 8vo. 8s. 6d.

—— INQUIRIES INTO HUMAN FACULTY AND
ITS DEVELOPMENT. 8vo. 16s.

—— RECORD OF FAMILY FACULTIES. Consisting of Tabular Forms and Directions for
Entering Data. 4to. 2s. 6d.

—— LIFE HISTORY ALBUM : Being a Personal
Note-book, combining the chief advantages
of a Diary, Photograph Album, a Register of
Height, Weight, and other Anthropometrical
Observations, and a Record of Illnesses.
4to. 3s. 6d.—Or, with Cards of Wools for
Testing Colour Vision. 4s. 6d.

—— NATURAL INHERITANCE. 8vo. 9s.

GAMGEE (Prof. Arthur).—A TEXT-BOOK OF
THE PHYSIOLOGICAL CHEMISTRY OF THE
ANIMAL BODY, including an account of the
Chemical Changes occurring in Disease.
Vol. I. Med. 8vo. 18s.

GANGUILLET (E.) and KUTTER (W. R.).
—A GENERAL FORMULA FOR THE UNIFORM
FLOW OF WATER IN RIVERS AND OTHER
CHANNELS. Translated by RUDOLPH HERING
and JOHN C. TRAUTWINE, Jun. 8vo. 17s.

GARDNER (Percy).—SAMOS AND SAMIAN
COINS. An Essay. 8vo. 7s. 6d.

GARNETT (R.).—IDYLLS AND EPIGRAMS.
Chiefly from the Greek Anthology. Fcp.
8vo. 2s. 6d.

GASKOIN (Mrs. Herman). — CHILDREN'S
TREASURY OF BIBLE STORIES. 18mo. 1s. each.
—Part I. Old Testament ; II. New Testa-
ment ; III. Three Apostles.

GEDDES (Prof. William D.).—THE PROBLEM
OF THE HOMERIC POEMS. 8vo. 14s.

—— FLOSCULI GRÆCI BOREALES, SIVE AN-
THOLOGIA GRÆCA ABERDONENSIS CON-
TEXUIT GULIELMUS D. GEDDES. Cr. 8vo. 6s.

—— THE PHAEDO OF PLATO. Edited, with
Introduction and Notes. 2nd Edition.
8vo 8s. 6d.

GEIKIE (Archibald).—PRIMER OF PHYSICAL
GEOGRAPHY. With Illustrations. 18mo. 1s.

—— PRIMER OF GEOLOGY. Illust. 18mo. 1s.

—— ELEMENTARY LESSONS IN PHYSICAL
GEOGRAPHY. With Illustrations. Fcp. 8vo.
4s. 6d.—QUESTIONS ON THE SAME. 1s. 6d.

—— OUTLINES OF FIELD GEOLOGY. With
numerous Illustrations. Crown 8vo. 3s. 6d.

GEIKIE (A.).—TEXT-BOOK OF GEOLOGY.
Illustrated. 2nd Edition. 7th Thousand.
Medium 8vo. 28s.

—— CLASS-BOOK OF GEOLOGY. Illustrated.
2nd Edition. Crown 8vo. 4s. 6d.

—— GEOLOGICAL SKETCHES AT HOME AND
ABROAD. With Illustrations. 8vo. 10s. 6d.

—— THE SCENERY OF SCOTLAND. Viewed in
connection with its Physical Geology. 2nd
Edition. Crown 8vo. 12s. 6d.

—— THE TEACHING OF GEOGRAPHY. A Practical Handbook for the use of Teachers.
Globe 8vo. 2s.

—— GEOGRAPHY OF THE BRITISH ISLES.
18mo. 1s.

GEOMETRY, SYLLABUS OF PLANE. Corresponding to Euclid I.—VI. Prepared by the
Association for the Improvement of Geometrical Teaching. New Edit. Cr. 8vo. 1s.

GEOMETRY, SYLLABUS OF MODERN PLANE.
Association for the Improvement of Geometrical Teaching. Crown 8vo, sewed. 1s.

GIBBINS (H. de B.).—COMMERCIAL HISTORY
OF EUROPE. 18mo. 2s. 6d.

GILES (P.).—A SHORT MANUAL OF PHI-
LOLOGY FOR CLASSICAL STUDENTS. Crown
8vo. [In the Press.

GILMAN (N. P.). — PROFIT-SHARING BE-
TWEEN EMPLOYER AND EMPLOYÉ. A
Study in the Evolution of the Wages System.
Crown 8vo. 7s. 6d.

GILMORE (Rev. John).—STORM WARRIORS ;
OR, LIFEBOAT WORK ON THE GOODWIN
SANDS. Crown 8vo. 3s. 6d.

GLADSTONE (Rt. Hon. W. E.).—HOMERIC
SYNCHRONISM. An Inquiry into the Time
and Place of Homer. Crown 8vo. 6s.

—— PRIMER OF HOMER. 18mo. 1s.

—— LANDMARKS OF HOMERIC STUDY, TO-
GETHER WITH AN ESSAY ON THE POINTS OF
CONTACT BETWEEN THE ASSYRIAN TABLETS
AND THE HOMERIC TEXT. Cr. 8vo. 2s. 6d.

GLADSTONE (J. H.).—SPELLING REFORM
FROM AN EDUCATIONAL POINT OF VIEW.
3rd Edition. Crown 8vo. 1s. 6d.

GLADSTONE (J. H.) and TRIBE (A.).—
THE CHEMISTRY OF THE SECONDARY BAT-
TERIES OF PLANTÉ AND FAURE. Crown
8vo. 2s. 6d.

GLOBE EDITIONS. Gl. 8vo. 3s. 6d. each.

THE COMPLETE WORKS OF WILLIAM
SHAKESPEARE. Edited by W. G. CLARK
and W. ALDIS WRIGHT.

MORTE D'ARTHUR. Sir Thomas Malory's
Book of King Arthur and of his Noble
Knights of the Round Table. The Edition
of Caxton, revised for modern use. By Sir
E. STRACHEY, Bart.

THE POETICAL WORKS OF SIR WALTER
SCOTT. With Essay by Prof. PALGRAVE.

THE POETICAL WORKS AND LETTERS OF
ROBERT BURNS. Edited, with Life and
Glossarial Index, by ALEXANDER SMITH.

THE ADVENTURES OF ROBINSON CRUSOE.
With Introduction by HENRY KINGSLEY.

GOLDSMITH'S MISCELLANEOUS WORKS.
Edited by Prof. MASSON.

POPE'S POETICAL WORKS. Edited, with
Memoir and Notes, by Prof. WARD.

GLOBE EDITIONS—*continued.*

SPENSER'S COMPLETE WORKS. Edited by R. MORRIS. Memoir by J. W. HALES.

DRYDEN'S POETICAL WORKS. A revised Text and Notes. By W. D. CHRISTIE.

COWPER'S POETICAL WORKS. Edited by the Rev. W. BENHAM, B.D.

VIRGIL'S WORKS. Rendered into English by JAMES LONSDALE and S. LEE.

HORACE'S WORKS. Rendered into English by JAMES LONSDALE and S. LEE.

MILTON'S POETICAL WORKS. Edited, with Introduction, &c., by Prof. MASSON.

GLOBE READERS, THE.—A New Series of Reading Books for Standards I.—VI. Selected, arranged, and Edited by A. F. MURISON, sometime English Master at Aberdeen Grammar School. With Original Illustrations. Globe 8vo.

Primer I.	...	...	(48 pp.)	3*d.*
Primer II.	...	...	(48 pp.)	3*d.*
Book I.	...	...	(132 pp.)	6*d.*
Book II.	...	...	(136 pp.)	9*d.*
Book III.	...	...	(232 pp.)	1*s.* 3*d.*
Book IV.	...	...	(328 pp.)	1*s.* 9*d.*
Book V.	...	...	(408 pp.)	2*s.*
Book VI.	...	...	(436 pp.)	2*s.* 6*d.*

GLOBE READERS, The Shorter.—A New Series of Reading Books for Standards I.—VI. Edited by A. F. MURISON. Gl. 8vo.

Primer I.	...	...	(48 pp.)	3*d.*
Primer II.	...	...	(48 pp.)	3*d.*
Standard I.	...	...	(90 pp.)	6*d.*
Standard II.	...	...	(124 pp.)	9*d.*
Standard III.	...	...	(178 pp.)	1*s.*
Standard IV.	...	...	(182 pp.)	1*s.*
Standard V.	...	...	(216 pp.)	1*s.* 3*d.*
Standard VI.	...	...	(228 pp.)	1*s.* 6*d.*

*** This Series has been abridged from the "Globe Readers" to meet the demand for smaller reading books.

GLOBE READINGS FROM STANDARD AUTHORS. Globe 8vo.

COWPER'S TASK: An Epistle to Joseph Hill, Esq.; TIROCINIUM, or a Review of the Schools; and the HISTORY OF JOHN GILPIN. Edited, with Notes, by Rev. WILLIAM BENHAM, B.D. 1*s.*

GOLDSMITH'S VICAR OF WAKEFIELD. With a Memoir of Goldsmith by Prof. MASSON. 1*s.*

LAMB'S (CHARLES) TALES FROM SHAKSPEARE. Edited, with Preface, by Rev. ALFRED AINGER, M.A. 2*s.*

SCOTT'S (SIR WALTER) LAY OF THE LAST MINSTREL; and the LADY OF THE LAKE. Edited by Prof. F. T. PALGRAVE. 1*s.*

— MARMION; and THE LORD OF THE ISLES. By the same Editor. 1*s.*

THE CHILDREN'S GARLAND FROM THE BEST POETS. Selected and arranged by COVENTRY PATMORE. 2*s.*

A BOOK OF GOLDEN DEEDS OF ALL TIMES AND ALL COUNTRIES. Gathered and narrated anew by CHARLOTTE M. YONGE. 2*s.*

GODFRAY (Hugh). — AN ELEMENTARY TREATISE ON LUNAR THEORY. 2nd Edition. Crown 8vo. 5*s.* 6*d.*

GODFRAY (H.).—A TREATISE ON ASTRONOMY, FOR THE USE OF COLLEGES AND SCHOOLS. 8vo. 12*s.* 6*d.*

GOETHE—CARLYLE.—CORRESPONDENCE BETWEEN GOETHE AND CARLYLE. Edited by C. E. NORTON. Crown 8vo. 9*s.*

GOETHE'S LIFE. By Prof. HEINRICH DÜNTZER. Translated by T. W. LYSTER. 2 vols. Crown 8vo. 21*s.*

GOETHE.—FAUST. Translated into English Verse by JOHN STUART BLACKIE. 2nd Edition. Crown 8vo. 9*s.*

— FAUST, Part I. Edited, with Introduction and Notes; followed by an Appendix on Part II., by JANE LEE. 18mo. 4*s.* 6*d.*

— REYNARD THE FOX. Trans. into English Verse by A. D. AINSLIE. Crn. 8vo. 7*s.* 6*d.*

— GÖTZ VON BERLICHINGEN. Edited by H. A. BULL, M.A. 18mo. 2*s.*

GOLDEN TREASURY SERIES. — Uniformly printed in 18mo, with Vignette Titles by Sir J. E. MILLAIS, Sir NOEL PATON, T. WOOLNER, W. HOLMAN HUNT, ARTHUR HUGHES, &c. Engraved on Steel. Bound in extra cloth. 4*s.* 6*d.* each.

THE GOLDEN TREASURY OF THE BEST SONGS AND LYRICAL POEMS IN THE ENGLISH LANGUAGE. Selected and arranged, with Notes, by Prof. F. T. PALGRAVE.

THE CHILDREN'S GARLAND FROM THE BEST POETS. Selected by COVENTRY PATMORE.

THE BOOK OF PRAISE. From the best English Hymn Writers. Selected by ROUNDELL, EARL OF SELBORNE.

THE FAIRY BOOK: THE BEST POPULAR FAIRY STORIES. Selected by the Author of "John Halifax, Gentleman."

THE BALLAD BOOK. A Selection of the Choicest British Ballads. Edited by WILLIAM ALLINGHAM.

THE JEST BOOK. The Choicest Anecdotes and Sayings. Arranged by MARK LEMON.

BACON'S ESSAYS, AND COLOURS OF GOOD AND EVIL. With Notes and Glossarial Index by W. ALDIS WRIGHT, M.A.

THE PILGRIM'S PROGRESS FROM THIS WORLD TO THAT WHICH IS TO COME. By JOHN BUNYAN.

THE SUNDAY BOOK OF POETRY FOR THE YOUNG. Selected by C. F. ALEXANDER.

A BOOK OF GOLDEN DEEDS OF ALL TIMES AND ALL COUNTRIES. By the Author of "The Heir of Redclyffe."

THE ADVENTURES OF ROBINSON CRUSOE. Edited by J. W. CLARK, M.A.

THE REPUBLIC OF PLATO. Translated by J. LL. DAVIES, M.A., and D. J. VAUGHAN.

THE SONG BOOK. Words and Tunes Selected and arranged by JOHN HULLAH.

LA LYRE FRANÇAISE. Selected and arranged, with Notes, by G. MASSON.

TOM BROWN'S SCHOOL DAYS. By AN OLD BOY.

A BOOK OF WORTHIES. By the Author of "The Heir of Redclyffe."

GUESSES AT TRUTH. By TWO BROTHERS.

2

GOLDEN TREASURY SERIES—*contd.*

THE CAVALIER AND HIS LADY. Selections from the Works of the First Duke and Duchess of Newcastle. With an Introductory Essay by EDWARD JENKINS.

SCOTTISH SONG. Compiled by MARY CARLYLE AITKEN.

DEUTSCHE LYRIK. The Golden Treasury of the best German Lyrical Poems. Selected by Dr. BUCHHEIM.

CHRYSOMELA. A Selection from the Lyrical Poems of Robert Herrick. By Prof. F. T. PALGRAVE.

POEMS OF PLACES—ENGLAND AND WALES. Edited by H. W. LONGFELLOW. 2 vols.

SELECTED POEMS OF MATTHEW ARNOLD.

THE STORY OF THE CHRISTIANS AND MOORS IN SPAIN. By CHARLOTTE M. YONGE.

LAMB'S TALES FROM SHAKSPEARE. Edited by Rev. ALFRED AINGER, M.A.

SHAKESPEARE'S SONGS AND SONNETS. Ed. with Notes, by Prof. F. T. PALGRAVE.

POEMS OF WORDSWORTH. Chosen and Edited by MATTHEW ARNOLD. Large Paper Edition. 9s.

POEMS OF SHELLEY. Ed. by S. A. BROOKE. Large Paper Edition. 12s. 6d.

THE ESSAYS OF JOSEPH ADDISON. Chosen and Edited by JOHN RICHARD GREEN.

POETRY OF BYRON. Chosen and arranged by MATTHEW ARNOLD. Large Paper Edition. 9s.

SIR THOMAS BROWNE'S RELIGIO MEDICI; LETTER TO A FRIEND, &c., AND CHRISTIAN MORALS. Ed. by W. A. GREENHILL, M.D.

THE SPEECHES AND TABLE-TALK OF THE PROPHET MOHAMMAD. Translated by STANLEY LANE-POOLE.

SELECTIONS FROM WALTER SAVAGE LANDOR. Edited by SIDNEY COLVIN.

SELECTIONS FROM COWPER'S POEMS. With an Introduction by Mrs. OLIPHANT.

LETTERS OF WILLIAM COWPER. Edited, With Introduction, by Rev. W. BENHAM.

THE POETICAL WORKS OF JOHN KEATS. Edited by Prof. F. T. PALGRAVE.

LYRICAL POEMS OF LORD TENNYSON. Selected and Annotated by Prof. FRANCIS T. PALGRAVE. Large Paper Edition. 9s.

IN MEMORIAM. By LORD TENNYSON, Poet Laureate. Large Paper Edition. 9s.

THE TRIAL AND DEATH OF SOCRATES. Being the Euthyphron, Apology, Crito, and Phaedo of Plato. Translated by F. J. CHURCH.

A BOOK OF GOLDEN THOUGHTS. By HENRY ATTWELL.

PLATO.—PHAEDRUS, LYSIS, AND PROTAGORAS. A New Translation, by J. WRIGHT.

THEOCRITUS, BION, AND MOSCHUS. Rendered into English Prose by ANDREW LANG. Large Paper Edition. 9s.

BALLADS, LYRICS, AND SONNETS. From the Works of HENRY W. LONGFELLOW.

GOLDEN TREASURY SERIES—*contd.*

DEUTSCHE BALLADEN UND ROMANZEN. The Golden Treasury of the Best German Ballads and Romances. Selected and arranged by Dr. BUCHHEIM. [*In the Press.*

GOLDEN TREASURY SERIES. Re-issue in uniform binding with Vignette Titles. Monthly volumes from May, 1891. 2s. 6d. each net.

THE GOLDEN TREASURY OF THE BEST SONGS AND LYRICAL POEMS IN THE ENGLISH LANGUAGE. Selected and arranged, with Notes, by Prof. F. T. PALGRAVE.

THE CHILDREN'S GARLAND FROM THE BEST POETS. Selected by COVENTRY PATMORE.

THE PILGRIM'S PROGRESS FROM THIS WORLD TO THAT WHICH IS TO COME. By JOHN BUNYAN.

THE BOOK OF PRAISE. From the best English Hymn Writers. Selected by ROUNDELL, EARL OF SELBORNE.

BACON'S ESSAYS, AND COLOURS OF GOOD AND EVIL. With Notes and Glossarial Index by W. ALDIS WRIGHT, M.A.

THE FAIRY BOOK: THE BEST POPULAR FAIRY STORIES. Selected by Mrs. CRAIK.

THE JEST BOOK. The Choicest Anecdotes and Sayings. Arranged by MARK LEMON.

THE BALLAD BOOK. A Selection of the Choicest British Ballads. Edited by WILLIAM ALLINGHAM.

THE SUNDAY BOOK OF POETRY FOR THE YOUNG. Selected by C. F. ALEXANDER.

A BOOK OF GOLDEN DEEDS OF ALL TIMES AND ALL COUNTRIES. By C. M. YONGE.

THE ADVENTURES OF ROBINSON CRUSOE. Edited by J. W. CLARK, M.A.

THE REPUBLIC OF PLATO. Translated by J. LL. DAVIES, M.A., and D. J. VAUGHAN.

Other Volumes to follow.

GOLDEN TREASURY PSALTER. THE STUDENT'S EDITION. Being an Edition with briefer Notes of "The Psalms Chronologically Arranged by Four Friends." 18mo. 3s. 6d.

GOLDSMITH.—ESSAYS OF OLIVER GOLDSMITH. Edited by C. D. YONGE, M.A. Fcp. 8vo. 2s. 6d.

—— THE TRAVELLER AND THE DESERTED VILLAGE. With Notes by J. W. HALES, M.A. Crown 8vo. 6d.

—— THE VICAR OF WAKEFIELD. With 182 Illustrations by HUGH THOMSON, and Preface by AUSTIN DOBSON. Crown 8vo. 6s. Also with uncut edges, paper label. 6s. *See also* ENGLISH CLASSICS, p. 12.

GONE TO TEXAS. LETTERS FROM OUR BOYS. Edited, with Preface, by THOMAS HUGHES, Q.C. Crown 8vo. 4s. 6d.

GOODALE (G. L.).—PHYSIOLOGICAL BOTANY. Part I. OUTLINES OF THE HISTORY OF PHÆNOGAMOUS PLANTS; II. VEGETABLE PHYSIOLOGY. 6th Edition. 8vo. 10s. 6d.

GOODWIN (Prof. W. W.).—SYNTAX OF THE GREEK MOODS AND TENSES. 8vo. 14s.

—— A GREEK GRAMMAR. Crown 8vo. 6s.

—— A SCHOOL GREEK GRAMMAR. Crown 8vo. 3s. 6d.

GORDON (General). A SKETCH. By REGI-NALD H. BARNES. Crown 8vo. 1s.

—— LETTERS OF GENERAL C. G. GORDON TO HIS SISTER, M. A. GORDON. 4th Edition. Crown 8vo. 3s. 6d.

GORDON (Lady Duff). — LAST LETTERS FROM EGYPT, TO WHICH ARE ADDED LETTERS FROM THE CAPE. 2nd Edition. Cr. 8vo. 9s.

GOSCHEN (Rt. Hon. George J.).—REPORTS AND SPEECHES ON LOCAL TAXATION. 8vo. 5s.

GOSSE (E.).—A HISTORY OF EIGHTEENTH CENTURY LITERATURE (1660—1780). Crn. 8vo. 7s. 6d.

GOW (Dr. James).—A COMPANION TO SCHOOL CLASSICS. Illustrated. 2nd Ed. Cr. 8vo. 6s.

GOYEN (P.).—HIGHER ARITHMETIC AND ELEMENTARY MENSURATION, for the Senior Classes of Schools and Candidates preparing for Public Examinations. Globe 8vo. 5s.

GRAHAM (David).—KING JAMES I. An Historical Tragedy. Globe 8vo. 7s.

GRAHAM (John W.).—NEÆRA : A TALE OF ANCIENT ROME. Crown 8vo. 6s.

GRAHAM (R. H.)—GEOMETRY OF POSITION. Crown 8vo. 7s. 6d.

GRAND'HOMME. — CUTTING OUT AND DRESSMAKING. From the French of Mdlle. E. GRAND'HOMME. 18mo. 1s.

GRAY (Prof. Andrew).—THE THEORY AND PRACTICE OF ABSOLUTE MEASUREMENTS IN ELECTRICITY AND MAGNETISM. 2 vols. Crown 8vo. Vol. I. 12s. 6d.

—— ABSOLUTE MEASUREMENTS IN ELECTRICITY AND MAGNETISM. 2nd Edit., revised. Fcp. 8vo. 5s. 6d.

GRAY (Prof. Asa).—STRUCTURAL BOTANY ; OR, ORGANOGRAPHY ON THE BASIS OF MORPHOLOGY. 8vo. 10s. 6d.

—— THE SCIENTIFIC PAPERS OF ASA GRAY. Selected by CHARLES S. SARGENT. 2 vols. 8vo. 21s.

GRAY (Tho.).—WORKS. Edited by E. GOSSE. In 4 vols. Globe 8vo. 20s.—Vol. I. POEMS, JOURNALS, AND ESSAYS.—II. LETTERS.—III. LETTERS. — IV. NOTES ON ARISTOPHANES ; AND PLATO.

GREAVES (John).—A TREATISE ON ELEMENTARY STATICS. 2nd Ed. Cr. 8vo. 6s. 6d.

—— STATICS FOR BEGINNERS. Gl. 8vo. 3s. 6d.

GREEK TESTAMENT. THE NEW TESTAMENT IN THE ORIGINAL GREEK. The Text revised by Bishop WESTCOTT, D.D., and Prof. F. J. A. HORT, D.D. 2 vols. Crn. 8vo. 10s. 6d. each.—Vol. I. Text ; II. Introduction and Appendix.

THE NEW TESTAMENT IN THE ORIGINAL GREEK, FOR SCHOOLS. The Text Revised by Bishop WESTCOTT, D.D., and F. J. A. HORT, D.D. 12mo. 4s. 6d.—18mo, roan, red edges. 5s. 6d. ; morocco, gilt, 6s. 6d.

SCHOOL READINGS IN THE GREEK TESTAMENT. Being the Outlines of the Life of our Lord as given by St. Mark, with additions from the Text of the other Evangelists. Edited, with Notes and Vocabulary, by A. CALVERT, M.A. Fcp. 8vo. 2s. 6d.

THE GREEK TESTAMENT AND THE ENGLISH VERSION, A COMPANION TO. By PHILIP SCHAFF, D.D. Crown 8vo. 12s.

GREEK TESTAMENT—continued.

THE GOSPEL ACCORDING TO ST. MATTHEW. Greek Text as Revised by Bishop WESTCOTT and Dr. HORT. With Introduction and Notes by Rev. A. SLOMAN, M.A. Fcp. 8vo. 2s. 6d.

THE GOSPEL ACCORDING TO ST. LUKE. The Greek Text as revised by Bp. WESTCOTT and Dr. HORT. With Introduction and Notes by Rev. J. BOND, M.A. Fcp. 8vo. 2s. 6d.

THE ACTS OF THE APOSTLES. Being the Greek Text as Revised by Bishop WESTCOTT and Dr. HORT. With Explanatory Notes by T. E. PAGE, M.A. Fcp. 8vo. 3s. 6d.

GREEN (John Richard).—A SHORT HISTORY OF THE ENGLISH PEOPLE. With Coloured Maps, Genealogical Tables, and Chronological Annals. New Edition, thoroughly revised. Cr. 8vo. 8s. 6d. 151st Thousand. Also the same in Four Parts. With the corresponding portion of Mr. Tait's "Analysis." 3s. each. Part I 607—1265. II. 1204—1553. III. 1540—1689. IV. 1660—1873.

—— HISTORY OF THE ENGLISH PEOPLE. In 4 vols. 8vo.—Vol. I. With 8 Coloured Maps. 16s.—II. 16s.—III. With 4 Maps. 16s.—IV. With Maps and Index. 16s.

—— THE MAKING OF ENGLAND. With Maps. 8vo. 16s.

—— THE CONQUEST OF ENGLAND. With Maps and Portrait. 8vo. 18s.

—— READINGS IN ENGLISH HISTORY. In 3 Parts. Fcp. 8vo. 1s. 6d. each.

GREEN (J. R.) and GREEN (Alice S.).— A SHORT GEOGRAPHY OF THE BRITISH ISLANDS. With 28 Maps. Fcp. 8vo. 3s. 6d.

GREEN (Mrs. J. R.).—HENRY II. Crown 8vo. 2s. 6d.

GREEN (W. S.).—AMONG THE SELKIRK GLACIERS. Crown 8vo. 7s. 6d.

GREENHILL (Prof. A. G.).—DIFFERENTIAL AND INTEGRAL CALCULUS. Crown 8vo.

GREENWOOD (Jessy E.). — THE MOON MAIDEN : AND OTHER STORIES. Crown 8vo. 3s. 6d.

GRIFFITHS (W. H.).—LESSONS ON PRESCRIPTIONS AND THE ART OF PRESCRIBING. New Edition. 18mo. 3s. 6d.

GRIMM'S FAIRY TALES. A Selection from the Household Stories. Translated from the German by LUCY CRANE, and done into Pictures by WALTER CRANE. Crown 8vo. 6s.

GROVE (Sir George).—A DICTIONARY OF MUSIC AND MUSICIANS, A.D. 1450—1889. Edited by Sir GEORGE GROVE, D.C.L. In 4 vols. 8vo, 21s. each. With Illustrations in Music Type and Woodcut.— Also published in Parts. Parts I.—XIV., XIX.—XXII. 3s. 6d. each ; XV. XVI. 7s. ; XVII. XVIII. 7s. ; XXIII.—XXV., Appendix, Edited by J. A. FULLER MAITLAND, M.A. 9s. [Cloth cases for binding the volumes, 1s. each.]

—— A COMPLETE INDEX TO THE ABOVE. By Mrs. E. WODEHOUSE. 8vo. 7s. 6d.

—— PRIMER OF GEOGRAPHY. Maps. 18mo. 1s.

GUEST (Dr. E.).—ORIGINES CELTICÆ (A Fragment) and other Contributions to the History of Britain. Maps. 2 vols. 8vo. 32s.

GUEST (M. J.).—LECTURES ON THE HISTORY OF ENGLAND. Crown 8vo. 6s.

GUIDE TO THE UNPROTECTED, In Every-day Matters relating to Property and Income. 5th Ed. Extra fcp. 8vo. 3s. 6d.

GUILLEMIN (Amédée).—THE FORCES OF NATURE. A Popular Introduction to the Study of Physical Phenomena. 455 Woodcuts. Royal 8vo. 21s.

—— THE APPLICATIONS OF PHYSICAL FORCES. With Coloured Plates and Illustrations. Royal 8vo. 21s.

—— ELECTRICITY AND MAGNETISM. A Popular Treatise. Translated and Edited, with Additions and Notes, by Prof. SYLVANUS P. THOMPSON. Royal 8vo. [In the Press.

GUIZOT.—GREAT CHRISTIANS OF FRANCE. ST. LOUIS AND CALVIN. Crown 8vo. 6s.

GUNTON (George).—WEALTH AND PROGRESS. Crown 8vo. 6s.

HADLEY (Prof. James).—ESSAYS, PHILOLOGICAL AND CRITICAL. 8vo. 16s.

HADLEY—ALLEN.—A GREEK GRAMMAR FOR SCHOOLS AND COLLEGES. By Prof. JAMES HADLEY. Revised and in part Rewritten by Prof. FREDERIC DE FOREST ALLEN. Crown 8vo. 6s.

HALES (Prof. J. W.).—LONGER ENGLISH POEMS, with Notes, Philological and Explanatory, and an Introduction on the Teaching of English. 12th Ed. Ext. fcp. 8vo. 4s. 6d.

HALL (H. S.) and KNIGHT (S. R.).—ELEMENTARY ALGEBRA FOR SCHOOLS. 6th Ed., revised. Gl. 8vo. 3s. 6d. With Answers, 4s. 6d. KEY. Crown 8vo. 8s. 6d.

—— ALGEBRAICAL EXERCISES AND EXAMINATION PAPERS to accompany "Elementary Algebra." 2nd Edition. Globe 8vo. 2s. 6d.

—— HIGHER ALGEBRA. A Sequel to "Elementary Algebra for Schools." 3rd Edition. Crown 8vo. 7s. 6d. KEY. Crown 8vo. 10s. 6d.

—— ARITHMETICAL EXERCISES AND EXAMINATION PAPERS. Globe 8vo. 2s. 6d.

HALL (H. S.) and STEVENS (F. H.).—A TEXT-BOOK OF EUCLID'S ELEMENTS. Globe 8vo. Complete, 4s. 6d.
Book I. 1s.
Books I. and II. 1s. 6d.
Books I.—IV. 3s.
Books III. and IV. 2s.
Books III.—VI. 3s.
Books V. VI. and XI. 2s. 6d.
Book XI. 1s.

HALLWARD (R. F.).—FLOWERS OF PARADISE. Music, Verse, Design, Illustration. Royal 4to. 6s.

HALSTED (G. B.).—THE ELEMENTS OF GEOMETRY. 8vo. 12s. 6d.

HAMERTON (P. G.).—THE INTELLECTUAL LIFE. 4th Edition. Crown 8vo. 10s. 6d.

—— ETCHING AND ETCHERS. 3rd Edition, revised. With 48 Plates. Colombier 8vo.

—— THOUGHTS ABOUT ART. New Edition. Crown 8vo. 8s. 6d.

HAMERTON (P. G.).—HUMAN INTERCOURSE. 4th Edition. Crown 8vo. 8s. 6d.

—— FRENCH AND ENGLISH: A COMPARISON. Crown 8vo. 10s. 6d.

HAMILTON (Prof. D. J.).—ON THE PATHOLOGY OF BRONCHITIS, CATARRHAL PNEUMONIA, TUBERCLE, AND ALLIED LESIONS OF THE HUMAN LUNG. 8vo. 8s. 6d.

—— A TEXT-BOOK OF PATHOLOGY, SYSTEMATIC AND PRACTICAL. Illustrated. Vol. I. 8vo. 25s.

HANBURY (Daniel). — SCIENCE PAPERS, CHIEFLY PHARMACOLOGICAL AND BOTANICAL. Medium 8vo. 14s.

HANDEL: LIFE OF. By W. S. ROCKSTRO Crown 8vo. 10s. 6d.

HARDWICK (Ven. Archdeacon). — CHRIST AND OTHER MASTERS. 6th Edition. Crown 8vo. 10s. 6d.

—— A HISTORY OF THE CHRISTIAN CHURCH. Middle Age. 6th Edition. Edit. by Bishop STUBBS. Crown 8vo. 10s. 6d.

—— A HISTORY OF THE CHRISTIAN CHURCH DURING THE REFORMATION. 9th Edition. Revised by Bishop STUBBS. Cr. 8vo. 10s. 6d.

HARDY (Arthur Sherburne).—BUT YET A WOMAN. A Novel. Crown 8vo. 4s. 6d.

—— THE WIND OF DESTINY. 2 vols. Globe 8vo. 12s.

HARDY (H. J.). — A LATIN READER FOR THE LOWER FORMS IN SCHOOLS. Globe 8vo. 2s. 6d.

HARDY (Thomas).—See p. 29.

HARE (Julius Charles).—THE MISSION OF THE COMFORTER. New Edition. Edited by Dean PLUMPTRE. Crown 8vo. 7s. 6d.

—— THE VICTORY OF FAITH. Edited by Dean PLUMPTRE, with Introductory Notices by Prof. MAURICE and by Dean STANLEY. Cr. 8vo. 6s. 6d.

—— GUESSES AT TRUTH. By Two Brothers, AUGUSTUS WILLIAM HARE and JULIUS CHARLES HARE. With a Memoir and Two Portraits. 18mo. 4s. 6d.

HARMONIA. By the Author of "Estelle Russell." 3 vols. Crown 8vo. 31s. 6d.

HARPER (Father Thomas). — THE METAPHYSICS OF THE SCHOOL. In 5 vols. Vols. I. and II. 8vo. 18s. each; Vol. III., Part I. 12s.

HARRIS (Rev. G. C.).—SERMONS. With a Memoir by CHARLOTTE M. YONGE, and Portrait. Extra fcp. 8vo. 6s.

HARRISON (Frederic).—THE CHOICE OF BOOKS. Globe 8vo. 6s.
Large Paper Edition. Printed on hand-made paper. 15s.

HARRISON (Miss Jane) and VERRALL (Mrs.).—MYTHOLOGY AND MONUMENTS OF ANCIENT ATHENS. Illustrated. Cr. 8vo. 16s.

HARTE (Bret).—See p. 29.

HARTLEY (Prof. W. Noel).—A COURSE OF QUANTITATIVE ANALYSIS FOR STUDENTS. Globe 8vo. 5s.

HARWOOD (George).—DISESTABLISHMENT; OR, A DEFENCE OF THE PRINCIPLE OF A NATIONAL CHURCH. 8vo. 12s.

—— THE COMING DEMOCRACY. Cr. 8vo. 6s.

HARWOOD (George).—FROM WITHIN. Cr. 8vo. 6s.

HAYWARD (R. B.).—THE ELEMENTS OF SOLID GEOMETRY. Globe 8vo. 3s.

HEARD (Rev. W. A.).—A SECOND GREEK EXERCISE BOOK. Globe 8vo. 2s. 6d.

HELLENIC STUDIES, THE JOURNAL OF.—8vo. Vol. I. With Plates of Illustrations. 30s.—Vol. II. 30s. With Plates of Illustrations. Or in 2 Parts, 15s. each.—Vol. III. 2 Parts. With Plates of Illustrations. 15s. each.—Vol. IV. 2 Parts. With Plates. Part I. 15s. Part II. 21s. Or complete, 30s.—Vol. V. With Plates. 30s.—Vol. VI. With Plates. Part I. 15s. Part II. 15s. Or complete, 30s.—Vol. VII. Part I. 15s. Part II. 15s. Or complete, 30s.—Vol. VIII. Part I. 15s. Part II. 15s.—Vol. IX. 2 Parts. 15s. each.—Vol. X. 30s.—Vol. XI. Pt. I. 15s. net.

The Journal will be sold at a reduced price to Libraries wishing to subscribe, but official application must in each case be made to the Council. Information on this point, and upon the conditions of Membership, may be obtained on application to the Hon. Sec., Mr. George Macmillan, 29, Bedford Street, Covent Garden.

HENSLOW (Rev. G.).—THE THEORY OF EVOLUTION OF LIVING THINGS, AND THE APPLICATION OF THE PRINCIPLES OF EVOLUTION TO RELIGION. Crown 8vo. 6s.

HERODOTUS.—THE HISTORY. Translated into English, with Notes and Indices, by G. C. MACAULAY, M.A. 2 vols. Cr. 8vo. 18s.

—— Books I.—III. Edited by A. H. SAYCE, M.A. 8vo. 16s.

See also p. 32.

HERTEL (Dr.).—OVERPRESSURE IN HIGH SCHOOLS IN DENMARK. With Introduction by Sir J. CRICHTON-BROWNE. Cr. 8vo. 3s. 6d.

HERVEY (Rt. Rev. Lord Arthur).—THE GENEALOGIES OF OUR LORD AND SAVIOUR JESUS CHRIST. 8vo. 10s. 6d.

HICKS (W. M.).—ELEMENTARY DYNAMICS OF PARTICLES AND SOLIDS. Cr. 8vo. 6s. 6d.

HILL (Florence D.).—CHILDREN OF THE STATE. Ed. by FANNY FOWKE. Cr. 8vo. 6s.

HILL (Octavia).—OUR COMMON LAND, AND OTHER ESSAYS. Extra fcp. 8vo. 3s. 6d.

—— HOMES OF THE LONDON POOR. Sewed. Crown 8vo. 1s.

HIORNS (Arthur H.).—PRACTICAL METALLURGY AND ASSAYING. A Text-Book for the use of Teachers, Students, and Assayers. With Illustrations. Globe 8vo. 6s.

—— A TEXT-BOOK OF ELEMENTARY METALLURGY FOR THE USE OF STUDENTS. Gl. 8vo 4s.

—— IRON AND STEEL MANUFACTURE. A Text-Book for Beginners. Illustr. Globe 8vo. 3s. 6d.

—— MIXED METALS OR METALLIC ALLOYS. Globe 8vo. 6s.

HISTORICAL COURSE FOR SCHOOLS. Ed. by EDW. A. FREEMAN, D.C.L. 18mo.
Vol. I. GENERAL SKETCH OF EUROPEAN HISTORY. By E. A. FREEMAN. With Maps, &c. 3s. 6d.
II. HISTORY OF ENGLAND. By EDITH THOMPSON. Coloured Maps. 2s. 6d.
III. HISTORY OF SCOTLAND. By MARGARET MACARTHUR. 2s.

HISTORICAL COURSE FOR SCHOOLS —*continued.*
IV. HISTORY OF ITALY. By the Rev. W. HUNT, M.A. Maps. 3s. 6d.
V. HISTORY OF GERMANY. By JAMES SIME, M.A. 3s.
VI. HISTORY OF AMERICA. By J. A. DOYLE. With Maps. 4s. 6d.
VII. HISTORY OF EUROPEAN COLONIES. By E. J. PAYNE, M.A. Maps. 4s. 6d.
VIII. HISTORY OF FRANCE. By CHARLOTTE M. YONGE. Maps. 3s. 6d.

HOBART. — ESSAYS AND MISCELLANEOUS WRITINGS OF VERE HENRY, LORD HOBART. With a Biographical Sketch. Edited by MARY, LADY HOBART. 2 vols. 8vo. 25s.

HOBDAY (E.). — VILLA GARDENING. A Handbook for Amateur and Practical Gardeners. Extra crown 8vo. 6s.

HODGSON (F.).—MYTHOLOGY FOR LATIN VERSIFICATION. 6th Edition. Revised by F. C. HODGSON, M.A. 18mo. 3s.

HODGSON. — MEMOIR OF REV. FRANCIS HODGSON, B.D., SCHOLAR, POET, AND DIVINE. By his Son, the Rev. JAMES T. HODGSON, M.A. 2 vols. Crown 8vo. 18s.

HÖFFDING (Dr. H.).—OUTLINES OF PSYCHOLOGY. Translated by M. E. LOWNDES. Crown 8vo. 6s.

HOFMANN (Prof. A. W.).—THE LIFE WORK OF LIEBIG IN EXPERIMENTAL AND PHILOSOPHIC CHEMISTRY. 8vo. 5s.

HOGAN, M.P. Globe 8vo. 2s.

HOLE (Rev. C.).—GENEALOGICAL STEMMA OF THE KINGS OF ENGLAND AND FRANCE. On a Sheet. 1s.

—— A BRIEF BIOGRAPHICAL DICTIONARY. 2nd Edition. 18mo. 4s. 6d.

HOLLAND (Prof. T. E.).—THE TREATY RELATIONS OF RUSSIA AND TURKEY, FROM 1774 TO 1853. Crown 8vo. 2s.

HOLMES (O. W., Jun.).—THE COMMON LAW. 8vo. 12s.

HOMER.—THE ODYSSEY OF HOMER DONE INTO ENGLISH PROSE. By S. H. BUTCHER, M.A., and A. LANG, M.A. 7th Edition. Crown 8vo. 6s.

—— THE ODYSSEY OF HOMER. Books I.— XII. Translated into English Verse by the EARL OF CARNARVON. Crown 8vo. 7s. 6d.

—— THE ILIAD. Edited, with English Notes and Introduction, by WALTER LEAF, Litt.D. 2 vols. 8vo. 14s. each.—Vol. I. Bks. I.—XII; Vol. II. Bks. XIII.—XXIV.

—— ILIAD. Translated into English Prose. By ANDREW LANG, WALTER LEAF, and ERNEST MYERS. Crown 8vo. 12s. 6d.

—— PRIMER OF HOMER. By Rt. Hon. W. E. GLADSTONE, M.P. 18mo. 1s.

See also pp. 31, 32.

HON. MISS FERRARD, THE. By the Author of "Hogan, M.P." Globe 8vo. 2s.

HOOKER (Sir J. D.). — THE STUDENT'S FLORA OF THE BRITISH ISLANDS. 3rd Edition. Globe 8vo. 10s. 6d.

—— PRIMER OF BOTANY. 18mo. 1s.

HOOKER (Sir Joseph D.) and BALL (J.).—JOURNAL OF A TOUR IN MAROCCO AND THE GREAT ATLAS. 8vo. 21s.

HOOLE (C. H.).—THE CLASSICAL ELEMENT IN THE NEW TESTAMENT. Considered as a Proof of its Genuineness. 8vo. 10s. 6d.

HOOPER (W. H.) and PHILLIPS (W. C.).—A MANUAL OF MARKS ON POTTERY AND PORCELAIN. 16mo. 4s. 6d.

HOPE (Frances J.).—NOTES AND THOUGHTS ON GARDENS AND WOODLANDS. Cr. 8vo. 6s.

HOPKINS (Ellice).—AUTUMN SWALLOWS: A Book of Lyrics. Extra fcp. 8vo. 6s.

HOPPUS (Mary).—A GREAT TREASON: A Story of the War of Independence. 2 vols. Crown 8vo. 9s.

HORACE.—THE WORKS OF HORACE RENDERED INTO ENGLISH PROSE. By J. LONSDALE and S. LEE. Globe 8vo. 3s. 6d.

—— STUDIES, LITERARY AND HISTORICAL, IN THE ODES OF HORACE. By A. W. VERRALL, Litt.D. 8vo. 8s. 6d.

—— THE ODES OF HORACE IN A METRICAL PARAPHRASE. By R. M. HOVENDEN, B.A. Extra fcap. 8vo. 4s. 6d.

—— LIFE AND CHARACTER: AN EPITOME OF HIS SATIRES AND EPISTLES. By R. M. HOVENDEN, B.A. Ext. fcp. 8vo. 4s. 6d.

—— WORD FOR WORD FROM HORACE: The Odes Literally Versified. By W. T. THORNTON, C.B. Crown 8vo. 7s. 6d.

See also pp. 31, 32.

HORT.—TWO DISSERTATIONS. I. On MONOΓENHΣ ΘEOΣ in Scripture and Tradition. II. On the "Constantinopolitan" Creed and other Eastern Creeds of the Fourth Century. By FENTON JOHN ANTHONY HORT, D.D. 8vo. 7s. 6d.

HORTON (Hon. S. Dana).—THE SILVER POUND AND ENGLAND'S MONETARY POLICY SINCE THE RESTORATION. With a History of the Guinea. 8vo. 14s.

HOWELL (George).—THE CONFLICTS OF CAPITAL AND LABOUR. 2nd Ed. Cr 8vo. 7s.6d.

HOWES (Prof. G. B.).—AN ATLAS OF PRACTICAL ELEMENTARY BIOLOGY. With a Preface by Prof. HUXLEY. 4to. 14s.

HOZIER (Lieut.-Colonel H. M.).—THE SEVEN WEEKS' WAR. 3rd Edition. Crown 8vo. 6s.

—— THE INVASIONS OF ENGLAND. 2 vols. 8vo. 28s.

HÜBNER (Baron von).—A RAMBLE ROUND THE WORLD. Crown 8vo. 6s.

HUGHES (Thomas).—ALFRED THE GREAT. Crown 8vo. 6s.

—— TOM BROWN'S SCHOOL DAYS. By AN OLD BOY. Illustrated Edition. Crown 8vo. 6s.—Golden Treasury Edition. 4s. 6d.—Uniform Edition. 3s.6d.—People's Edition. 2s.—People's Sixpenny Edition, Illustrated. Med. 4to. 6d.—Uniform with Sixpenny Kingsley. Medium 8vo. 6d.

—— TOM BROWN AT OXFORD. Crown 8vo. 6s.—Uniform Edition. 3s. 6d.

—— MEMOIR OF DANIEL MACMILLAN. With Portrait. Cr. 8vo. 4s. 6d.—Cheap Edition. Sewed. Crown 8vo. 1s.

HUGHES (T.).—RUGBY, TENNESSEE. Crn. 8vo. 4s. 6d.

—— GONE TO TEXAS. Edited by THOMAS HUGHES, Q.C. Crown 8vo. 4s. 6d.

—— THE SCOURING OF THE WHITE HORSE, AND THE ASHEN FAGGOT. Uniform Edit. 3s. 6d.

—— JAMES FRASER, Second Bishop of Manchester. A Memoir, 1818—85. Cr. 8vo. 6s.

—— FIFTY YEARS AGO: Rugby Address, 1891. 8vo, sewed. 6d. net.

HULL (E.).—A TREATISE ON ORNAMENTAL AND BUILDING STONES OF GREAT BRITAIN AND FOREIGN COUNTRIES. 8vo. 12s.

HULLAH (M. E.).—HANNAH TARNE. A Story for Girls. Globe 8vo. 2s. 6d.

HUMPHRY (Prof. Sir G. M.).—THE HUMAN SKELETON (INCLUDING THE JOINTS). With 260 Illustrations drawn from Nature. Med. 8vo. 14s.

—— THE HUMAN FOOT AND THE HUMAN HAND. With Illustrations. Fcp. 8vo. 4s. 6d.

—— OBSERVATIONS IN MYOLOGY. 8vo. 6s.

—— OLD AGE. The Results of Information received respecting nearly nine hundred persons who had attained the age of eighty years, including seventy-four centenarians. Crown 8vo. 4s. 6d.

HUNT (W.).—TALKS ABOUT ART. With a Letter from Sir J. E. MILLAIS, Bart., R.A. Crown 8vo. 3s. 6d.

HUSS (Hermann).—A SYSTEM OF ORAL INSTRUCTION IN GERMAN. Crown 8vo. 5s.

HUTTON (R. H.).—ESSAYS ON SOME OF THE MODERN GUIDES OF ENGLISH THOUGHT IN MATTERS OF FAITH. Globe 8vo. 6s.

—— ESSAYS. 2 vols. Globe 8vo. 6s. each.
—Vol. I. Literary Essays; II. Theological Essays.

HUXLEY (Thomas Henry).—LESSONS IN ELEMENTARY PHYSIOLOGY. With numerous Illustrations. New Edit. Fcp. 8vo. 4s. 6d.

—— LAY SERMONS, ADDRESSES, AND REVIEWS. 9th Edition. 8vo. 7s. 6d.

—— ESSAYS SELECTED FROM LAY SERMONS, ADDRESSES, AND REVIEWS. 3rd Edition. Crown 8vo. 1s.

—— CRITIQUES AND ADDRESSES. 8vo. 10s. 6d.

—— PHYSIOGRAPHY. AN INTRODUCTION TO THE STUDY OF NATURE. 13th Ed. Cr.8vo. 6s.

—— AMERICAN ADDRESSES, WITH A LECTURE ON THE STUDY OF BIOLOGY. 8vo. 6s. 6d.

—— SCIENCE AND CULTURE, AND OTHER ESSAYS. 8vo. 10s. 6d.

—— SOCIAL DISEASES AND WORSE REMEDIES: LETTERS TO THE "TIMES" ON MR. BOOTH'S SCHEMES. With a Preface and Introductory Essay. 2nd Ed. Cr. 8vo, sewed. 1s. net.

HUXLEY'S PHYSIOLOGY, QUESTIONS ON, FOR SCHOOLS. By T. ALCOCK, M.D. 5th Edition. 18mo. 1s. 6d.

HUXLEY (T. H.) and MARTIN (H. N.).—A COURSE OF PRACTICAL INSTRUCTION IN ELEMENTARY BIOLOGY. New Edition, Revised and Extended by Prof. G. B. HOWES and D. H SCOTT, M.A., Ph.D. With Preface by T. H. HUXLEY, F.R.S. Cr. 8vo. 10s. 6d.

IBBETSON (W. J.). — AN ELEMENTARY TREATISE ON THE MATHEMATICAL THEORY OF PERFECTLY ELASTIC SOLIDS. 8vo. 21s.

ILLINGWORTH (Rev. J. R.).—SERMONS PREACHED IN A COLLEGE CHAPEL. Crown 8vo. 5s.

IMITATIO CHRISTI, LIBRI IV. Printed in Borders after Holbein, Dürer, and other old Masters, containing Dances of Death, Acts of Mercy, Emblems, &c. Cr. 8vo. 7s.6d.

INDIAN TEXT-BOOKS.—PRIMER OF ENGLISH GRAMMAR. By R. MORRIS, LL.D. 18mo. 1s.; sewed, 10d.

PRIMER OF ASTRONOMY. By J. N. LOCKYER. 18mo. 1s.; sewed, 10d.

EASY SELECTIONS FROM MODERN ENGLISH LITERATURE. For the use of the Middle Classes in Indian Schools. With Notes. By Sir ROPER LETHBRIDGE. Cr.8vo. 1s.6d.

SELECTIONS FROM MODERN ENGLISH LITERATURE. For the use of the Higher Classes in Indian Schools. By Sir ROPER LETHBRIDGE, M.A. Crown 8vo. 3s. 6d.

SERIES OF SIX ENGLISH READING BOOKS FOR INDIAN CHILDREN. By P. C. SIRCAR. Revised by Sir ROPER LETHBRIDGE. Cr. 8vo. Book I. 5d.; Nagari Characters, 5d.; Persian Characters, 5d.; Book II. 6d.; Book III. 8d.; Book IV. 1s.; Book V. 1s. 2d.; Book VI. 1s. 3d.

HIGH SCHOOL READER. By ERIC ROBERTSON. Crown 8vo. 2s.

NOTES ON THE HIGH SCHOOL READER. By the same. Crown 8vo. 1s.

THE ORIENT READERS. Books I.—VI. By the same.

A GEOGRAPHICAL READER AND COMPANION TO THE ATLAS. By C. B. CLARKE, F.R.S. Crown 8vo. 2s.

A CLASS-BOOK OF GEOGRAPHY. By the same. Fcap. 8vo. 3s.; sewed, 2s. 6d.

THE WORLD'S HISTORY. Compiled under direction of Sir ROPER LETHBRIDGE. Crown 8vo. 1s.

EASY INTRODUCTION TO THE HISTORY OF INDIA. By Sir ROPER LETHBRIDGE. Crown 8vo. 1s. 6d.

HISTORY OF ENGLAND. Compiled under direction of Sir ROPER LETHBRIDGE. Crown 8vo. 1s. 6d.

EASY INTRODUCTION TO THE HISTORY AND GEOGRAPHY OF BENGAL. By Sir ROPER LETHBRIDGE. Crown 8vo. 1s. 6d.

ARITHMETIC. With Answers. By BARNARD SMITH. 18mo. 2s.

ALGEBRA. By I. TODHUNTER. 18mo, sewed. 2s. 3d.

EUCLID. First Four Books. With Notes, &c. By I. TODHUNTER. 18mo. 2s.

ELEMENTARY MENSURATION AND LAND SURVEYING. By the same Author. 18mo. 2s.

EUCLID. Books I.—IV. By H. S. HALL and F. H. STEVENS. Gl. 8vo. 3s.; sewed, 2s.6d.

PHYSICAL GEOGRAPHY. By H. F. BLANFORD. Crown 8vo. 2s. 6d.

ELEMENTARY GEOMETRY AND CONIC SECTIONS. By J. M. WILSON. Ex. fcp. 8vo. 6s.

INGRAM (T. Dunbar).—A HISTORY OF THE LEGISLATIVE UNION OF GREAT BRITAIN AND IRELAND. 8vo. 10s. 6d.

—— TWO CHAPTERS OF IRISH HISTORY: I. The Irish Parliament of James II.; II. The Alleged Violation of the Treaty of Limerick. 8vo. 6s.

IRVING (Joseph).—ANNALS OF OUR TIME. A Diurnal of Events, Social and Political, Home and Foreign. From the Accession of Queen Victoria to Jubilee Day, being the First Fifty Years of Her Majesty's Reign. In 2 vols. 8vo.—Vol. I. June 20th, 1837, to February 28th, 1871. Vol. II. February 24th, 1871, to June 24th, 1887. 18s. each. The Second Volume may also be had in Three Parts: Part I. February 24th, 1871, to March 19th, 1874, 4s. 6d. Part II. March 20th, 1874, to July 22nd, 1878, 4s. 6d. Part III. July 23rd, 1878, to June 24th, 1887, 9s.

IRVING (Washington).—OLD CHRISTMAS. From the Sketch Book. With 100 Illustrations by RANDOLPH CALDECOTT. Crown 8vo, gilt edges. 6s.
Also with uncut edges, paper label. 6s.
People's Edition. Medium 4to. 6d.

—— BRACEBRIDGE HALL. With 120 Illustrations by RANDOLPH CALDECOTT. Cloth elegant, gilt edges. Crown 8vo. 6s.
Also with uncut edges, paper label. 6s.
People's Edition. Medium 4to. 6d.

—— OLD CHRISTMAS AND BRACEBRIDGE HALL. Illustrations by RANDOLPH CALDECOTT. *Edition de Luxe.* Royal 8vo. 21s.

ISMAY'S CHILDREN. By the Author of "Hogan, M.P." Globe 8vo. 2s.

JACKSON (Rev. Blomfield).—FIRST STEPS TO GREEK PROSE COMPOSITION. 12th Edit. 18mo. 1s. 6d.
KEY (supplied to Teachers only). 3s. 6d.

—— SECOND STEPS TO GREEK PROSE COMPOSITION. 18mo. 2s. 6d.
KEY (supplied to Teachers only). 3s. 6d.

JACOB (Rev. J. A.).—BUILDING IN SILENCE, AND OTHER SERMONS. Extra fcp. 8vo. 6s.

JAMES (Hen.).—NOVELS AND TALES. Pocket Edition. 18mo. 14 vols. 2s. each vol.: THE PORTRAIT OF A LADY. 3 vols.—RODERICK HUDSON. 2 vols.—THE AMERICAN. 2 vols.—WASHINGTON SQUARE. 1 vol.—THE EUROPEANS. 1 vol.—CONFIDENCE. 1 vol.—THE SIEGE OF LONDON; MADAME DE MAUVES. 1 vol.—AN INTERNATIONAL EPISODE; THE PENSION BEAUREPAS; THE POINT OF VIEW. 1 vol.—DAISY MILLER, A STUDY; FOUR MEETINGS; LONGSTAFF'S MARRIAGE; BENVOLIO. 1 vol.—THE MADONNA OF THE FUTURE; A BUNDLE OF LETTERS; THE DIARY OF A MAN OF FIFTY; EUGENE PICKERING. 1 vol.

—— FRENCH POETS AND NOVELISTS. New Edition. Crown 8vo. 4s. 6d.

—— TALES OF THREE CITIES. Cr. 8vo. 4s.6d.

—— PORTRAITS OF PLACES. Cr. 8vo. 7s.6d.

—— PARTIAL PORTRAITS. Crown 8vo. 6s.
See also pp. 28, 29.

JAMES (Rev. Herbert). — THE COUNTRY CLERGYMAN AND HIS WORK. Cr. 8vo. 6s.

JAMES (Right Hon. Sir William Milbourne).—THE BRITISH IN INDIA. 8vo. 12s. 6d.

JAMES (Wm.).—THE PRINCIPLES OF PSYCHO-LOGY. 2 vols. 8vo. 25s. net.

JARDINE (Rev. Robert).—THE ELEMENTS OF THE PSYCHOLOGY OF COGNITION. Third Edition. Crown 8vo. 6s. 6d.

JEANS (Rev. G. E.).—HAILEYBURY CHAPEL, AND OTHER SERMONS. Fcp. 8vo. 3s. 6d.

JEBB (Prof. R. C.).—THE ATTIC ORATORS, FROM ANTIPHON TO ISAEOS. 2 vols. 8vo. 25s.

—— MODERN GREECE. Two Lectures. Crown 8vo. 5s.

JELLETT (Rev. Dr.).—THE ELDER SON, AND OTHER SERMONS. Crown 8vo. 6s.

—— THE EFFICACY OF PRAYER. 3rd Edition. Crown 8vo. 5s.

JENNINGS (A. C.).—CHRONOLOGICAL TA-BLES OF ANCIENT HISTORY. With Index. 8vo. 5s.

JENNINGS (A. C.) and LOWE (W. H.).—THE PSALMS, WITH INTRODUCTIONS AND CRITICAL NOTES. 2 vols. 2nd Edition. Crown 8vo. 10s. 6d. each.

JEVONS (W. Stanley).—THE PRINCIPLES OF SCIENCE: A TREATISE ON LOGIC AND SCIENTIFIC METHOD. Crown 8vo. 12s. 6d.

JEVONS (W. S.).—ELEMENTARY LESSONS IN LOGIC: DEDUCTIVE AND INDUCTIVE. 18mo. 3s. 6d.

—— THE THEORY OF POLITICAL ECONOMY. 3rd Edition. 8vo. 10s. 6d.

—— STUDIES IN DEDUCTIVE LOGIC. 2nd Edition. Crown 8vo. 6s.

—— INVESTIGATIONS IN CURRENCY AND FI-NANCE. Edited, with an Introduction, by H. S. FOXWELL, M.A. Illustrated by 20 Diagrams. 8vo. 21s.

—— METHODS OF SOCIAL REFORM. 8vo. 10s. 6d.

—— THE STATE IN RELATION TO LABOUR. Crown 8vo. 3s. 6d.

—— LETTERS AND JOURNAL. Edited by His Wife. 8vo. 14s.

—— PURE LOGIC, AND OTHER MINOR WORKS. Edited by R. ADAMSON, M.A., and HAR-RIET A. JEVONS. With a Preface by Prof. ADAMSON. 8vo. 10s. 6d.

JEX-BLAKE (Dr. Sophia).—THE CARE OF INFANTS: A Manual for Mothers and Nurses. 18mo. 1s.

JOHNSON (W. E.).—A TREATISE ON TRIGO-NOMETRY. Crown 8vo. 8s. 6d.

JOHNSON (Prof. W. Woolsey).—CURVE TRACING IN CARTESIAN CO-ORDINATES. Crown 8vo. 4s. 6d.

—— A TREATISE ON ORDINARY AND DIFFER-ENTIAL EQUATIONS. Crown 8vo. 15s.

—— AN ELEMENTARY TREATISE ON THE IN-TEGRAL CALCULUS. Crown 8vo. 9s.

JOHNSON'S LIVES OF THE POETS. The Six Chief Lives. Edited by MATTHEW ARNOLD. Crown 8vo. 4s. 6d.

JONES (D. E.).—EXAMPLES IN PHYSICS. Containing 1000 Problems, with Answers and numerous solved Examples. Fcp. 8vo. 3s. 6d.

—— ELEMENTARY LESSONS IN HEAT, LIGHT, AND SOUND. Globe 8vo. 2s. 6d.

JONES (F.).—THE OWENS COLLEGE JUNIOR COURSE OF PRACTICAL CHEMISTRY. With Preface by Sir HENRY E. ROSCOE. New Edition. 18mo. 2s. 6d.

—— QUESTIONS ON CHEMISTRY. A Series of Problems and Exercises in Inorganic and Organic Chemistry. 18mo. 3s.

JONES (Rev. C. A.) and CHEYNE (C. H.). —ALGEBRAICAL EXERCISES. Progressively arranged. 18mo. 2s. 6d.

—— SOLUTIONS OF SOME OF THE EXAMPLES IN THE ALGEBRAICAL EXERCISES OF MESSRS. JONES AND CHEYNE. By the Rev. W. FAILES. Crown 8vo. 7s. 6d.

JUVENAL. THIRTEEN SATIRES OF JUVE-NAL. With a Commentary by Prof. J. E. B. MAYOR, M.A. 4th Edition. Vol. I. Crown 8vo. 10s. 6d.—Vol. II. Crown 8vo. 10s. 6d.

SUPPLEMENT to Third Edition, containing the Principal Changes made in the Fourth Edition. 5s.

—— THIRTEEN SATIRES. Translated into English after the Text of J. E. B. MAYOR by ALEX. LEEPER, M.A. Cr. 8vo. 3s. 6d.

See also p. 32.

KANT.—KANT'S CRITICAL PHILOSOPHY FOR ENGLISH READERS. By JOHN P. MAHAFFY, D.D., and JOHN H. BERNARD, B.D. New Edition. 2 vols. Crown 8vo. Vol. I. THE KRITIK OF PURE REASON EXPLAINED AND DEFENDED. 7s. 6d.—Vol. II. THE "PRO-LEGOMENA." Translated, with Notes and Appendices. 6s.

KANT—MAX MÜLLER.—CRITIQUE OF PURE REASON BY IMMANUEL KANT. Trans-lated by F. MAX MÜLLER. With Intro-duction by LUDWIG NOIRÉ. 2 vols. 8vo. 16s. each. Sold separately. Vol. I. HIS-TORICAL INTRODUCTION, by LUDWIG NOIRÉ, etc., etc.; Vol. II. CRITIQUE OF PURE REASON.

KAVANAGH (Rt. Hon. A. McMURROUGH): A Biography compiled by his Cousin, SARAH L. STEELE. With Portrait. 8vo. 14s. net.

KAY (Rev. W.).—A COMMENTARY ON ST. PAUL'S TWO EPISTLES TO THE CORINTHIANS. Greek Text, with Commentary. 8vo. 9s.

KEARY (Annie).—NATIONS AROUND. Crn. 8vo. 4s. 6d. See also pp. 28, 29.

KEARY (Eliza).—THE MAGIC VALLEY; OR, PATIENT ANTOINE. With Illustrations by "E.V.B." Globe 8vo. 2s. 6d.

KEARY (A. and E.).—THE HEROES OF ASGARD. Tales from Scandinavian My-thology. Globe 8vo. 2s. 6d.

KEATS. LETTERS OF KEATS. Edited by SIDNEY COLVIN. Globe 8vo.

KELLAND (P.) and TAIT (P. G.).—INTRO-DUCTION TO QUATERNIONS, WITH NUMEROUS EXAMPLES. 2nd Edition. Cr. 8vo. 7s. 6d.

KELLOGG (Rev. S. H.).—THE LIGHT OF ASIA AND THE LIGHT OF THE WORLD. Cr. 8vo. 7s. 6d.

KENNEDY (Prof. Alex. W. B.).—THE MECHANICS OF MACHINERY. With Illus-trations. Crown 8vo. 12s. 6d.

KERNEL AND THE HUSK (THE): LET-TERS ON SPIRITUAL CHRISTIANITY. By the Author of "Philochristus." Crown 8vo. 5s.

KEYNES (J. N.).—STUDIES AND EXERCISES IN FORMAL LOGIC. 2nd Ed. Cr. 8vo. 10s. 6d.

—— THE SCOPE AND METHOD OF POLITICAL ECONOMY. Crown 8vo. 7s. net.

KIEPERT (H.).—MANUAL OF ANCIENT GEOGRAPHY. Crown 8vo. 5s.

KILLEN (W. D.).—ECCLESIASTICAL HISTORY OF IRELAND, FROM THE EARLIEST DATE TO THE PRESENT TIME. 2 vols. 8vo. 25s.

KINGSLEY (Charles): HIS LETTERS, AND MEMORIES OF HIS LIFE. Edited by HIS WIFE. 2 vols. Crown 8vo. 12s.—Cheap Edition, 6s.

—— NOVELS AND POEMS. Eversley Edition. 13 vols. Globe 8vo. 5s. each.

WESTWARD HO! 2 vols.—TWO YEARS AGO. 2 vols.—HYPATIA. 2 vols.—YEAST. 1 vol.—ALTON LOCKE. 2 vols.—HEREWARD THE WAKE. 2 vols.—POEMS. 2 vols.

—— Complete Edition OF THE WORKS OF CHARLES KINGSLEY. Cr. 8vo. 3s. 6d. each.

WESTWARD HO! With a Portrait.
HYPATIA. | YEAST.
ALTON LOCKE. | TWO YEARS AGO.
HEREWARD THE WAKE. | POEMS.
THE HEROES; OR, GREEK FAIRY TALES FOR MY CHILDREN.
THE WATER BABIES: A FAIRY TALE FOR A LAND-BABY.
MADAM HOW AND LADY WHY; OR, FIRST LESSONS IN EARTH-LORE FOR CHILDREN.
AT LAST: A CHRISTMAS IN THE WEST INDIES.
PROSE IDYLLS. | PLAYS AND PURITANS.
THE ROMAN AND THE TEUTON. With Preface by Professor MAX MÜLLER.
SANITARY AND SOCIAL LECTURES.
HISTORICAL LECTURES AND ESSAYS.
SCIENTIFIC LECTURES AND ESSAYS.
LITERARY AND GENERAL LECTURES.
THE HERMITS.
GLAUCUS; OR, THE WONDERS OF THE SEA-SHORE. With Coloured Illustrations.
VILLAGE AND TOWN AND COUNTRY SERMONS.
THE WATER OF LIFE, AND OTHER SERMONS.
SERMONS ON NATIONAL SUBJECTS, AND THE KING OF THE EARTH.
SERMONS FOR THE TIMES.
GOOD NEWS OF GOD.
THE GOSPEL OF THE PENTATEUCH, AND DAVID.
DISCIPLINE, AND OTHER SERMONS.
WESTMINSTER SERMONS.
ALL SAINTS' DAY, AND OTHER SERMONS.

—— A Sixpenny Edition OF CHARLES KINGSLEY'S NOVELS. Med. 8vo. 6d. each.
WESTWARD HO! — HYPATIA. — YEAST. — ALTON LOCKE. — TWO YEARS AGO. — HEREWARD THE WAKE.

—— THE WATER BABIES: A FAIRY TALE FOR A LAND BABY. New Edition, with 100 New Pictures by LINLEY SAMBOURNE; engraved by J. SWAIN. Fcp. 4to. 12s. 6d.

—— THE HEROES; OR, GREEK FAIRY TALES FOR MY CHILDREN. Extra cloth, gilt edges. Presentation Edition. Crown 8vo. 7s. 6d.

—— GLAUCUS; OR, THE WONDERS OF THE SEA SHORE. With Coloured Illustrations, extra cloth, gilt edges. Presentation Edition. Crown 8vo. 7s. 6d.

KINGSLEY (C.).—HEALTH AND EDUCATION. Crown 8vo. 6s.

—— POEMS. Pocket Edition. 18mo. 1s. 6d.

—— SELECTIONS FROM SOME OF THE WRITINGS OF CHARLES KINGSLEY. Crown 8vo. 6s.

—— OUT OF THE DEEP: WORDS FOR THE SORROWFUL. From the Writings of CHARLES KINGSLEY. Extra fcp. 8vo. 3s. 6d.

—— DAILY THOUGHTS. Selected from the Writings of CHARLES KINGSLEY. By HIS WIFE. Crown 8vo. 6s.

—— FROM DEATH TO LIFE. Fragments of Teaching to a Village Congregation. With Letters on the "Life after Death." Edited by HIS WIFE. Fcp. 8vo. 2s. 6d.

—— TRUE WORDS FOR BRAVE MEN. Crown 8vo. 2s. 6d.

KINGSLEY (Henry). — TALES OF OLD TRAVEL. Crown 8vo. 3s. 6d.

KIPLING (Rudyard).—PLAIN TALES FROM THE HILLS. Crown 8vo. 6s.

—— THE LIGHT THAT FAILED. Cr. 8vo. 6s.

KITCHENER (F. E.). — GEOMETRICAL NOTE-BOOK. Containing Easy Problems in Geometrical Drawing, preparatory to the Study of Geometry. 4to. 2s.

KLEIN (Dr. E.).—MICRO-ORGANISMS AND DISEASE. An Introduction into the Study of Specific Micro-Organisms. With 121 Engravings. 3rd Edition. Crown 8vo. 6s.

—— THE BACTERIA IN ASIATIC CHOLERA. Crown 8vo. 5s.

KNOX (A.).—DIFFERENTIAL CALCULUS FOR BEGINNERS. Fcp. 8vo. 3s. 6d.

KTESIAS.—THE FRAGMENTS OF THE PERSIKA OF KTESIAS. Edited, with Introduction and Notes, by J. GILMORE, M.A. 8vo. 8s. 6d.

KUENEN (Prof. A.). — AN HISTORICO-CRITICAL INQUIRY INTO THE ORIGIN AND COMPOSITION OF THE HEXATEUCH (PENTATEUCH AND BOOK OF JOSHUA). Translated by PHILIP H. WICKSTEED, M.A. 8vo. 14s.

KYNASTON (Herbert, D.D.). — SERMONS PREACHED IN THE COLLEGE CHAPEL, CHELTENHAM. Crown 8vo. 6s.

—— PROGRESSIVE EXERCISES IN THE COMPOSITION OF GREEK IAMBIC VERSE. Extra fcp. 8vo. 5s.
KEY (supplied to Teachers only). 4s. 6d.

—— EXEMPLARIA CHELTONIENSIA. Sive quae discipulis suis Carmina identidem Latine reddenda proposuit ipse reddidit ex cathedra dictavit HERBERT KYNASTON, M.A. Extra fcp. 8vo. 5s.

LABBERTON (R. H.).—NEW HISTORICAL ATLAS AND GENERAL HISTORY. 4to. 15s.

LAFARGUE (Philip).—THE NEW JUDGMENT OF PARIS: A Novel. 2 vols. Gl. 8vo. 12s.

LAMB.—COLLECTED WORKS. Edited, with Introduction and Notes, by the Rev. ALFRED AINGER, M.A. Globe 8vo. 5s. each volume.
I. ESSAYS OF ELIA.—II. PLAYS, POEMS, AND MISCELLANEOUS ESSAYS.—III. MRS. LEICESTER'S SCHOOL; THE ADVENTURES OF ULYSSES; AND OTHER ESSAYS.—IV. TALES FROM SHAKSPEARE.—V. and VI. LETTERS. Newly arranged, with additions.

LAMB. The Life of Charles Lamb. By Rev. Alfred Ainger, M.A. Uniform with above. Globe 8vo. 5s.

—— Tales from Shakspeare. 18mo. 4s. 6d. *Globe Readings Edition.* For Schools. Globe 8vo. 2s.

LANCIANI(Prof. R.)—Ancient Rome in the Light of Recent Discoveries. 4to. 24s.

LAND OF DARKNESS (THE). With some further Chapters in the Experiences of The Little Pilgrim. By the Author of "A Little Pilgrim in the Unseen." Cr. 8vo. 5s.'

LANDAUER (J.).—Blowpipe Analysis. Authorised English Edition by James Taylor and Wm. E. Kay. Ext. fcp. 8vo. 4s. 6d.

LANG (Andrew).—The Library. With a Chapter on Modern Illustrated Books, by Austin Dobson. Crown 8vo. 3s. 6d.

LANG (Prof. Arnold).—Text-Book of Comparative Anatomy. Translated by H. M. Bernard, M.A., F.Z.S., and Matilda Bernard. With Preface by Professor E. Haeckel. 2 vols. Illustrated. 8vo

LANKESTER (Prof. E. Ray).—The Advancement of Science: Occasional Essays and Addresses. 8vo. 10s. 6d.

—— Comparative Longevity in Man and the Lower Animals. Crn. 8vo. 4s. 6d.

LASLETT (Thomas).—Timber and Timber Trees, Native and Foreign. Cr. 8vo. 8s. 6d.

LEAHY (Sergeant).—The Art of Swimming in the Eton Style. With Preface by Mrs. Oliphant. Crown 8vo. 2s.

LECTURES ON ART. By Regd. Stuart Poole, Professor W. B. Richmond, E. J. Poynter, R.A., J. T. Micklethwaite, and William Morris. Crown 8vo. 4s. 6d.

LEPROSY INVESTIGATION COMMITTEE, JOURNAL OF THE. Ed. by P. S. Abraham, M.A. Nos. I. II. 2s. 6d. each net.

LETHBRIDGE (Sir Roper).—A Short Manual of the History of India. With Maps. Crown 8vo. 5s. For other Works by this Author, see *Indian Text-Books Series*, p. 27.

LEVETT (R.) and DAVISON (A. F.).—Elements of Trigonometry. Crown 8vo.

LEWIS (Richard).—History of the Life-boat and its Work. Crown 8vo. 5s.

LIGHTFOOT (Bishop).—St. Paul's Epistle to the Galatians. A Revised Text, with Introduction, Notes, and Dissertations. 10th Edition. 8vo. 12s.

—— St. Paul's Epistle to the Philippians. A Revised Text, with Introduction, Notes and Dissertations. 9th Edition. 8vo. 12s.

—— St. Paul's Epistles to the Colossians and to Philemon. A Revised Text with Introductions, etc. 9th Edition. 8vo. 12s.

—— The Apostolic Fathers. Part I. St. Clement of Rome. A Revised Text, with Introductions, Notes, Dissertations, and Translations. 2 vols. 8vo. 32s.

—— The Apostolic Fathers. Part II. St. Ignatius to St. Polycarp. Revised Texts, with Introductions, Notes, Dissertations, and Translations. 2nd Edit. 3 vols. 8vo. 48s.

LIGHTFOOT (Bishop). —— The Apostolic Fathers. Abridged Edition. With Short Introductions, Greek Text, and English Translation. 8vo.

—— Essays on the Work entitled "Supernatural Religion." 8vo. 10s. 6d.

—— A Charge delivered to the Clergy of the Diocese of Durham, Nov. 25th, 1886. Demy 8vo. 2s.

—— Leaders in the Northern Church. 2nd Edition. Crown 8vo. 6s.

—— Ordination Addresses and Counsels to Clergy. Crown 8vo. 6s.

—— Cambridge Sermons. Crown 8vo. 6s.

—— Sermons Preached in St. Paul's Cathedral. Crown 8vo. 6s.

—— Sermons Preached on Special Occasions. Crown 8vo.

—— On the Revision of the New Testament. Crown 8vo.

LIGHTWOOD (J. M.)—The Nature of Positive Law. 8vo. 12s. 6d.

LINDSAY (Dr. J. A.).—The Climatic Treatment of Consumption. Cr. 8vo. 5s.

LITTLE PILGRIM IN THE UNSEEN. 24th Thousand. Crown 8vo. 2s. 6d.

LIVY.—Books XXI.—XXV. The Second Punic War. Translated by A. J. Church, M.A., and W. J. Brodribb, M.A. With Maps. Cr. 8vo. 7s. 6d. *See also* pp. 31, 32.

LOCK (Rev. J. B.)—Arithmetic for Schools. 4th Edition, revised. Globe 8vo. Complete with Answers, 4s. 6d. Without Answers, 4s. 6d.

—— Key to "Arithmetic for Schools." By the Rev. R. G. Watson. Cr. 8vo. 10s. 6d.

—— Arithmetic for Beginners. A School Class-Book of Commercial Arithmetic. Globe 8vo. 2s. 6d.

—— Key to "Arithmetic for Beginners." By Rev. R. G. Watson. Crown 8vo. 8s. 6d.

—— A Shilling Book of Arithmetic for Elementary Schools. 18mo. 1s.—With Answers, 1s. 6d.

—— Trigonometry. Globe 8vo. Part I. Elementary Trigonometry. 4s. 6d.—Part II. Higher Trigonometry. 4s. 6d. Complete, 7s. 6d.

—— Key to "Elementary Trigonometry." By H. Carr, B.A. Crown 8vo. 8s. 6d.

—— Trigonometry for Beginners. As far as the Solution of Triangles. Gl. 8vo. 2s. 6d.

—— Key to "Trigonometry for Beginners." Crown 8vo. 6s. 6d.

—— Trigonometry of one Angle. Globe 8vo. 2s. 6d.

—— Elementary Statics. Gl. 8vo. 4s. 6d.

—— Dynamics for Beginners. 3rd Edit. Globe 8vo. 4s. 6d.

LOCKYER (J. Norman, F.R.S.).—Elementary Lessons in Astronomy. Illustrations and Diagram. New Edit. 18mo. 5s. 6d.

—— Primer of Astronomy. 18mo. 1s.

—— Outlines of Physiography: The Movements of the Earth. Cr. 8vo. 1s. 6d.

—— The Chemistry of the Sun. 8vo. 14s.

LOCKYER (J. Norman, F.R.S.).—THE METEORITIC HYPOTHESIS OF THE ORIGIN OF COSMICAL SYSTEMS. 8vo. 17s. net.

LOCKYER'S ASTRONOMY, QUESTIONS ON. By J. FORBES-ROBERTSON. 18mo. 1s. 6d.

LOCKYER—SEABROKE.—STAR-GAZING PAST AND PRESENT. By J. NORMAN LOCKYER, F.R.S., with the assistance of G. M. SEABROKE, F.R.A.S. Roy. 8vo. 21s.

LODGE (Prof. Oliver J.).—MODERN VIEWS OF ELECTRICITY. Crown 8vo. 6s. 6d.

LOEWY (B.).—QUESTIONS AND EXAMPLES IN EXPERIMENTAL PHYSICS, SOUND, LIGHT, HEAT, ELECTRICITY, AND MAGNETISM. Fcp. 8vo. 2s.

—— A GRADUATED COURSE OF NATURAL SCIENCE, EXPERIMENTAL AND THEORETICAL, FOR SCHOOLS AND COLLEGES. Part I. FIRST YEAR'S COURSE FOR ELEMENTARY SCHOOLS AND THE JUNIOR CLASSES OF TECHNICAL SCHOOLS AND COLLEGES. Globe 8vo. 2s.

LONGINUS.—ON THE SUBLIME. Translated by H. L. HAVELL, B.A. With Introduction by ANDREW LANG. Crown 8vo. 4s. 6d.

LOWE (W. H.).—THE HEBREW STUDENT'S COMMENTARY ON ZECHARIAH, HEBREW AND LXX. 8vo. 10s. 6d.

LOWELL (James Russell). — COMPLETE POETICAL WORKS. 18mo. 4s. 6d.

—— DEMOCRACY, AND OTHER ADDRESSES. Crown 8vo. 5s.

—— HEARTSEASE AND RUE. Crown 8vo. 5s.

—— POLITICAL ESSAYS. Ext. cr. 8vo. 7s. 6d.

—— COMPLETE WORKS. 10 vols. Crn. 8vo. 6s. each.

Vols. I.—IV. LITERARY ESSAYS; Vol. V. POLITICAL ESSAYS; Vol. VI. LITERARY AND POLITICAL ADDRESSES; Vols. VII.—X. POETICAL WORKS.

LUBBOCK (Sir John, Bart.).—THE ORIGIN AND METAMORPHOSES OF INSECTS. With Illustrations. Crown 8vo. 3s. 6d.

—— ON BRITISH WILD FLOWERS CONSIDERED IN THEIR RELATION TO INSECTS. With Illustrations. Crown 8vo. 4s. 6d.

—— FLOWERS, FRUITS, AND LEAVES. With Illustrations. Crown 8vo. 4s. 6d.

—— SCIENTIFIC LECTURES. With Illustrations. 2nd Edition, revised. 8vo. 8s. 6d.

—— POLITICAL AND EDUCATIONAL ADDRESSES. 8vo. 8s. 6d.

—— THE PLEASURES OF LIFE. New Edition. Gl. 8vo. 1s. 6d.; swd., 1s. 60th Thousand. *Library Edition.* Globe 8vo. 3s. 6d.

Part II. Globe 8vo. 1s. 6d.; sewed, 1s. *Library Edition.* Globe 8vo. 3s. 6d.

—— Two Parts in one vol. Gl. 8vo. 2s. 6d.

—— FIFTY YEARS OF SCIENCE: Address to the British Association, 1881. 5th Edition. Crown 8vo. 2s. 6d.

LUCAS (F.).—SKETCHES OF RURAL LIFE. Poems. Globe 8vo. 5s.

LUCIAN.—*See* p. 31.

LUCRETIUS.—*See* p. 32.

LUPTON (J. H.).—AN INTRODUCTION TO LATIN ELEGIAC VERSE COMPOSITION. Globe 8vo. 2s. 6d.

—— LATIN RENDERING OF THE EXERCISES IN PART II. (XXV.-C.) TO LUPTON'S "INTRODUCTION TO LATIN ELEGIAC VERSE COMPOSITION." Globe 8vo. 3s. 6d.

—— AN INTRODUCTION TO LATIN LYRIC VERSE COMPOSITION. Globe 8vo. 3s.—Key, 4s. 6d.

LUPTON (Sydney).—CHEMICAL ARITHMETIC. With 1200 Examples. Fcp. 8vo. 4s. 6d.

—— NUMERICAL TABLES AND CONSTANTS IN ELEMENTARY SCIENCE. Ex. fcp. 8vo. 2s. 6d.

LYSIAS.—*See* p. 33.

LYTE (H. C. Maxwell).—ETON COLLEGE, HISTORY OF, 1440—1884. With Illustrations. 2nd Edition. 8vo. 21s.

—— THE UNIVERSITY OF OXFORD, A HISTORY OF, FROM THE EARLIEST TIMES TO THE YEAR 1530. 8vo. 16s.

LYTTON (Rt. Hon. Earl of).—THE RING OF AMASIS: A ROMANCE. Crown 8vo. 3s. 6d.

M'CLELLAND (W. J.).—GEOMETRY OF THE CIRCLE. Crown 8vo.

M'CLELLAND (W. J.) and PRESTON (T.). —A TREATISE ON SPHERICAL TRIGONOMETRY. With numerous Examples. Crown 8vo. 8s. 6d.—Or Part I. 4s. 6d.; Part II. 5s.

McCOSH (Rev. Dr. James).—THE METHOD OF THE DIVINE GOVERNMENT, PHYSICAL AND MORAL. 8vo. 10s. 6d.

—— THE SUPERNATURAL IN RELATION TO THE NATURAL. Crown 8vo. 7s. 6d.

—— THE INTUITIONS OF THE MIND. New Edition. 8vo. 10s. 6d.

—— AN EXAMINATION OF MR. J. S. MILL'S PHILOSOPHY. 8vo. 10s. 6d.

—— THE LAWS OF DISCURSIVE THOUGHT. A Text-Book of Formal Logic. Crn. 8vo. 5s.

—— CHRISTIANITY AND POSITIVISM. Lectures on Natural Theology and Apologetics. Crown 8vo. 7s. 6d.

—— THE SCOTTISH PHILOSOPHY, FROM HUTCHESON TO HAMILTON, BIOGRAPHICAL, EXPOSITORY, CRITICAL. Royal 8vo. 16s.

—— THE EMOTIONS. 8vo. 9s.

—— REALISTIC PHILOSOPHY DEFENDED IN A PHILOSOPHIC SERIES. 2 vols. Vol. I. EXPOSITORY. Vol. II. HISTORICAL AND CRITICAL. Crown 8vo. 14s.

—— PSYCHOLOGY. - Crown 8vo. I. THE COGNITIVE POWERS. 6s. 6d. — II. THE MOTIVE POWERS. 6s. 6d.

—— FIRST AND FUNDAMENTAL TRUTHS. Being a Treatise on Metaphysics. 8vo. 9s.

—— THE PREVAILING TYPES OF PHILOSOPHY: CAN THEY LOGICALLY REACH REALITY? 8vo. 3s. 6d.

MACDONALD (George).—ENGLAND'S ANTIPHON. Crown 8vo. 4s. 6d.

MACDONELL (John).—THE LAND QUESTION. 8vo. 10s. 6d.

MACFARLANE (Alexander). — PHYSICAL ARITHMETIC. Crown 8vo. 7s. 6d.

MACGREGOR (James Gordon).—AN ELE-
MENTARY TREATISE ON KINEMATICS AND
DYNAMICS. Crown 8vo. 10s. 6d.

MACKENZIE (Sir Morell).—THE HYGIENE
OF THE VOCAL ORGANS. 7th Ed. Crn. 8vo. 6s.

MACKIE (Rev. Ellis).—PARALLEL PASSAGES
FOR TRANSLATION INTO GREEK AND ENG-
LISH. Globe 8vo. 4s. 6d.

MACLAGAN (Dr. T.).—THE GERM THEORY.
8vo. 10s. 6d.

MACLAREN (Rev. Alexander).—SERMONS
PREACHED AT MANCHESTER. 11th Edition.
Fcp. 8vo. 4s. 6d.

—— A SECOND SERIES OF SERMONS. 7th
Edition. Fcp. 8vo. 4s. 6d.

—— A THIRD SERIES. 6th Ed. Fcp. 8vo. 4s. 6d.

—— WEEK-DAY EVENING ADDRESSES. 4th
Edition. Fcp. 8vo. 2s. 6d.

—— THE SECRET OF POWER, AND OTHER
SERMONS. Fcp. 8vo. 4s. 6d.

MACLAREN (Arch.).—THE FAIRY FAMILY.
A Series of Ballads and Metrical Tales.
Crown 8vo, gilt. 5s.

MACLEAN (Surgeon-Gen. W. C.).—DISEASES
OF TROPICAL CLIMATES. Cr. 8vo. 10s. 6d.

MACLEAR (Rev. Canon).—A CLASS-BOOK
OF OLD TESTAMENT HISTORY. With Four
Maps. 18mo. 4s. 6d.

—— A CLASS-BOOK OF NEW TESTAMENT
HISTORY. Including the connection of the
Old and New Testament. 18mo. 5s. 6d.

—— A SHILLING BOOK OF OLD TESTAMENT
HISTORY. 18mo. 1s.

—— A SHILLING BOOK OF NEW TESTAMENT
HISTORY. 18mo. 1s.

—— A CLASS-BOOK OF THE CATECHISM OF
THE CHURCH OF ENGLAND. 18mo. 1s. 6d.

—— A FIRST CLASS-BOOK OF THE CATE-
CHISM OF THE CHURCH OF ENGLAND, WITH
SCRIPTURE PROOFS FOR JUNIOR CLASSES
AND SCHOOLS. 18mo. 6d.

—— A MANUAL OF INSTRUCTION FOR CON-
FIRMATION AND FIRST COMMUNION, WITH
PRAYERS AND DEVOTIONS. 32mo. 2s.

—— FIRST COMMUNION, WITH PRAYERS AND
DEVOTIONS FOR THE NEWLY CONFIRMED.
32mo. 6d.

—— THE ORDER OF CONFIRMATION, WITH
PRAYERS AND DEVOTIONS. 32mo. 6d.

—— THE HOUR OF SORROW; OR, THE OFFICE
FOR THE BURIAL OF THE DEAD. 32mo. 2s.

—— APOSTLES OF MEDIÆVAL EUROPE. Crn.
8vo. 4s. 6d.

—— AN INTRODUCTION TO THE CREEDS.
18mo. 2s. 6d.

—— AN INTRODUCTION TO THE THIRTY-NINE
ARTICLES. 18mo.

M'LENNAN (J. F.).—THE PATRIARCHAL
THEORY. Edited and completed by DONALD
M'LENNAN, M.A. 8vo. 14s.

—— STUDIES IN ANCIENT HISTORY. Comprising a Reprint of "Primitive Marriage."
New Edition. 8vo. 16s.

MACMILLAN (D.). MEMOIR OF DANIEL
MACMILLAN. By THOMAS HUGHES, Q.C.
With Portrait. Crown 8vo. 4s. 6d.
Cheap Edition. Crown 8vo, sewed. 1s.

MACMILLAN (Rev. Hugh).—BIBLE TEACH-
INGS IN NATURE. 15th Ed. Gl. 8vo. 6s.

—— HOLIDAYS ON HIGH LANDS; OR, RAM-
BLES AND INCIDENTS IN SEARCH OF ALPINE
PLANTS. 2nd Edition. Globe 8vo. 6s.

—— THE TRUE VINE; OR, THE ANALOGIES
OF OUR LORD'S ALLEGORY. 5th Edition.
Globe 8vo. 6s.

—— THE MINISTRY OF NATURE. 8th Edition.
Globe 8vo. 6s.

—— THE SABBATH OF THE FIELDS. 6th
Edition. Globe 8vo. 6s.

—— THE MARRIAGE IN CANA. Globe 8vo. 6s.

—— TWO WORLDS ARE OURS. 3rd Edition.
Globe 8vo. 6s.

—— THE OLIVE LEAF. Globe 8vo. 6s.

—— ROMAN MOSAICS; OR, STUDIES IN ROME
AND ITS NEIGHBOURHOOD. Globe 8vo. 6s.

MACMILLAN (M. C.)—FIRST LATIN GRAM-
MAR. Extra fcp. 8vo. 1s. 6d.

MACMILLAN'S MAGAZINE. Published
Monthly. 1s.—Vols. I.—LXII. 7s. 6d. each.
[Cloth covers for binding, 1s. each.]

MACMILLAN'S SIX-SHILLING NO-
VELS. Crown 8vo. 6s. each volume.

By William Black.
A PRINCESS OF THULE.
STRANGE ADVENTURES OF A PHAETON.
THE MAID OF KILLEENA, and other Tales.
MADCAP VIOLET.
GREEN PASTURES AND PICCADILLY.
THE BEAUTIFUL WRETCH; THE FOUR
MACNICOLS; THE PUPIL OF AURELIUS.
MACLEOD OF DARE. Illustrated.
WHITE WINGS: A YACHTING ROMANCE.
SHANDON BELLS. | YOLANDE.
JUDITH SHAKESPEARE.
THE WISE WOMEN OF INVERNESS, A TALE:
AND OTHER MISCELLANIES.
WHITE HEATHER. | SABINA ZEMBRA.

By J. H. Shorthouse.
JOHN INGLESANT. | SIR PERCIVAL.
A TEACHER OF THE VIOLIN, ETC.
THE COUNTESS EVE.

By Rudyard Kipling.
PLAIN TALES FROM THE HILLS.
THE LIGHT THAT FAILED.

By Henry James.
THE AMERICAN. | THE EUROPEANS.
DAISY MILLER; AN INTERNATIONAL EPI-
SODE; FOUR MEETINGS.
THE MADONNA OF THE FUTURE, AND
OTHER TALES.
RODERICK HUDSON.
WASHINGTON SQUARE; THE PENSION BEAU-
REPAS; A BUNDLE OF LETTERS.
THE PORTRAIT OF A LADY.
STORIES REVIVED. Two Series. 6s. each.
THE BOSTONIANS.
THE REVERBERATOR.

A DOUBTING HEART. By ANNIE KEARY.
REALMAH. By the Author of "Friends in
Council."
OLD SIR DOUGLAS. By Hon. Mrs. NORTON.
VIRGIN SOIL. By TOURGENIEF.
THE HARBOUR BAR.
BENGAL PEASANT LIFE. By LAL BEHARI
DAY.

MACMILLAN'S SIX-SHILLING NO-
VELS—*continued.*

VIDA : STUDY OF A GIRL. By AMY DUNS-
MUIR.
JILL. By E. A. DILLWYN.
NEÆRA : A TALE OF ANCIENT ROME. By
J. W. GRAHAM.
THE NEW ANTIGONE : A ROMANCE.
A LOVER OF THE BEAUTIFUL. By the
MARCHIONESS OF CARMARTHEN.
A SOUTH SEA LOVER. By A. ST. JOHNSTON.
A CIGARETTE MAKER'S ROMANCE. By
F. MARION CRAWFORD.

MACMILLAN'S THREE - AND - SIX-
PENNY SERIES. Cr. 8vo. 3s. 6d. each

By Rolf Boldrewood.

ROBBERY UNDER ARMS : A Story of Life and
Adventure in the Bush and in the Gold-
fields of Australia.
THE MINER'S RIGHT.
THE SQUATTER'S DREAM.

*By Mrs. Craik, Author of " John Halifax,
Gentleman."*

OLIVE. | THE OGILVIES.
AGATHA'S HUSBAND.
THE HEAD OF THE FAMILY.
TWO MARRIAGES. | THE LAUREL BUSH.
MY MOTHER AND I.
MISS TOMMY : A MEDIÆVAL ROMANCE.
KING ARTHUR : NOT A LOVE STORY.

By F. Marion Crawford.

MR. ISAACS : A TALE OF MODERN INDIA.
DR. CLAUDIUS : A TRUE STORY.
A ROMAN SINGER. | ZOROASTER.
A TALE OF A LONELY PARISH.
MARZIO'S CRUCIFIX. | PAUL PATOFF.
WITH THE IMMORTALS.
GREIFENSTEIN. | SANT' ILARIO.

By Sir H. S. Cunningham.

THE CŒRULEANS : A VACATION IDYLL.
THE HERIOTS. | WHEAT AND TARES.

By Thomas Hardy.

THE WOODLANDERS. | WESSEX TALES.

By Bret Harte.

CRESSY.
THE HERITAGE OF DEDLOW MARSH, AND
OTHER TALES.

By Thomas Hughes. See p. 22.

By Henry James.

A LONDON LIFE. | THE ASPERN PAPERS, etc.
THE TRAGIC MUSE.

By Annie Keary.

CASTLE DALY. | JANET'S HOME.
A YORK AND A LANCASTER ROSE.
OLDBURY.

By Charles Kingsley. See p. 25.

By D. Christie Murray.

AUNT RACHEL. | SCHWARTZ.
THE WEAKER VESSEL.
JOHN VALE'S GUARDIAN.

By Mrs. Oliphant.

NEIGHBOURS ON THE GREEN.
JOYCE. | A BELEAGUERED CITY.
KIRSTEEN.

By Charlotte M. Yonge. See p. 54.

MACMILLAN'S THREE - AND - SIX-
PENNY SERIES —*continued.*

FAITHFUL AND UNFAITHFUL. By M. LEE.
REUBEN SACHS. By AMY LEVY.
MISS BRETHERTON. By Mrs. H. WARD.
LOUISIANA, AND THAT LASS O' LOWRIE'S.
By FRANCES HODGSON BURNETT.
THE RING OF AMASIS. By Lord LYTTON.
MAROONED. By W. CLARK RUSSELL.

Uniform with the above.

STORM WARRIORS ; OR, LIFEBOAT WORK
ON THE GOODWIN SANDS. By the Rev.
JOHN GILMORE.
TALES OF OLD JAPAN. By A. B. MITFORD.
A YEAR WITH THE BIRDS. By W. WARDE
FOWLER. Illustrated by BRYAN HOOK.
TALES OF THE BIRDS. By the same. Illus-
trated by BRYAN HOOK.
LEAVES OF A LIFE. By MONTAGU WIL-
LIAMS, Q.C.
TRUE TALES FOR MY GRANDSONS. By Sir
SAMUEL W. BAKER, F.R.S.
TALES OF OLD TRAVEL. By HENRY
KINGSLEY.

MACMILLAN'S TWO-SHILLING NO-
VELS. Globe 8vo. 2s. each.

*By Mrs. Craik, Author of " John Halifax,
Gentleman."*

TWO MARRIAGES. | AGATHA'S HUSBAND.
THE OGILVIES.

By Mrs. Oliphant.

THE CURATE IN CHARGE.
A SON OF THE SOIL. | YOUNG MUSGRAVE.
HE THAT WILL NOT WHEN HE MAY.
A COUNTRY GENTLEMAN.
HESTER. | SIR TOM.
THE SECOND SON. | THE WIZARD'S SON.

By the Author of " Hogan, M.P."

HOGAN, M.P.
THE HONOURABLE MISS FERRARD.
FLITTERS, TATTERS, AND THE COUNSELLOR,
WEEDS, AND OTHER SKETCHES.
CHRISTY CAREW. | ISMAY'S CHILDREN.

By George Fleming.

A NILE NOVEL. | MIRAGE.
THE HEAD OF MEDUSA. | VESTIGIA.

By Mrs. Macquoid.

PATTY.

By Annie Keary.

JANET'S HOME. | OLDBURY.
CLEMENCY FRANKLYN.
A YORK AND A LANCASTER ROSE.

By W. E. Norris.

MY FRIEND JIM. | CHRIS.

By Henry James.

DAISY MILLER ; AN INTERNATIONAL EPI-
SODE ; FOUR MEETINGS.
RODERICK HUDSON.
THE MADONNA OF THE FUTURE, AND OTHER
TALES.
WASHINGTON SQUARE.
PRINCESS CASAMASSIMA.

By Frances Hodgson Burnett.

LOUISIANA, AND THAT LASS O' LOWRIE'S.
Two Stories.
HAWORTH'S.

MACMILLAN'S TWO-SHILLING NO-
VELS—*continued.*

By Hugh Conway.
A FAMILY AFFAIR. | LIVING OR DEAD.

By D. Christie Murray.
AUNT RACHEL.

By Helen Jackson.
RAMONA : A STORY.

A SLIP IN THE FENS.

MACMILLAN'S HALF-CROWN SERIES
OF JUVENILE BOOKS. Globe 8vo,
cloth, extra. 2s. 6d. each.

OUR YEAR. By the Author of ";John
Halifax, Gentleman."

LITTLE SUNSHINE'S HOLIDAY. By the
Author of " John Halifax, Gentleman."

WHEN I WAS A LITTLE GIRL. By the
Author of " St. Olave's."

NINE YEARS OLD. By the Author of
"When I was a Little Girl," etc.

A STOREHOUSE OF STORIES. Edited by
CHARLOTTE M. YONGE. 2 vols.

AGNES HOPETOUN'S SCHOOLS AND HOLI-
DAYS. By Mrs. OLIPHANT.

THE STORY OF A FELLOW SOLDIER. By
FRANCES AWDRY. (A Life of Bishop
Patteson for the Young.)

RUTH AND HER FRIENDS : A STORY FOR
GIRLS.

THE HEROES OF ASGARD : TALES FROM
SCANDINAVIAN MYTHOLOGY. By A. and
E. KEARY.

THE RUNAWAY. By the Author of " Mrs.
Jerningham's Journal."

WANDERING WILLIE. By the Author of
" Conrad the Squirrel."

PANSIE'S FLOUR BIN. Illustrated by ADRIAN
STOKES.

MILLY AND OLLY. By Mrs. T. H. WARD.
Illustrated by Mrs. ALMA TADEMA.

THE POPULATION OF AN OLD PEAR TREE ;
OR, STORIES OF INSECT LIFE. From the
French of E. VAN BRUYSSEL. Edited by
CHARLOTTE M. YONGE. Illustrated.

HANNAH TARNE. By MARY E. HULLAH.
Illustrated by W. J. HENNESSY.

*By Mrs. Molesworth. Illustrated by Walter
Crane. See p. 37.*

MACMILLAN'S READING BOOKS.
Adapted to the English and Scotch Codes.
Pr.mer . . . . . .   (48 pp.) 18mo, 2d.
Book   I. for Standard   I. (96 pp.) 18mo, 4d.
Book II. for Standard II. (144 pp.) 18mo, 5d.
Book III. for Standard III. (160 pp.) 18mo, 6d.
Book IV. for Standard IV. (176 pp.) 18mo, 8d.
Book V. for Standard V. (380 pp.) 18mo, 1s.
Book VI. for Standard VI. (430 pp.) Cr.8vo, 2s.

MACMILLAN'S COPY-BOOKS.
*1. Initiatory Exercises and Short Letters.
*2. Words consisting of Short Letters.
*3. Long Letters, with words containing Long
    Letters. Figures.
*4. Words containing Long Letters.
4A. Practising and Revising Copybook for
    Nos. 1 to 4.

MACMILLAN'S COPY-BOOKS—*contd.*
*5. Capitals, and Short Half-text Words be-
    ginning with a Capital.
*6. Half-text Words beginning with a Capital.
    Figures.
*7. Small-hand and Half-text, with Capitals
    and Figures.
*8. Small-hand and Half-text, with Capitals
    and Figures.
8A. Practising and Revising Copybook for
    Nos. 5 to 8.
*9. Small-hand Single Head Lines. Figures.
10. Small-hand Single Head Lines. Figures.
*11. Small-hand Double Head Lines. Figures.
12. Commercial and Arithmetical Examples,
    etc.
12A. Practising and Revising Copybook for
    Nos. 8 to 12.
    The Copybooks may be had in two sizes :
      (1) Large Post 4to, 4d. each ;
      (2) Post oblong, 2d. each.
    The numbers marked * may also be had in
    Large Post 4to, with GOODMAN'S PATENT
    SLIDING COPIES. 6d. each.

MACMILLAN'S LATIN COURSE. Part I.
By A. M. COOK, M.A. 2nd Edition,
enlarged. Globe 8vo. 3s. 6d.
Part II. By the same. Gl. 8vo. 2s. 6d.

MACMILLAN'S SHORTER LATIN
COURSE. By A. M. COOK, M.A. Being
an Abridgment of " Macmillan's Latin
Course, Part I." Globe 8vo. 1s. 6d.

MACMILLAN'S LATIN READER. A
Latin Reader for the Lower Forms in
Schools. By H. J. HARDY. Gl. 8vo. 2s. 6d.

MACMILLAN'S GREEK COURSE. Edit.
by Rev. W. G. RUTHERFORD, LL.D. Gl. 8vo.
I. FIRST GREEK GRAMMAR. By the Rev.
W. G. RUTHERFORD, M.A. Part I. Acci-
dence, 2s. ; Part II. Syntax, 2s. ; or in
1 vol. 3s. 6d.
II. EASY EXERCISES IN GREEK ACCIDENCE.
By H. G. UNDERHILL, M.A. 2s.
III. SECOND GREEK EXERCISE BOOK. By
Rev. W. A. HEARD, M.A. 2s. 6d.

MACMILLAN'S GREEK READER.
Stories and Legends. A First Greek Reader.
With Notes, Vocabulary, and Exercises, by
F. H. COLSON, M.A. Globe 8vo. 3s.

MACMILLAN'S ELEMENTARY CLAS-
SICS. 18mo. 1s. 6d. each.
This Series falls into two classes :—
  (1) First Reading Books for Beginners,
provided not only with *Introductions and
Notes*, but with *Vocabularies*, and in some
cases with *Exercises* based upon the Text.
  (2) Stepping-stones to the study of particular authors, intended for more advanced
students, who are beginning to read such
authors as Terence, Plato, the Attic Drama-
tists, and the harder parts of Cicero, Horace,
Virgil, and Thucydides.
  These are provided with Introductions and
Notes, but no *Vocabulary*. The Publishers
have been led to provide the more strictly
Elementary Books with Vocabularies by the
representations of many teachers, who hold
that beginners do not understand the use of
a Dictionary, and of others who, in the case
of middle-class schools where the cost of
books is a serious consideration, advocate the
Vocabulary system on grounds of economy.

MACMILLAN'S ELEMENTARY CLAS-
SICS—*continued.*

It is hoped that the two parts of the Series,
fitting into one another, may together fulfil
all the requirements of Elementary and
Preparatory Schools, and the Lower Forms
of Public Schools.

The following Elementary Books, *with
Introductions, Notes, and Vocabularies,* and
in some cases with *Exercises,* are either
ready or in preparation:

LATIN ACCIDENCE AND EXERCISES AR-
RANGED FOR BEGINNERS. By WILLIAM
WELCH, M.A., and C. G. DUFFIELD, M.A.

ÆSCHYLUS.—PROMETHEUS VINCTUS. Edit.
by Rev. H. M. STEPHENSON, M.A.

ARRIAN.—SELECTIONS. Edited by JOHN
BOND, M.A., and A. S. WALPOLE, M.A.

AULUS GELLIUS, STORIES FROM. By Rev.
G. H. NALL, M.A.

CÆSAR. — THE INVASION OF BRITAIN.
Being Selections from Books IV. and V.
of the "De Bello Gallico." Adapted for
Beginners by W. WELCH, and C. G. DUF-
FIELD.

— THE HELVETIAN WAR. Selected from
Book I. of "The Gallic War," arranged
for the use of Beginners by W. WELCH,
M.A., and C. G. DUFFIELD, M.A.

— THE GALLIC WAR. Scenes from Books V.
and VI. Edited by C. COLBECK, M.A.

— THE GALLIC WAR. Book I. Edited by
Rev. A. S. WALPOLE, M.A.

— THE GALLIC WAR. Books II. and III.
Ed. by Rev. W. G. RUTHERFORD, LL.D.

— THE GALLIC WAR. Book IV. Edited
by C. BRYANS, M.A.

— THE GALLIC WAR. Books V. and VI.
(separately). By the same Editor.

— THE GALLIC WAR. Book VII. Ed. by J.
BOND, M.A., and A. S. WALPOLE, M.A.

CICERO.—DE SENECTUTE. Edited by E. S.
SHUCKBURGH, M.A.

— DE AMICITIA. Ed. by E. S. SHUCKBURGH.

— STORIES OF ROMAN HISTORY. Edited
by Rev. G. E. JEANS and A. V. JONES.

EURIPIDES.—ALCESTIS. By the Rev. M. A.
BAYFIELD, M.A.

— HECUBA. Edited by Rev. J. BOND, M.A.,
and A. S. WALPOLE, M.A.

— MEDEA. Edited by A. W. VERRALL,
Litt.D., and Rev. M. A. BAYFIELD, M.A.

EUTROPIUS. Adapted for the use of Beginners by W. WELCH and C. G. DUFFIELD.

HOMER.—ILIAD. Book I. Ed. by Rev. J.
BOND, M.A., and A. S. WALPOLE, M.A.

— ILIAD. Book XVIII. THE ARMS OF
ACHILLES. Edited by S. R. JAMES, M.A.

—.ODYSSEY. Book I. Edited by Rev. J.
BOND, M.A., and A. S. WALPOLE, M.A.

HORACE.—ODES. Books I.—IV. Edited by
T. E. PAGE, M.A. 1s. 6d. each.

LIVY. Book I. Ed. by H. M. STEPHENSON.

— THE HANNIBALIAN WAR. Being part of
the 21st and 22nd Books of Livy. Adapted
for Beginners by G. C. MACAULAY, M.A.

MACMILLAN'S ELEMENTARY CLAS-
SICS—*continued.*

LIVY.—THE SIEGE OF SYRACUSE. Being
part of the 24th and 25th Books of Livy.
Adapted for Beginners by G. RICHARDS,
M.A., and Rev. A. S. WALPOLE, M.A.

— Book XXI. With Notes adapted from
Mr. Capes' Edition for Junior Students, by
Rev. W. W. CAPES, M.A., and J. E.
MELHUISH, M.A.

— Book XXII. By the same Editors.

— LEGENDS OF ANCIENT ROME, FROM LIVY.
Adapted for Beginners. With Notes, by
H. WILKINSON, M.A.

LUCIAN, EXTRACTS FROM. Edited by J.
BOND, M.A., and A. S. WALPOLE, M.A.

NEPOS.—SELECTIONS ILLUSTRATIVE OF
GREEK AND ROMAN HISTORY. Edited
by G. S. FARNELL, B.A.

OVID.—SELECTIONS. Edited by E. S.
SHUCKBURGH, M.A.

— EASY SELECTIONS FROM OVID IN ELE-
GIAC VERSE. Arranged for the use of
Beginners by H. WILKINSON, M.A.

— STORIES FROM THE METAMORPHOSES.
Arranged for the use of Beginners by J.
BOND, M.A., and A. S. WALPOLE, M.A.

PHÆDRUS.—SELECT FABLES. Adapted for
use of Beginners by Rev. A. S. WAL-
POLE, M.A.

THUCYDIDES.—THE RISE OF THE ATHENIAN
EMPIRE. Book I. Ch. 89—117 and 128—
138. Edited by F. H. COLSON, M.A.

VIRGIL.—GEORGICS. Book I. Edited by
T. E. PAGE, M.A.

— GEORGICS. Book II. Edited by Rev.
J. H. SKRINE, M.A.

— ÆNEID. Book I. Edited by Rev. A. S.
WALPOLE, M.A.

— ÆNEID. Book II. Ed. by T. E. PAGE.

— ÆNEID. Book III. Edited by T. E.
PAGE, M.A.

— ÆNEID. Book IV. Edit. by Rev. H. M.
STEPHENSON, M.A.

— ÆNEID. Book V. Edited by Rev. A.
CALVERT, M.A.

— ÆNEID. Book VI. Ed. by T. E. PAGE.

— ÆNEID. Book VII. THE WRATH OF
TURNUS. Edited by A. CALVERT, M.A.

— ÆNEID. Book VIII. Edited by Rev.
A. CALVERT, M.A.

— ÆNEID. Book IX. Edited by Rev.
H. M. STEPHENSON, M.A.

— ÆNEID. Book X. Ed. by S.G.OWEN, M.A.

-- SELECTIONS. Edited by E. S. SHUCK-
BURGH, M.A.

XENOPHON.—ANABASIS: Selections. Edit.
by W. WELCH, M.A., and C. G. DUF-
FIELD, M.A.

— ANABASIS. Book I., Chaps. i.—viii.
Edited by E. A. WELLS, M.A.

— ANABASIS. Book I. Edited by Rev.
A. S. WALPOLE, M.A.

— ANABASIS. Book II. Edited by Rev.
A. S. WALPOLE, M.A.

MACMILLAN'S ELEMENTARY CLASSICS—*continued.*

XENOPHON.—ANABASIS. Book III. Edit. by Rev. G. H. NALL, M.A.

— ANABASIS. Book IV. Edited by Rev. E. D. STONE, M.A.

— SELECTIONS FROM BOOK IV. OF "THE ANABASIS." Edit. by Rev. E. D. STONE.

— SELECTIONS FROM "THE CYROPAEDIA." Edited by Rev. A. H. COOKE, M.A.

The following more advanced books have *Introductions, Notes,* but no *Vocabularies*:

CICERO.—SELECT LETTERS. Edit. by Rev. G. E. JEANS, M.A.

HERODOTUS.—SELECTIONS FROM BOOKS VII. AND VIII. THE EXPEDITION OF XERXES. Edited by A. H. COOKE, M.A.

HORACE.—SELECTIONS FROM THE SATIRES AND EPISTLES. Edited by Rev. W. J. V. BAKER, M.A.

— SELECT EPODES AND ARS POETICA. Edited by H. A. DALTON, M.A.

PLATO.—EUTHYPHRO AND MENEXENUS. Edited by C. E. GRAVES, M.A.

TERENCE.—SCENES FROM THE ANDRIA. Edited by F. W. CORNISH, M.A.

THE GREEK ELEGIAC POETS, FROM CALLINUS TO CALLIMACHUS. Selected and Edited by Rev. H. KYNASTON.

THUCYDIDES. Book IV., Chaps. i.—lxi. THE CAPTURE OF SPHACTERIA. Edited by C. E. GRAVES, M.A.

Other Volumes to follow.

MACMILLAN'S CLASSICAL SERIES FOR COLLEGES AND SCHOOLS.

Fcp. 8vo. Being select portions of Greek and Latin authors, edited, with Introductions and Notes, for the use of Middle and Upper Forms of Schools, or of Candidates for Public Examinations at the Universities and elsewhere.

ÆSCHINES.—IN CTESIPHONTA. Edited by Rev. T. GWATKIN, M.A., and E. S. SHUCKBURGH, M.A. 5s.

ÆSCHYLUS. — PERSÆ. Edited by A. O. PRICKARD, M.A. With Map. 2s. 6d.

— THE "SEVEN AGAINST THEBES." Edit. by A. W. VERRALL, Litt.D., and M. A. BAYFIELD, M.A. 2s. 6d.

ANDOCIDES.—DE MYSTERIIS. Edited by W. J. HICKIE, M.A. 2s. 6d.

ATTIC ORATORS, SELECTIONS FROM THE. Antiphon, Andocides, Lysias, Isocrates, and Isæus. Ed. by R.C. JEBB, Litt.D. 5s.

CÆSAR.—THE GALLIC WAR. Edited after Kraner by Rev. J. BOND, M.A., and Rev. A. S. WALPOLE, M.A. With Maps. 4s. 6d.

CATULLUS.—SELECT POEMS. Edited by F. P. SIMPSON, B.A. 3s. 6d. [The Text of this Edition is carefully adapted to School use.]

CICERO.—THE CATILINE ORATIONS. From the German of Karl Halm. Edited by A. S. WILKINS, Litt.D. 2s. 6d.

— PRO LEGE MANILIA. Edited, after Halm, by Prof. A. S. WILKINS, Litt.D. 2s. 6d.

MACMILLAN'S CLASSICAL SERIES—*continued.*

CICERO.—THE SECOND PHILIPPIC ORATION. From the German of Karl Halm. Edited, with Corrections and Additions, by Prof. J. E. B. MAYOR. 3s. 6d.

— PRO ROSCIO AMERINO. Edited, after Halm, by E. H. DONKIN, M.A. 2s. 6d.

— PRO P. SESTIO. Edited by Rev. H. A. HOLDEN, M.A. 3s. 6d.

— SELECT LETTERS. Edited by Prof. R. Y. TYRRELL, M.A.

DEMOSTHENES.—DE CORONA. Edited by B. DRAKE, M.A. Revised by E. S. SHUCKBURGH, M.A. 3s. 6d.

— ADVERSUS LEPTINEM. Edited by Rev. J. R. KING, M.A. 2s. 6d.

— THE FIRST PHILIPPIC. Edited, after C. Rehdantz, by Rev. T. GWATKIN. 2s. 6d.

EURIPIDES.—HIPPOLYTUS. Edited by Prof. J. P. MAHAFFY and J. B. BURY. 2s. 6d.

— MEDEA. Edited by A. W. VERRALL, Litt.D. 2s. 6d.

— IPHIGENIA IN TAURIS. Edited by E. B. ENGLAND, M.A. 3s.

— ION. Ed. by M. A. BAYFIELD, M.A. 2s. 6d.

HERODOTUS. Book III. Edited by G. C. MACAULAY, M.A. 2s. 6d.

— Book VI. Edited by Prof. J. STRACHAN, M.A. 3s. 6d.

— Book VII. Edited by Mrs. MONTAGU BUTLER. 3s. 6d.

HOMER.—ILIAD. Books I. IX. XI. XVI.-XXIV. THE STORY OF ACHILLES. Ed. by J. H. PRATT, M.A., and W. LEAF, Litt.D. 5s.

— ODYSSEY. Book IX. Edited by Prof. J. E. B. MAYOR, M.A. 2s. 6d.

— ODYSSEY. Books XXI.—XXIV. THE TRIUMPH OF ODYSSEUS. Edited by S. G. HAMILTON, B.A. 2s. 6d.

HORACE.—THE ODES. Edited by T. E. PAGE, M.A. 5s. (Books I. II. III. and IV. separately, 2s. each.)

— THE SATIRES. Edited by Prof. A. PALMER, M.A. 5s.

— THE EPISTLES AND ARS POETICA. Edit. by Prof. A. S. WILKINS, Litt.D. 5s.

JUVENAL.—THIRTEEN SATIRES. Edited, for the use of Schools, by E. G. HARDY, M.A. 5s. [The Text of this Edition is carefully adapted to School use.]

— SELECT SATIRES. Edited by Prof. J. E. B. MAYOR. X. XI. 3s. 6d.; XII.—XVI. 4s. 6d.

LIVY. Books II. and III. Edited by Rev. H. M. STEPHENSON, M.A. 3s. 6d.

— Books XXI. and XXII. Edited by Rev. W. W. CAPES, M.A. 4s. 6d.

— Books XXIII. and XXIV. Ed. by G. C. MACAULAY. With Maps. 3s. 6d.

— THE LAST TWO KINGS OF MACEDON. Extracts from the Fourth and Fifth Decades of Livy. Selected and Edit. by F. H. RAWLINS, M.A. With Maps. 2s. 6d.

LUCRETIUS. Books I.—III. Edited by J. H. WARBURTON LEE, M.A. 3s. 6d.

MACMILLAN'S CLASSICAL SERIES—
continued.

LYSIAS.—SELECT ORATIONS. Edited by
E. S. SHUCKBURGH, M.A. 5s.

MARTIAL.—SELECT EPIGRAMS. Edited by
Rev. H. M. STEPHENSON, M.A. 5s.

OVID.—FASTI. Edited by G. H. HALLAM,
M.A. With Maps. 3s. 6d.

— HEROIDUM EPISTULÆ XIII. Edited by
E. S. SHUCKBURGH, M.A. 3s. 6d.

— METAMORPHOSES. Books XIII. and XIV.
Edited by C. SIMMONS, M.A. 3s. 6d.

PLATO.—THE REPUBLIC. Books I.—V.
Edited by T. H. WARREN, M.A. 5s.

— LACHES. Edited by M. T. TATHAM,
M.A. 2s. 6d.

PLAUTUS.—MILES GLORIOSUS. Edited by
Prof. R. Y. TYRRELL, M.A. 3s. 6d.

— AMPHITRUO. Edited by A. PALMER,
M.A. 3s. 6d.

— CAPTIVI. Ed. by A. RHYS-SMITH, M.A.

PLINY.—LETTERS. Books I. and II. Edited
by J. COWAN, M.A. 3s.

— LETTERS. Book III. Edited by Prof.
J. E. B. MAYOR. With Life of Pliny by
G. H. RENDALL. 3s. 6d.

PLUTARCH. — LIFE OF THEMISTOKLES.
Edited by Rev. H. A. HOLDEN, M.A.,
LL.D. 3s. 6d.

— LIVES OF GALBA AND OTHO. Edited by
E. G. HARDY, M.A. 5s.

POLYBIUS.—The History of the Achæan
League as contained in the remains of
Polybius. Edited by W. W. CAPES. 5s.

PROPERTIUS.—SELECT POEMS. Edited by
Prof. J. P. POSTGATE, M.A. 5s.

SALLUST.—CATILINE AND JUGURTHA. Ed.
by C. MERIVALE, D.D. 3s. 6d.—Or separately, 2s. each.

— BELLUM CATULINAE. Edited by A. M.
COOK, M.A. 2s. 6d.

TACITUS.—AGRICOLA AND GERMANIA. Ed.
by A. J. CHURCH, M.A., and W. J.
BRODRIBB, M.A. 3s. 6d.—Or separately,
2s. each.

— THE ANNALS. Book VI. By the same
Editors. 2s.

— THE HISTORIES. Books I. and II.
Edited by A. D. GODLEY, M.A. 3s. 6d.

— THE HISTORIES. Books III.—V. By
the same Editor. 3s. 6d.

TERENCE.—HAUTON TIMORUMENOS. Edit.
by E. S. SHUCKBURGH, M.A. 2s. 6d.—With
Translation, 3s. 6d.

— PHORMIO. Ed. by Rev. J. BOND, M.A.,
and Rev. A. S. WALPOLE, M.A. 2s. 6d.

THUCYDIDES. Book II. Edited by E. C.
MARCHANT, M.A.

— Book IV. Ed. by C. E. GRAVES. 3s. 6d.

— Book V. By the same Editor.

— Books VI. and VII. THE SICILIAN EX-
PEDITION. Edited by Rev. P. FROST,
M.A. With Map. 3s. 6d.

VIRGIL.—ÆNEID. Books II. and III. THE
NARRATIVE OF ÆNEAS. Edited by E. W.
HOWSON, M.A. 2s.

MACMILLAN'S CLASSICAL SERIES—
continued.

XENOPHON.—HELLENICA. Books I. and II.
Edited by H. HAILSTONE, M.A. 2s. 6d.

— CYROPÆDIA. Books VII. and VIII. Ed.
by Prof. A. GOODWIN, M.A. 2s. 6d.

— MEMORABILIA SOCRATIS. Edited by
A. R. CLUER, B.A. 5s.

— THE ANABASIS. Books I.—IV. Edited
by Professors W. W. GOODWIN and J. W.
WHITE. Adapted to Goodwin's Greek
Grammar. With a Map. 3s. 6d.

— HIERO. Edited by Rev. H. A. HOLDEN,
M.A., LL.D. 2s. 6d.

— OECONOMICUS. By the same Editor.
With Introduction, Explanatory Notes
Critical Appendix, and Lexicon. 5s.

The following are in preparation:

DEMOSTHENES.—IN MIDIAM. Edited by
Prof. A. S. WILKINS, Litt.D., and HER-
MAN HAGER, Ph.D.

EURIPIDES.—BACCHAE. Edited by Prof.
R. Y. TYRRELL, M.A.

HERODOTUS. Book V. Edited by Prof.
J. STRACHAN, M.A.

ISÆOS.—THE ORATIONS. Edited by Prof
WM. RIDGEWAY, M.A.

OVID.—METAMORPHOSES. Books I.—III.
Edited by C. SIMMONS, M.A.

SALLUST.—JUGURTHA. Edited by A. M.
COOK, M.A.

TACITUS.—THE ANNALS. Books I. and II.
Edited by J. S. REID, Litt.D.

Other Volumes will follow.

MACMILLAN'S GEOGRAPHICAL
SERIES. Edited by ARCHIBALD GEIKIE,
F.R.S., Director-General of the Geological
Survey of the United Kingdom.

THE TEACHING OF GEOGRAPHY. A Practical
Handbook for the use of Teachers. Globe
8vo. 2s.

GEOGRAPHY OF THE BRITISH ISLES. By
ARCHIBALD GEIKIE, F.R.S. 18mo. 1s.

THE ELEMENTARY SCHOOL ATLAS. 24 Maps
in Colours. By JOHN BARTHOLOMEW,
F.R.G.S. 4to. 1s.

AN ELEMENTARY CLASS-BOOK OF GENERAL
GEOGRAPHY. By HUGH ROBERT MILL,
D.Sc. Edin. Illustrated. Cr. 8vo. 3s. 6d.

MAPS AND MAP DRAWING. By W. A.
ELDERTON. 18mo. 1s.

GEOGRAPHY OF EUROPE. By JAMES SIME,
M.A. With Illustrations. Gl. 8vo. 3s.

ELEMENTARY GEOGRAPHY OF INDIA,
BURMA, AND CEYLON. By H. F. BLAN-
FORD, F.G.S. Globe 8vo. 2s. 6d.

MACMILLAN'S SCIENCE CLASS-
BOOKS. Fcp. 8vo.

LESSONS IN APPLIED MECHANICS. By J. H.
COTTERILL and J. H. SLADE. 5s. 6d.

LESSONS IN ELEMENTARY PHYSICS. By
Prof. BALFOUR STEWART, F.R.S. New
Edition. 4s. 6d. (Questions on, 2s.)

EXAMPLES IN PHYSICS. By Prof. D. E.
JONES, B.Sc. 3s. 6d.

MACMILLAN'S SCIENCE CLASS-BOOKS—*continued.*

ELEMENTARY LESSONS IN HEAT, LIGHT, AND SOUND. By Prof. D. E. JONES, B.Sc. Globe 8vo. 2s. 6d.

QUESTIONS AND EXAMPLES ON EXPERIMENTAL PHYSICS: Sound, Light, Heat, Electricity, and Magnetism. By B. LOEWV, F.R.A.S. 2s.

A GRADUATED COURSE OF NATURAL SCIENCE FOR ELEMENTARY AND TECHNICAL SCHOOLS AND COLLEGES. Part I. First Year's Course. By the same. Gl. 8vo. 2s.

ELEMENTARY LESSONS ON SOUND. By Dr. W. H. STONE. 3s. 6d.

ELECTRIC LIGHT ARITHMETIC. By R. E. DAY, M.A. 2s.

A COLLECTION OF EXAMPLES ON HEAT AND ELECTRICITY. By H. H. TURNER. 2s. 6d.

AN ELEMENTARY TREATISE ON STEAM. By Prof. J. PERRY, C.E. 4s. 6d.

ELECTRICITY AND MAGNETISM. By Prof. SILVANUS P. THOMPSON. 4s. 6d.

POPULAR ASTRONOMY. By Sir G. B. AIRY, K.C.B., late Astronomer-Royal. 4s. 6d.

ELEMENTARY LESSONS ON ASTRONOMY. By J. N. LOCKYER, F.R.S. New Edition. 5s. 6d. (Questions on 1s. 6d.)

LESSONS IN ELEMENTARY CHEMISTRY. By Sir H. ROSCOE, F.R.S. 4s. 6d.—Problems adapted to the same, by Prof. THORPE and W. TATE. With Key. 2s.

OWENS COLLEGE JUNIOR COURSE OF PRACTICAL CHEMISTRY. By F. JONES. With Preface by Sir H. ROSCOE, F.R.S. 2s. 6d.

QUESTIONS ON CHEMISTRY. A Series of Problems and Exercises in Inorganic and Organic Chemistry. By F. JONES. 3s.

OWENS COLLEGE COURSE OF PRACTICAL ORGANIC CHEMISTRY. By JULIUS B. COHEN, Ph.D. With Preface by Sir H. ROSCOE and Prof. SCHORLEMMER. 2s. 6d.

ELEMENTS OF CHEMISTRY. By Prof. IRA REMSEN. 2s. 6d.

EXPERIMENTAL PROOFS OF CHEMICAL THEORY FOR BEGINNERS. By WILLIAM RAMSAY, Ph.D. 2s. 6d.

NUMERICAL TABLES AND CONSTANTS IN ELEMENTARY SCIENCE. By SYDNEY LUPTON, M.A. 2s. 6d.

ELEMENTARY LESSONS IN PHYSICAL GEOGRAPHY. By ARCHIBALD GEIKIE, F.R.S. 4s. 6d. (Questions on, 1s. 6d.)

ELEMENTARY LESSONS IN PHYSIOLOGY. By T. H. HUXLEY, F.R.S. 4s. 6d. (Questions on, 1s. 6d.)

LESSONS IN ELEMENTARY ANATOMY. By ST. G. MIVART, F.R.S. 6s. 6d.

LESSONS IN ELEMENTARY BOTANY. By Prof. D. OLIVER, F.R.S. 4s. 6d.

DISEASES OF FIELD AND GARDEN CROPS. By W. G. SMITH. 4s. 6d.

LESSONS IN LOGIC, INDUCTIVE AND DEDUCTIVE. By W. S. JEVONS, LL.D. 3s. 6d.

THE ECONOMICS OF INDUSTRY. By Prof. A. MARSHALL and M. P. MARSHALL. 2s. 6d.

MACMILLAN'S SCIENCE CLASS-BOOKS—*continued.*

POLITICAL ECONOMY FOR BEGINNERS. By Mrs. FAWCETT. With Questions. 2s. 6d.

ELEMENTARY LESSONS IN THE SCIENCE OF AGRICULTURAL PRACTICE. By Prof. H. TANNER. 3s. 6d.

CLASS-BOOK OF GEOGRAPHY. By C. B. CLARKE, F.R.S. 3s.; sewed, 2s. 6d.

SHORT GEOGRAPHY OF THE BRITISH ISLANDS. By J. R. GREEN and ALICE S. GREEN. With Maps. 3s. 6d.

MACMILLAN'S PROGRESSIVE FRENCH COURSE. By G. EUGÈNE FASNACHT. Extra fcp. 8vo.

I. FIRST YEAR, CONTAINING EASY LESSONS IN THE REGULAR ACCIDENCE. Thoroughly revised Edition. 1s.

II. SECOND YEAR, CONTAINING AN ELEMENTARY GRAMMAR. With copious Exercises, Notes, and Vocabularies. New Edition, enlarged. 2s.

III. THIRD YEAR, CONTAINING A SYSTEMATIC SYNTAX AND LESSONS IN COMPOSITION. 2s. 6d.

THE TEACHER'S COMPANION TO THE SAME. With copious Notes, Hints for different renderings, Synonyms, Philological Remarks, etc. 1st Year, 4s. 6d. 2nd Year, 4s. 6d. 3rd Year, 4s. 6d.

MACMILLAN'S PROGRESSIVE FRENCH READERS. By G. EUGÈNE FASNACHT. Extra fcp. 8vo.

I. FIRST YEAR, CONTAINING TALES, HISTORICAL EXTRACTS, LETTERS, DIALOGUES, FABLES, BALLADS, NURSERY SONGS, etc. With Two Vocabularies: (1) In the Order of Subjects; (2) In Alphabetical Order. 2s. 6d.

II. SECOND YEAR, CONTAINING FICTION IN PROSE AND VERSE, HISTORICAL AND DESCRIPTIVE EXTRACTS, ESSAYS, LETTERS, etc. 2s. 6d.

MACMILLAN'S FRENCH COMPOSITION. By G. Eugène Fasnacht. Extra fcp. 8vo.—Part I. ELEMENTARY. 2s. 6d.—Part II. ADVANCED.

THE TEACHER'S COMPANION TO THE SAME. Part I. 4s. 6d.

MACMILLAN'S FRENCH READINGS FOR CHILDREN. By G. E. FASNACHT. Illustrated. Globe 8vo.

MACMILLAN'S PROGRESSIVE GERMAN COURSE. By G. EUGÈNE FASNACHT. Extra fcp. 8vo.

I. FIRST YEAR, CONTAINING EASY LESSONS ON THE REGULAR ACCIDENCE. 1s. 6d.

II. SECOND YEAR, CONTAINING CONVERSATIONAL LESSONS ON SYSTEMATIC ACCIDENCE AND ELEMENTARY SYNTAX, WITH PHILOLOGICAL ILLUSTRATIONS AND ETYMOLOGICAL VOCABULARY. New Edition, enlarged. 3s. 6d.

THE TEACHER'S COMPANION TO THE SAME. 1st Year, 4s. 6d.; 2nd Year, 4s. 6d.

MACMILLAN'S PROGRESSIVE GERMAN READERS. By G. Eugène Fasnacht. Extra fcap. 8vo.

I, First Year, containing an Introduction to the German order of Words, with Copious Examples, Extracts from German Authors in Prose and Poetry, Notes, Vocabularies. 2s. 6d.

MACMILLAN'S GERMAN COMPOSITION. By G. E. Fasnacht. Extra fcp. 8vo.—Part I. First Course: Parallel German-English Extracts, Parallel English-German Syntax. 2s. 6d.

The Teacher's Companion to the same. Part I. 4s. 6d.

MACMILLAN'S SERIES OF FOREIGN SCHOOL CLASSICS. Edited by G. E. Fasnacht. 18mo.

Select works of the best foreign Authors, with suitable Notes and Introductions based on the latest researches of French and German Scholars by practical masters and teachers.

FRENCH.

CORNEILLE.—Le Cid. Edited by G. E. Fasnacht. 1s.

DUMAS.—Les Demoiselles de St. Cyr. Edited by Victor Oger. 1s. 6d.

FRENCH Readings from Roman History. Selected from various Authors. Edited by C. Colbeck, M.A. 4s. 6d.

La Fontaine's Fables. Books I.—VI. Ed. by L. M. Moriarty. [In preparation.

MOLIÈRE.—Les Femmes Savantes. By G. E. Fasnacht. 1s.

— Le Misanthrope. By the same. 1s.

— Le Médecin Malgré Lui. By the same. 1s.

— Les Precieuses Ridicules. By the same. [In the Press.

— L'Avare. Edited by L. M. Moriarty. 1s.

— Le Bourgeois Gentilhomme. By the same. 1s. 6d.

RACINE.—Britannicus. Edited by Eugène Pellissier. 2s.

SAND (George).—La Mare au Diable. Edited by W. E. Russell, M.A. 1s.

SANDEAU (Jules).—Mademoiselle de la Seiglière. Edit. by H. C. Steel. 1s. 6d.

THIERS'S History of the Egyptian Expedition. Edited by Rev. H. A. Bull, M.A. [In preparation.

VOLTAIRE.—Charles XII. Edited by G. E. Fasnacht. 3s. 6d.

GERMAN.

FREYTAG.—Doktor Luther. Edited by Francis Storr, M.A. [In preparation.

GOETHE.—Götz von Berlichingen. Edit. by H. A. Bull, M.A. 2s.

— Faust. Part I. Ed. by Miss J. Lee. 4s. 6d.

HEINE.—Selections from the Reisebilder and other Prose Works. Edit. by C. Colbeck, M.A. 2s. 6d.

LESSING.—Minna von Barnhelm. Edited by J. Sime, M.A. [In preparation.

MACMILLAN'S FOREIGN SCHOOL CLASSICS –German—continued.

SCHILLER.—Die Jungfrau Von Orleans. Edited by Joseph Gostwick. 2s. 6d.

SCHILLER.—Wallenstein. Part I. Das Läger. Edited by H. B. Cotterill, M.A. 2s.

— Maria Stuart. Edited by C. Sheldon, M.A., D.Lit. 2s. 6d.

— Wilhelm Tell. Edited by G. E. Fasnacht. 2s. 6d.

— Selections from Schiller's Lyrical Poems. Edited by E. J. Turner, M.A., and E. D. A. Morshead, M.A. 2s. 6d.

UHLAND.—Select Ballads. Adapted as a First Easy Reading Book for Beginners. Edited by G. E. Fasnacht. 1s.

MACMILLAN'S PRIMARY SERIES OF FRENCH AND GERMAN READING BOOKS. Edited by G. Eugène Fasnacht. With Illustrations. Globe 8vo.

CORNAZ.—Nos Enfants et Leurs Amis. Edited by Edith Harvey. 1s. 6d.

DE MAISTRE.—La Jeune Sibérienne et le Lépreux de la Cité d'Aoste. Edit. by S. Barlet, B.Sc. 1s. 6d.

FLORIAN.—Select Fables. Edited by Charles Yeld, M.A. 1s. 6d.

GRIMM.—Kinder- und Hausmärchen. Selected and Edited by G. E. Fasnacht. Illustrated. 2s. 6d.

HAUFF.—Die Karavane. Edited by Herman Hager, Ph.D. With Exercises by G. E. Fasnacht. 3s.

La Fontaine.—Fables. A Selection, by L. M. Moriarty, M.A. With Illustrations by Randolph Caldecott. 2s. 6d.

LAMARTINE.—Jeanne d'Arc. Edited by M. de G. Verrall. [In the Press.

MOLESWORTH.—French Life in Letters. By Mrs. Molesworth. 1s. 6d.

PERRAULT.—Contes de Fées. Edited by G. E. Fasnacht. 1s. 6d.

SCHMID.—Heinrich von Eichenfels. Ed. by G. E. Fasnacht. 2s. 6d.

MACNAMARA (C.).—A History of Asiatic Cholera. Crown 8vo. 10s. 6d.·

MADAGASCAR : An Historical and Descriptive Account of the Island and its former Dependencies. By Captain S. Oliver, F.S.A. 2 vols. Med. 8vo. 2l.12s.6d.

MADAME TABBY'S ESTABLISHMENT. By Kari. Illus. by L. Wain. Cr. 8vo. 4s. 6d.

MADOC (Fayr).—The Story of Melicent. Crown 8vo. 4s. 6d.

MAHAFFY (Rev. Prof. J. P.).—Social Life in Greece, from Homer to Menander. 6th Edition. Crown 8vo. 9s.

—— Greek Life and Thought from the Age of Alexander to the Roman Conquest. Crown 8vo. 12s. 6d.

—— Rambles and Studies in Greece. Illustrated. 3rd Edition. Crn. 8vo. 10s. 6d.

—— A History of Classical Greek Literature. Crown 8vo. Vol. I. The Poets. With an Appendix on Homer by Prof. Sayce. In 2 Parts.—Vol. II. The Prose Writers. In 2 Parts, 4s. 6d. each.

MAHAFFY (Rev. Prof. J. P.).—THE GREEK WORLD UNDER ROMAN SWAY, FROM POLYBIUS TO PLUTARCH. Cr. 8vo. 10s. 6d.

—— GREEK ANTIQUITIES. Illust. 18mo. 1s.

—— EURIPIDES. 18mo. 1s. 6d.

—— THE DECAY OF MODERN PREACHING: AN ESSAY. Crown 8vo. 3s. 6d.

—— THE PRINCIPLES OF THE ART OF CONVERSATION. 2nd Ed. Crown 8vo. 4s. 6d.

MAHAFFY (Rev. Prof. J. P.) and ROGERS (J. E.).—SKETCHES FROM A TOUR THROUGH HOLLAND AND GERMANY. Illustrated by J. E. ROGERS. Extra crown 8vo. 10s. 6d.

MAHAFFY (Prof. J. P.) and BERNARD (J. H.).—See p. 24 under KANT.

MAITLAND (F. W.).—PLEAS OF THE CROWN FOR THE COUNTY OF GLOUCESTER, A.D. 1221. Edited by F. W. MAITLAND. 8vo. 7s. 6d.

—— JUSTICE AND POLICE. Cr. 8vo. 3s. 6d.

MALET (Lucas).—MRS. LORIMER: A SKETCH IN BLACK AND WHITE. Cr. 8vo. 4s. 6d.

MANCHESTER SCIENCE LECTURES FOR THE PEOPLE. Eighth Series, 1876—77. With Illustrations. Cr. 8vo. 2s.

MANSFIELD (C. B.).—AERIAL NAVIGATION. Cr. 8vo. 10s. 6d.

MARCUS AURELIUS ANTONINUS.—BOOK IV. OF THE MEDITATIONS. The Greek Text Revised. With Translation and Commentary, by HASTINGS CROSSLEY, M.A. 8vo. 6s.

MARRIOTT (J. A. R.).—THE MAKERS OF MODERN ITALY: MAZZINI, CAVOUR, GARIBALDI. Three Oxford Lectures. Crown 8vo. 1s. 6d.

MARSHALL (Prof. Alfred).—PRINCIPLES OF ECONOMICS. 2 vols. 8vo. Vol. 1. 12s.6d. net.

MARSHALL (Prof. A. and Mary P.).—THE ECONOMICS OF INDUSTRY. Ex.fcp.8vo. 2s.6d.

MARSHALL (J. M.).—A TABLE OF IRREGULAR GREEK VERBS. 8vo. 1s.

MARTEL (Chas.).—MILITARY ITALY. With Map. 8vo. 12s. 6d.

MARTIAL.—SELECT EPIGRAMS FOR ENGLISH READERS. Translated by W. T. WEBB, M.A. Ext. fcp. 8vo. 4s. 6d.—See also p. 33

MARTIN (Frances).—THE POET'S HOUR. Poetry Selected and Arranged for Children. 12mo. 2s. 6d.

—— SPRING-TIME WITH THE POETS. Fcp. 8vo. 3s. 6d.

—— ANGELIQUE ARNAULD, Abbess of Port Royal. Crown 8vo. 4s. 6d.

MARTIN (Frederick).—THE HISTORY OF LLOYDS, AND OF MARINE INSURANCE IN GREAT BRITAIN. 8vo. 14s.

MARTINEAU (Miss C. A.).—EASY LESSONS ON HEAT. Globe 8vo. 2s. 6d.

MARTINEAU (Harriet). — BIOGRAPHICAL SKETCHES, 1852—75. Crown 8vo. 6s.

MARTINEAU (Dr. James).—SPINOZA. 2nd Edition. Crown 8vo. 6s.

MASSON (Prof. David).—RECENT BRITISH PHILOSOPHY. 3rd Edition. Cr. 8vo. 6s.

—— DRUMMOND OF HAWTHORNDEN. Crown 8vo. 10s. 6d.

MASSON (Prof. D.).—WORDSWORTH, SHELLEY, KEATS, AND OTHER ESSAYS. Crown 8vo. 5s.

—— CHATTERTON: A STORY OF THE YEAR 1770. Crown 8vo. 5s.

—— LIFE OF MILTON. See "Milton."

—— MILTON'S POEMS. See "Milton."

MASSON (Gustave).—A COMPENDIOUS DICTIONARY OF THE FRENCH LANGUAGE (FRENCH-ENGLISH AND ENGLISH-FRENCH). Crown 8vo. 6s.

MASSON (Mrs.).—THREE CENTURIES OF ENGLISH POETRY. Being Selections from Chaucer to Herrick. Globe 8vo. 3s. 6d.

MATTHEWS (G. F.).—MANUAL OF LOGARITHMS. 8vo. 5s. net.

MATURIN (Rev. W.).—THE BLESSEDNESS OF THE DEAD IN CHRIST. Cr. 8vo. 7s. 6d.

MAUDSLEY (Dr. Henry).—THE PHYSIOLOGY OF MIND. Crown 8vo. 10s. 6d.

—— THE PATHOLOGY OF MIND. 8vo. 18s.

—— BODY AND MIND. Crown 8vo. 6s. 6d.

MAURICE.—LIFE OF FREDERICK DENISON MAURICE. By his Son, FREDERICK MAURICE, Two Portraits. 3rd Ed. 2 vols. Demy 8vo. 36s. *Cheap Edition* (4th Thousand) 2 vols. Crown 8vo. 16s.

MAURICE (Frederick Denison).—THE KINGDOM OF CHRIST. 3rd Edition. 2 vols. Crn. 8vo. 12s.

—— LECTURES ON THE APOCALYPSE. 2nd Edition. Crown 8vo. 6s.

—— SOCIAL MORALITY. 3rd Ed. Cr. 8vo. 6s.

—— THE CONSCIENCE. Lectures on Casuistry. 3rd Edition. Crown 8vo. 4s. 6d.

—— DIALOGUES ON FAMILY WORSHIP. Crown 8vo. 4s. 6d.

—— THE PATRIARCHS AND LAWGIVERS OF THE OLD TESTAMENT. 7th Ed. Cr. 8vo. 4s. 6d.

—— THE PROPHETS AND KINGS OF THE OLD TESTAMENT. 5th Edition. Crn. 8vo. 6s.

—— THE GOSPEL OF THE KINGDOM OF HEAVEN. 3rd Edition. Crown 8vo. 6s.

—— THE GOSPEL OF ST. JOHN. 8th Edition. Crown 8vo. 6s.

—— THE EPISTLES OF ST. JOHN. 4th Edit. Crown 8vo. 6s.

—— EXPOSITORY SERMONS ON THE PRAYERBOOK; AND ON THE LORD'S PRAYER. New Edition. Crown 8vo. 6s.

—— THEOLOGICAL ESSAYS. 4th Edition. Crn. 8vo. 6s.

—— THE DOCTRINE OF SACRIFICE DEDUCED FROM THE SCRIPTURES. 2nd Edition. Crown 8vo. 6s.

—— MORAL AND METAPHYSICAL PHILOSOPHY. 4th Edition. 2 vols. 8vo. 16s.

—— THE RELIGIONS OF THE WORLD. 6th Edition. Crown 8vo. 4s. 6d.

—— ON THE SABBATH DAY; THE CHARACTER OF THE WARRIOR; AND ON THE INTERPRETATION OF HISTORY. Fcp. 8vo. 2s. 6d.

—— LEARNING AND WORKING. Crown 8vo. 4s. 6d.

—— THE LORD'S PRAYER, THE CREED, AND THE COMMANDMENTS. 18mo. 1s.

MAURICE (F. D.).—SERMONS PREACHED IN COUNTRY CHURCHES. 2nd Edition. Cr. 8vo. 6s.

—— THE FRIENDSHIP OF BOOKS, AND OTHER LECTURES. 3rd Edition. Cr. 8vo. 4s. 6d.

—— THE UNITY OF THE NEW TESTAMENT. 2nd Edition. 2 vols. Crown 8vo. 12s.

—— LESSONS OF HOPE. Readings from the Works of F. D. MAURICE. Selected by Rev. J. LL. DAVIES, M.A. Crown 8vo. 5s.

—— THE COMMUNION SERVICE FROM THE BOOK OF COMMON PRAYER, WITH SELECT READINGS FROM THE WRITINGS OF THE REV. F. D. MAURICE. Edited by Bishop COLENSO. 16mo. 2s. 6d.

MAURICE (Col. F.).—WAR. 8vo. 5s. net.

MAXWELL. PROFESSOR CLERK MAXWELL, A LIFE OF. By Prof. L. CAMPBELL, M.A., and W. GARNETT, M.A. 2nd Edition. Crown 8vo. 7s. 6d.

MAYER (Prof. A. M.).—SOUND. A Series of Simple, Entertaining, and Inexpensive Experiments in the Phenomena of Sound. With Illustrations. Crown 8vo. 3s. 6d.

MAYER (Prof. A. M.) and BARNARD (C.)—LIGHT. A Series of Simple, Entertaining, and Useful Experiments in the Phenomena of Light. Illustrated. Crown 8vo. 2s. 6d.

MAYOR (Prof. John E. B.).—A FIRST GREEK READER. New Edition. Fcp. 8vo. 4s. 6d.

—— AUTOBIOGRAPHY OF MATTHEW ROBINSON. Fcp. 8vo. 5s.

—— A BIBLIOGRAPHICAL CLUE TO LATIN LITERATURE. Crown 8vo. 10s. 6d. [See also under "Juvenal."]

MAYOR (Prof. Joseph B.).—GREEK FOR BEGINNERS. Fcp. 8vo. Part I. 1s. 6d.—Parts II. and III. 3s. 6d.—Complete, 4s. 6d.

MAZINI (Linda).—IN THE GOLDEN SHELL. With Illustrations. Globe 8vo. 4s. 6d.

MELDOLA (Prof. R.)—THE CHEMISTRY OF PHOTOGRAPHY. Crown 8vo. 6s.

MELDOLA (Prof. R.) and WHITE (Wm.).—REPORT ON THE EAST ANGLIAN EARTHQUAKE OF 22ND APRIL, 1884. 8vo. 3s. 6d.

MELEAGER: FIFTY POEMS OF. Translated by WALTER HEADLAM. Fcp. 4to. 7s. 6d.

MERCIER (Dr. C.).—THE NERVOUS SYSTEM AND THE MIND. 8vo. 12s. 6d.

MERCUR (Prof. J.).—ELEMENTS OF THE ART OF WAR. 8vo. 17s.

MEREDITH (George).— A READING OF EARTH. Extra fcp. 8vo. 5s.

—— POEMS AND LYRICS OF THE JOY OF EARTH. Extra fcp. 8vo. 6s.

—— BALLADS AND POEMS OF TRAGIC LIFE. Crown 8vo. 6s.

MEYER (Ernst von).—HISTORY OF CHEMISTRY. Trans. by G. MACGOWAN, Ph.D. 8vo. 14s. net.

MIALL.—LIFE OF EDWARD MIALL. By his Son, ARTHUR MIALL. 8vo. 10s. 6d.

MICHELET (M.).—A SUMMARY OF MODERN HISTORY. Translated by M. C. M. SIMPSON. Globe 8vo. 4s. 6d.

MILL (H. R.).—ELEMENTARY CLASS-BOOK OF GENERAL GEOGRAPHY. Cr. 8vo. 3s. 6d.

MILLAR (J. B.)—ELEMENTS OF DESCRIPTIVE GEOMETRY. 2nd Edition. Crown 8vo. 6s.

MILLER (R. Kalley).—THE ROMANCE OF ASTRONOMY. 2nd Ed. Cr. 8vo. 4s. 6d.

MILLIGAN (Rev. Prof. W.).—THE RESURRECTION OF OUR LORD. 2nd Ed. Cr. 8vo. 5s.

—— THE REVELATION OF ST. JOHN. 2nd Edition. Crown 8vo. 7s. 6d.

MILNE (Rev. John J.).—WEEKLY PROBLEM PAPERS. Fcp. 8vo. 4s. 6d.

—— COMPANION TO WEEKLY PROBLEMS. Cr. 8vo. 10s. 6d.

—— SOLUTIONS OF WEEKLY PROBLEM PAPERS. Crown 8vo. 10s. 6d.

MILNE (Rev. J. J.) and DAVIS (R. F.).—GEOMETRICAL CONICS. Part I. THE PARABOLA. Crown 8vo. 2s.

MILTON.—THE LIFE OF JOHN MILTON. By Prof. DAVID MASSON. Vol. I., 21s.; Vol. III., 18s.; Vols. IV. and V., 32s.; Vol. VI., with Portrait, 21s.

—— POETICAL WORKS. Edited, with Introductions and Notes, by Prof. DAVID MASSON, M.A. 3 vols. 8vo. 2l. 2s.

—— POETICAL WORKS. Ed. by Prof. MASSON. 3 vols. Fcp. 8vo. 15s.

—— POETICAL WORKS. (Globe Edition.) Ed. by Prof. MASSON. Globe 8vo. 3s. 6d. See also ENGLISH CLASSICS, p. 12.

MINCHIN (Rev. Prof. G. M.).—NATURÆ VERITAS. Fcp. 8vo. 2s. 6d.

MINTO (W.).—THE MEDIATION OF RALPH HARDELOT. 3 vols. Crown 8vo. 31s. 6d.

MITFORD (A. B.).—TALES OF OLD JAPAN. With Illustrations. Crown 8vo. 3s. 6d.

MIVART (St. George).—LESSONS IN ELEMENTARY ANATOMY. Fcp. 8vo. 6s. 6d.

MIXTER (Prof. W. G.).—AN ELEMENTARY TEXT-BOOK OF CHEMISTRY. 2nd Edition. Crown 8vo. 7s. 6d.

MIZ MAZE (THE); OR, THE WINKWORTH PUZZLE. A Story in Letters by Nine Authors. Crown 8vo. 4s. 6d.

MOLESWORTH (Mrs.). Illustrated by WALTER CRANE.

HERR BABY. Globe 8vo. 2s. 6d.

GRANDMOTHER DEAR. Globe 8vo. 2s. 6d.

THE TAPESTRY ROOM. Globe 8vo. 2s. 6d.

A CHRISTMAS CHILD. Globe 8vo. 2s. 6d.

ROSY. Globe 8vo. 2s. 6d.

TWO LITTLE WAIFS. Globe 8vo. 2s. 6d.

CHRISTMAS TREE LAND. Gl. 8vo. 2s. 6d.

"US": AN OLD-FASHIONED STORY. Globe 8vo. 2s. 6d.

"CARROTS," JUST A LITTLE BOY. Globe 8vo. 2s. 6d.

TELL ME A STORY. Globe 8vo. 2s. 6d.

THE CUCKOO CLOCK. Globe 8vo. 2s. 6d.

FOUR WINDS FARM. Globe 8vo. 2s. 6d.

LITTLE MISS PEGGY. Globe 8vo. 2s. 6d.

THE RECTORY CHILDREN. Gl. 8vo. 2s. 6d.

A CHRISTMAS POSY. Crown 8vo. 4s. 6d.

MOLESWORTH (Mrs.)—*continued*.

THE CHILDREN OF THE CASTLE. Crown 8vo. 4s. 6d.

SUMMER STORIES. Crown 8vo. 4s. 6d.

FOUR GHOST STORIES. Crown 8vo. 6s.

FRENCH LIFE IN LETTERS. With Notes on Idioms, etc. Globe 8vo. 1s. 6d.

MOLIÈRE.—LE MALADE IMAGINAIRE. Edit. by F. TARVER, M.A. Fcp. 8vo. 2s. 6d. *See also* p. 35.

MOLLOY (Rev. G.).—GLEANINGS IN SCIENCE : A SERIES OF POPULAR LECTURES ON SCIENTIFIC SUBJECTS. 8vo. 7s. 6d.

MONAHAN (James H.).—THE METHOD OF LAW. Crown 8vo. 6s.

MONTELIUS—WOODS.—THE CIVILISATION OF SWEDEN IN HEATHEN TIMES. By Prof. OSCAR MONTELIUS. Translated by Rev. F. H. WOODS, B.D. With Illustrations. 8vo. 14s.

MOORE (Prof. C. H.).—THE DEVELOPMENT AND CHARACTER OF GOTHIC ARCHITECTURE. Illustrated. Medium 8vo. 18s.

MOORHOUSE (Rt. Rev. Bishop).—JACOB : THREE SERMONS. Extra fcp. 8vo. 3s. 6d.

—— THE TEACHING OF CHRIST. Crown 8vo. 3s. net.

MORISON (J. C.).—THE LIFE AND TIMES OF SAINT BERNARD. 4th Edition. Crown 8vo. 6s

MORISON (Jeanie).—THE PURPOSE OF THE AGES. Crown 8vo. 9s.

MORLEY (John). - WORKS. Collected Edit. In 11 vols. Globe 8vo. 5s. each.

VOLTAIRE. 1 vol.—ROUSSEAU. 2 vols.—DIDEROT AND THE ENCYCLOPÆDISTS. 2 vols.—ON COMPROMISE. 1 vol.—MISCELLANIES. 3 vols.—BURKE. 1 vol.—STUDIES IN LITERATURE. 1 vol.

MORRIS (Rev. Richard, LL.D.).—HISTORICAL OUTLINES OF ENGLISH ACCIDENCE. Fcp. 8vo. 6s.

—— ELEMENTARY LESSONS IN HISTORICAL ENGLISH GRAMMAR. 18mo. 2s. 6d.

—— PRIMER OF ENGLISH GRAMMAR. 18mo, cloth. 1s.

MORRIS (R.) and BOWEN (H. C.).—ENGLISH GRAMMAR EXERCISES. 18mo. 1s.

MORRIS (R.) and KELLNER (L.).—HISTORICAL OUTLINES OF ENGLISH SYNTAX. Extra fcp. 8vo.

MORTE D'ARTHUR. THE EDITION OF CAXTON REVISED FOR MODERN USE. By Sir EDWARD STRACHEY. Gl. 8vo. 3s. 6d.

MOULTON (Louise Chandler).—SWALLOW-FLIGHTS. Extra fcp. 8vo. 4s. 6d.

—— IN THE GARDEN OF DREAMS: LYRICS AND SONNETS. Crown 8vo. 6s.

MUDIE (C. E.).—STRAY LEAVES : POEMS. 4th Edition. Extra fcp. 8vo. 3s. 6d.

MUIR (T.).—THE THEORY OF DETERMINANTS IN THE HISTORICAL ORDER OF ITS DEVELOPMENT. Part I. DETERMINANTS IN GENERAL. Leibnitz (1693) to Cayley (1841). 8vo. 10s. 6d.

MUIR (M. M. Pattison).—PRACTICAL CHEMISTRY FOR MEDICAL STUDENTS. Fcp. 8vo. 1s. 6d.

MUIR (M. M. P.) and WILSON (D. M.).—THE ELEMENTS OF THERMAL CHEMISTRY. 8vo. 12s. 6d.

MÜLLER—THOMPSON.—THE FERTILISATION OF FLOWERS. By Prof. HERMANN MÜLLER. Translated by D'ARCY W. THOMPSON. With a Preface by CHARLES DARWIN, F.R.S. Medium 8vo. 21s.

MULLINGER (J. B.).—CAMBRIDGE CHARACTERISTICS IN THE SEVENTEENTH CENTURY. Crown 8vo. 4s. 6d.

MURPHY (J. J.).—HABIT AND INTELLIGENCE. 2nd Ed. Illustrated. 8vo. 16s.

MURRAY (E. C. Grenville).—ROUND ABOUT FRANCE. Crown 8vo. 7s. 6d.

MURRAY (D. Christie).—*See* p. 29.

MURRAY (D. Christie) and HERMAN (Henry).—HE FELL AMONG THIEVES. 2 vols. Globe 8vo. 12s.

MUSIC.—A DICTIONARY OF MUSIC AND MUSICIANS, A.D. 1450—1889. Edited by Sir GEORGE GROVE, D.C.L. In 4 vols. 8vo. 21s. each.—Parts I.—XIV., XIX.—XXII. 3s. 6d. each.—Parts XV. XVI. 7s.—Parts XVII. XVIII. 7s.—Parts XXIII.—XXV. APPENDIX. Ed. J. A. F. MAITLAND, M.A. 9s.

—— A COMPLETE INDEX TO THE ABOVE. By Mrs. E. WODEHOUSE. 8vo. 7s. 6d.

MYERS (E.).—THE PURITANS : A POEM. Extra fcap. 8vo. 2s. 6d.

—— PINDAR'S ODES. Translated, with Introduction and Notes. Crown 8vo. 5s.

—— POEMS. Extra fcp. 8vo. 4s. 6d.

—— THE DEFENCE OF ROME, AND OTHER POEMS. Extra fcp. 8vo. 5s.

—— THE JUDGMENT OF PROMETHEUS, AND OTHER POEMS. Extra fcp. 8vo. 3s. 6d.

MYERS (F. W. H.).—THE RENEWAL OF YOUTH, AND OTHER POEMS. Crown 8vo. 7s. 6d.

—— ST. PAUL : A POEM. Ex. fcp. 8vo. 2s. 6d.

—— ESSAYS. 2 vols.—I. Classical. II. Modern. Crown 8vo. 4s. 6d. each.

MYLNE (The Rt. Rev. Bishop).—SERMONS PREACHED IN ST. THOMAS'S CATHEDRAL, BOMBAY. Crown 8vo. 6s.

NADAL (E. S.).—ESSAYS AT HOME AND ELSEWHERE. Crown 8vo. 6s.

NAPOLEON I., HISTORY OF. By P. LANFREY. 4 vols. Crown 8vo. 30s.

NATURAL RELIGION. By the Author of "Ecce Homo." 3rd Edit. Globe 8vo. 6s.

NATURE : A WEEKLY ILLUSTRATED JOURNAL OF SCIENCE. Published every Thursday. Price 6d. Monthly Parts, 2s. and 2s. 6d.; Current Half-yearly vols., 15s. each. Vols. I.—XLI. [Cases for binding vols. 1s. 6d. each.]

NATURE PORTRAITS. A Series of Portraits of Scientific Worthies engraved by JEENS and others in Portfolio. India Proofs, 5s. each. [Portfolio separately, 6s. net.]

NATURE SERIES. Crown 8vo:

THE ORIGIN AND METAMORPHOSES OF INSECTS. By Sir JOHN LUBBOCK, M.P., F.R.S. With Illustrations. 3s. 6d.

THE TRANSIT OF VENUS. By Prof. G. FORBES. With Illustrations. 3s. 6d.

POLARISATION OF LIGHT. By W. SPOTTISWOODE, LL.D. Illustrated. 3s. 6d.

ON BRITISH WILD FLOWERS CONSIDERED IN RELATION TO INSECTS. By Sir JOHN LUBBOCK, M.P., F.R.S. Illustrated. 4s.6d.

FLOWERS, FRUITS, AND LEAVES. By Sir JOHN LUBBOCK. Illustrated. 4s. 6d.

HOW TO DRAW A STRAIGHT LINE: A LECTURE ON LINKAGES. By A. B. KEMPE, B.A. Illustrated. 1s. 6d.

LIGHT: A SERIES OF SIMPLE, ENTERTAINING, AND USEFUL EXPERIMENTS. By A. M. MAYER and C. BARNARD. Illustrated. 2s. 6d.

SOUND: A SERIES OF SIMPLE, ENTERTAINING, AND INEXPENSIVE EXPERIMENTS. By A. M. MAYER. 3s. 6d.

SEEING AND THINKING. By Prof. W. K. CLIFFORD, F.R.S. Diagrams. 3s. 6d.

CHARLES DARWIN. Memorial Notices reprinted from "Nature." By THOMAS H. HUXLEY, F.R.S., G. J. ROMANES, F.R.S., ARCHIBALD GEIKIE, F.R.S., and W. T. DYER, F.R.S. 2s. 6d.

ON THE COLOURS OF FLOWERS. By GRANT ALLEN. Illustrated. 3s. 6d.

THE CHEMISTRY OF THE SECONDARY BATTERIES OF PLANTÉ AND FAURE. By J. H. GLADSTONE and A. TRIBE. 2s. 6d.

A CENTURY OF ELECTRICITY. By T. C. MENDENHALL. 4s. 6d.

ON LIGHT. The Burnett Lectures. By Sir GEORGE GABRIEL STOKES, M.P., F.R.S. Three Courses: I. On the Nature of Light. II. On Light as a Means of Investigation. III. On Beneficial Effects of Light. 7s. 6d.

THE SCIENTIFIC EVIDENCES OF ORGANIC EVOLUTION. By GEORGE J. ROMANES, M.A., LL.D. 2s. 6d.

POPULAR LECTURES AND ADDRESSES. By Sir WM. THOMSON. In 3 vols. Vol. I. Constitution of Matter. Illustrated. 6s.— Vol. III. Navigation.

THE CHEMISTRY OF PHOTOGRAPHY. By Prof. R. MELDOLA, F.R.S. Illustrated. 6s.

MODERN VIEWS OF ELECTRICITY. By Prof. O. J. LODGE, LL.D. Illustrated. 6s. 6d.

TIMBER AND SOME OF ITS DISEASES. By Prof. H. M. WARD, M.A. Illustrated. 6s.

ARE THE EFFECTS OF USE AND DISUSE INHERITED? An Examination of the View held by Spencer and Darwin. By W. PLATT BALL. 3s. 6d.

NEW ANTIGONE (THE): A ROMANCE. Crown 8vo. 6s.

NEWCOMB (Prof. Simon).—POPULAR ASTRONOMY. With 112 Engravings and Maps of the Stars. 2nd Edition. 8vo. 18s.

NEWMAN (F. W.). — MATHEMATICAL TRACTS. 8vo. Part I. 5s.—Part II. 4s.

—— ELLIPTIC INTEGRALS. 8vo. 9s.

NEWTON (Sir C. T.).—ESSAYS ON ART AND ARCHÆOLOGY. 8vo. 12s. 6d.

NEWTON'S PRINCIPIA. Edited by Prof. Sir W. THOMSON and Prof. BLACKBURN. 4to. 31s. 6d.

—— FIRST BOOK. Sections I. II. III. With Notes, Illustrations, and Problems. By P. FROST, M.A. 3rd Edition. 8vo. 12s.

NIXON (J. E.).—PARALLEL EXTRACTS. Arranged for Translation into English and Latin, with Notes on Idioms. Part I. Historical and Epistolary. 2nd Ed. Cr.8vo. 3s.6d.

—— PROSE EXTRACTS. Arranged for Translation into English and Latin, with General and Special Prefaces on Style and Idiom. I. Oratorical. II. Historical. III. Philosophical. IV. Anecdotes and Letters. 2nd Edition, enlarged to 280 pages. Crown 8vo. 4s. 6d.—SELECTIONS FROM THE SAME. Globe 8vo. 3s.

NOEL (Lady Augusta).—WANDERING WILLIE. Globe 8vo. 2s. 6d.

—— HITHERSEA MERE. 3 vols. Cr.8vo. 31s.6d.

NORDENSKIÖLD. — VOYAGE OF THE "VEGA" ROUND ASIA AND EUROPE. By Baron A. E. VON NORDENSKIÖLD. Translated by ALEXANDER LESLIE. 400 Illustrations, Maps, etc. 2 vols. Medium 8vo. 45s. Cheap Edition. With Portrait, Maps, and Illustrations. Crown 8vo. 6s.

NORGATE (Kate).—ENGLAND UNDER THE ANGEVIN KINGS. 2 vols. With Maps and Plans. 8vo. 32s.

NORRIS (W. E.).—MY FRIEND JIM. Globe 8vo. 2s.

—— CHRIS. Globe 8vo. 2s.

NORTON (the Hon. Mrs.).—THE LADY OF LA GARAYE. 9th Ed. Fcp. 8vo. 4s. 6d.

—— OLD SIR DOUGLAS. Crown 8vo. 6s.

OLD SONGS. With Drawings by E. A. ABBEY and A. PARSONS. 4to. Morocco gilt. 1l. 11s. 6d.

OLIPHANT (Mrs. M. O. W.).—FRANCIS OF ASSISI. Crown 8vo. 6s.

—— THE MAKERS OF VENICE: DOGES, CONQUERORS, PAINTERS, AND MEN OF LETTERS. Illustrated. Crown 8vo. 10s. 6d.

—— THE MAKERS OF FLORENCE: DANTE, GIOTTO, SAVONAROLA, AND THEIR CITY. Illustrated. Cr. 8vo. 10s. 6d.

—— ROYAL EDINBURGH: HER SAINTS, KINGS, PROPHETS, AND POETS. Illustrated by G. REID, R.S.A. Crn. 8vo. 10s. 6d.

—— THE LITERARY HISTORY OF ENGLAND IN THE END OF THE XVIII. AND BEGINNING OF THE XIX. CENTURY. 3 vols. 8vo. 21s.

See also p. 29

OLIPHANT (T. L. Kington).—THE OLD AND MIDDLE ENGLISH. Globe 8vo. 9s.

OLIPHANT (T. L. Kington). —THE DUKE AND THE SCHOLAR, AND OTHER ESSAYS. 8vo. 7s. 6d.

—— THE NEW ENGLISH. 2 vols. Cr. 8vo. 21s.

OLIVER (Prof. Daniel).—LESSONS IN ELEMENTARY BOTANY. Illustr. Fcp. 8vo. 4s. 6d.

—— FIRST BOOK OF INDIAN BOTANY. Illustrated. Extra fcp. 8vo. 6s. 6d.

OLIVER (Capt. S. P.).—MADAGASCAR: AN HISTORICAL AND DESCRIPTIVE ACCOUNT OF THE ISLAND AND ITS FORMER DEPENDENCIES. 2 vols. Medium 8vo. 2l. 12s. 6d.

ORCHIDS : BEING THE REPORT ON THE ORCHID CONFERENCE HELD AT SOUTH KENSINGTON, 1885. 8vo. 2s. 6d. net.

OSTWALD (Prof. W.). — OUTLINES OF GENERAL CHEMISTRY. Translated by Dr. J. WALKER. 8vo. 10s. net.

OTTÉ (E. C.).—SCANDINAVIAN HISTORY. With Maps. Globe 8vo. 6s.

OVERING (H.).—TIM : A STORY OF SCHOOL LIFE. Crown 8vo.

OVID.—See pp. 31, 33.

OWENS COLLEGE CALENDAR, 1889—90. Crown 8vo. 3s. net.

OWENS COLLEGE ESSAYS AND ADDRESSES. By Professors and Lecturers of the College. 8vo. 14s.

OXFORD, A HISTORY OF THE UNIVERSITY OF. From the Earliest Times to the Year 1530. By H. C. MAXWELL LYTE, M.A. 8vo. 16s.

PALGRAVE (Sir Francis). — HISTORY OF NORMANDY AND OF ENGLAND. 4 vols. 8vo. 4l. 4s.

PALGRAVE (William Gifford).—A NARRATIVE OF A YEAR'S JOURNEY THROUGH CENTRAL AND EASTERN ARABIA, 1862—63. 9th Edition. Crown 8vo. 6s.

—— ESSAYS ON EASTERN QUESTIONS. 8vo. 10s. 6d.

—— DUTCH GUIANA. 8vo. 9s.

—— ULYSSES; OR, SCENES AND STUDIES IN MANY LANDS. 8vo. 12s. 6d.

PALGRAVE (Prof. Francis Turner).—THE FIVE DAYS' ENTERTAINMENTS AT WENTWORTH GRANGE. A Book for Children. Small 4to. 6s.

—— ESSAYS ON ART. Extra fcp. 8vo. 6s.

—— ORIGINAL HYMNS. 3rd Ed. 18mo. 1s. 6d.

—— LYRICAL POEMS. Extra fcp. 8vo. 6s.

—— VISIONS OF ENGLAND : A SERIES OF LYRICAL POEMS ON LEADING EVENTS AND PERSONS IN ENGLISH HISTORY. Crown 8vo. 7s. 6d.

—— THE GOLDEN TREASURY OF THE BEST SONGS AND LYRICAL POEMS IN THE ENGLISH LANGUAGE. 18mo. 2s. 6d. net. (Large Type.) Crown 8vo. 10s. 6d.

—— THE CHILDREN'S TREASURY OF LYRICAL POETRY. 18mo. 2s. 6d.—Or in Two Parts, 1s. each.

PALGRAVE (Reginald F. D.).—THE HOUSE OF COMMONS : ILLUSTRATIONS OF ITS HISTORY AND PRACTICE. Crown 8vo. 2s. 6d.

PALGRAVE (R. H. Inglis).—DICTIONARY OF POLITICAL ECONOMY. Ed. by R. H. INGLIS PALGRAVE. 3s. 6d. each Part. [Part I. shortly.

PALMER (Lady Sophia).—MRS. PENICOTT'S LODGER, AND OTHER STORIES. Cr. 8vo. 2s. 6d.

PALMER (J. H.).—TEXT-BOOK OF PRACTICAL LOGARITHMS AND TRIGONOMETRY. Crown 8vo. 4s. 6d.

PANTIN (W. E. P.).—A FIRST LATIN VERSE BOOK. Globe 8vo. 1s. 6d.

PARADOXICAL PHILOSOPHY : A SEQUEL TO "THE UNSEEN UNIVERSE." Cr. 8vo. 7s. 6d.

PARKER (Prof. T. Jeffery).—A COURSE OF INSTRUCTION IN ZOOTOMY (VERTEBRATA). With 74 Illustrations. Crown 8vo. 8s. 6d.

—— LESSONS IN ELEMENTARY BIOLOGY. Illustrated. Crown 8vo.

PARKINSON (S.).—A TREATISE ON ELEMENTARY MECHANICS. Crown 8vo. 9s. 6d.

—— A TREATISE ON OPTICS. 4th Edition, revised. Crown 8vo. 10s. 6d.

PARKMAN (Francis). — MONTCALM AND WOLFE. Library Edition. Illustrated with Portraits and Maps. 2 vols. 8vo. 12s. 6d. each.

—— THE COLLECTED WORKS OF FRANCIS PARKMAN. Popular Edition. In 10 vols. Crown 8vo. 7s. 6d. each; or complete, 3l. 13s. 6d.—PIONEERS OF FRANCE IN THE NEW WORLD. 1 vol.—THE JESUITS IN NORTH AMERICA. 1 vol.—LA SALLE AND THE DISCOVERY OF THE GREAT WEST. 1 vol.—THE OREGON TRAIL. 1 vol.—THE OLD RÉGIME IN CANADA UNDER LOUIS XIV. 1 vol.—COUNT FRONTENAC AND NEW FRANCE UNDER LOUIS XIV. 1 vol.—MONTCALM AND WOLFE. 2 vols.—THE CONSPIRACY OF PONTIAC. 2 vols.

PASTEUR — FAULKNER. — STUDIES ON FERMENTATION : THE DISEASES OF BEER, THEIR CAUSES, AND THE MEANS OF PREVENTING THEM. By L. PASTEUR. Translated by FRANK FAULKNER. 8vo. 21s.

PATER (W.).—THE RENAISSANCE : STUDIES IN ART AND POETRY. 4th Ed. Cr. 8vo. 10s. 6d.

—— MARIUS THE EPICUREAN : HIS SENSATIONS AND IDEAS. 3rd Edition. 2 vols. 8vo. 12s.

—— IMAGINARY PORTRAITS. 3rd Edition. Crown 8vo. 6s.

—— APPRECIATIONS. With an Essay on Style. 2nd Edition. Crown 8vo. 8s. 6d.

PATERSON (James).—COMMENTARIES ON THE LIBERTY OF THE SUBJECT, AND THE LAWS OF ENGLAND RELATING TO THE SECURITY OF THE PERSON. 2 vols. Cr. 8vo. 21s.

—— THE LIBERTY OF THE PRESS, SPEECH, AND PUBLIC WORSHIP. Crown 8vo. 12s.

PATMORE (C.).—THE CHILDREN'S GARLAND FROM THE BEST POETS. With a Vignette. 18mo. 2s. 6d. net.
    Globe Readings Edition. For Schools. Globe 8vo. 2s.

PATTESON.—LIFE AND LETTERS OF JOHN COLERIDGE PATTESON, D.D., MISSIONARY BISHOP. By CHARLOTTE M. YONGE. 8th Edition. 2 vols. Crown 8vo. 12s.

PATTISON (Mark).—MEMOIRS. Crown 8vo. 8s. 6d.

—— SERMONS. Crown 8vo. 6s.

PAUL OF TARSUS. 8vo. 10s. 6d.

PEABODY (Prof. C. H.).—THERMODYNAMICS OF THE STEAM ENGINE AND OTHER HEAT-ENGINES. 8vo. 21s.

PEDLEY (S.).—EXERCISES IN ARITHMETIC. With upwards of 7000 Examples and Answers. Crown 8vo. 5s.—Also in Two Parts. 2s. 6d. each.

PELLISSIER (Eugène).—FRENCH ROOTS AND THEIR FAMILIES. Globe 8vo. 6s.

PENNELL (Joseph).—PEN DRAWING AND PEN DRAUGHTSMEN. With 158 Illustrations. 4to. 3l. 13s. 6d. net.

PENNINGTON (Rooke).—NOTES ON THE BARROWS AND BONE CAVES OF DERBYSHIRE. 8vo. 6s.

PENROSE (Francis).—ON A METHOD OF PREDICTING, BY GRAPHICAL CONSTRUCTION, OCCULTATIONS OF STARS BY THE MOON AND SOLAR ECLIPSES FOR ANY GIVEN PLACE. 4to. 12s.

—— AN INVESTIGATION OF THE PRINCIPLES OF ATHENIAN ARCHITECTURE. Illustrated. Folio. 7l. 7s. net.

PERRY (Prof. John).—AN ELEMENTARY TREATISE ON STEAM. 18mo. 4s. 6d.

PERSIA, EASTERN. AN ACCOUNT OF THE JOURNEYS OF THE PERSIAN BOUNDARY COMMISSION, 1870—71—72. 2 vols. 8vo. 42s.

PETTIGREW (J. Bell).—THE PHYSIOLOGY OF THE CIRCULATION. 8vo. 12s.

PHAEDRUS.—See p. 31.

PHILLIMORE (John G.).—PRIVATE LAW AMONG THE ROMANS. 8vo. 16s.

PHILLIPS (J. A.).—A TREATISE ON ORE DEPOSITS. Illustrated. Medium 8vo. 25s.

PHILOCHRISTUS.—MEMOIRS OF A DISCIPLE OF THE LORD. 3rd Ed. 8vo. 12s.

PHILOLOGY. THE JOURNAL OF SACRED AND CLASSICAL PHILOLOGY. 4 vols. 8vo. 12s. 6d. each net.

—— THE JOURNAL OF PHILOLOGY. New Series. Edited by W. A. WRIGHT, M.A., I. BYWATER, M.A., and H. JACKSON, M.A. 4s. 6d. each number (half-yearly) net.

—— THE AMERICAN JOURNAL OF PHILOLOGY. Edited by Prof. BASIL L. GILDERSLEEVE. 4s. 6d. each (quarterly) net.

—— TRANSACTIONS OF THE AMERICAN PHILOLOGICAL ASSOCIATION. Vols. I.—XX. 8s. 6d. per vol. net, except Vols. XV. and XX., which are 10s. 6d. net.

PHRYNICHUS. THE NEW PHRYNICHUS. A revised text of "The Ecloga" of the Grammarian PHRYNICHUS. With Introductions and Commentary. By W. GUNION RUTHERFORD, LL.D. 8vo. 18s.

PICKERING (Prof. Edward C.).—ELEMENTS OF PHYSICAL MANIPULATION. Medium 8vo. Part I., 12s. 6d.; Part II., 14s.

PICTON (J. A.).—THE MYSTERY OF MATTER, AND OTHER ESSAYS. Crown 8vo. 6s.

PINDAR'S EXTANT ODES. Translated by ERNEST MYERS. Crown 8vo. 5s.

—— THE OLYMPIAN AND PYTHIAN ODES. Edited, with Notes, by Prof. BASIL GILDERSLEEVE. Crown 8vo. 7s. 6d.

—— THE NEMEAN ODES. Edited by J. B. BURY, M.A. 8vo. 12s.

PIRIE (Prof. G.).—LESSONS ON RIGID DYNAMICS. Crown 8vo. 6s.

PLATO.—PHÆDO. Edited by R. D. ARCHER-HIND, M.A. 8vo. 8s. 6d.

—— TIMÆUS. With Introduction, Notes, and Translation, by the same Editor. 8vo. 16s.

—— PHÆDO. Ed. by Principal W. D. GEDDES, LL.D. 2nd Edition. 8vo. 8s. 6d.

See also pp. 17, 32, 33.

PLAUTUS.—THE MOSTELLARIA. With Notes, Prolegomena, and Excursus. By the late Prof. RAMSAY. Ed. by G. G. RAMSAY, M.A. 8vo. 14s. See also p. 33.

PLINY.—CORRESPONDENCE WITH TRAJAN. Edit. by E. G. HARDY, M.A. 8vo. 10s. 6d. See also p. 33.

PLUMPTRE (Very Rev. E. H.).—MOVEMENTS IN RELIGIOUS THOUGHT. Fcp. 8vo. 3s. 6d.

PLUTARCH. Being a Selection from the Lives in North's Plutarch which illustrate Shakespeare's Plays. Edited by Rev. W. W. SKEAT, M.A. Crn. 8vo. 6s. See p. 33.

POLLOCK (Prof. Sir F., Bart.).—ESSAYS IN JURISPRUDENCE AND ETHICS. 8vo. 10s. 6d.

—— THE LAND LAWS. 2nd Edition. Crown 8vo. 3s. 6d.

—— INTRODUCTION TO THE HISTORY OF THE SCIENCE OF POLITICS. Crown 8vo. 2s. 6d.

—— OXFORD LECTURES AND OTHER DISCOURSES. 8vo. 9s.

POLLOCK (Sir Frederick).—PERSONAL REMEMBRANCES. 2 vols. Crown 8vo. 16s.

POLYBIUS.—THE HISTORIES OF POLYBIUS. Translated by E. S. SHUCKBURGH. 2 vols. Crown 8vo. 24s. See also p. 33.

POOLE (M. E.).—PICTURES OF COTTAGE LIFE IN THE WEST OF ENGLAND. 2nd Ed. Crown 8vo. 3s. 6d.

POOLE (Reginald Lane).—A HISTORY OF THE HUGUENOTS OF THE DISPERSION AT THE RECALL OF THE EDICT OF NANTES. Crown 8vo. 6s.

POOLE, THOMAS, AND HIS FRIENDS. By Mrs. SANDFORD. 2 vols. Crn. 8vo. 15s.

POSTGATE (Prof. J. P.).—SERMO LATINUS. A Short Guide to Latin Prose Composition. Part I. Introduction. Part II. Selected Passages for Translation. Gl. 8vo. 2s. 6d.—Key to "Selected Passages." Crown 8vo. 3s. 6d.

POTTER (Louisa).—LANCASHIRE MEMORIES. Crown 8vo. 6s.

POTTER (R.).—THE RELATION OF ETHICS TO RELIGION. Crown 8vo. 2s. 6d.

POTTS (A. W.).—HINTS TOWARDS LATIN PROSE COMPOSITION. Globe 8vo. 3s.

—— PASSAGES FOR TRANSLATION INTO LATIN PROSE. 4th Ed. Extra fcp. 8vo. 2s. 6d.

—— LATIN VERSIONS OF PASSAGES FOR TRANSLATION INTO LATIN PROSE. Extra fcp. 8vo. 2s. 6d. (For Teachers only.)

PRACTICAL POLITICS. Published under the auspices of the National Liberal Federation. 8vo. 6s.

PRACTITIONER (THE): A MONTHLY JOURNAL OF THERAPEUTICS AND PUBLIC HEALTH. Edited by T. LAUDER BRUNTON, M.D., F.R.C.P., F.R.S., Assistant Physician to St. Bartholomew's Hospital, etc.; DONALD MACALISTER, M.A., M.D., B.Sc., F.R.C.P., Fellow and Medical Lecturer, St. John's College, Cambridge, Physician to Addenbrooke's Hospital and University Lecturer in Medicine; and J. MITCHELL BRUCE, M.A., M.D., F.R.C.P., Physician and Lecturer on Therapeutics at Charing Cross Hospital. 1s. 6d. monthly. Vols. I.—XLIII. Half-yearly vols. 10s. 6d. [Cloth covers for binding, 1s. each.]

PRESTON (Rev. G.).—EXERCISES IN LATIN VERSE OF VARIOUS KINDS. Globe 8vo. 2s. 6d.—Key. Globe 8vo. 5s.

PRESTON (T.).—THE THEORY OF LIGHT. Illustrated. 8vo. 12s. 6d.

PRICE (L. L. F. R.).—INDUSTRIAL PEACE: ITS ADVANTAGES, METHODS, AND DIFFICULTIES. Medium 8vo. 6s.

PRICKARD (A. O.).—ARISTOTLE AND THE ART OF POETRY. Globe 8vo.

PRIMERS.—HISTORY. Edited by JOHN R. GREEN, Author of "A Short History of the English People," etc. 18mo. 1s. each:

EUROPE. By E. A. FREEMAN, M.A.

GREECE. By C. A. FYFFE, M.A.

ROME. By Bishop CREIGHTON.

GREEK ANTIQUITIES. By Prof. MAHAFFY.

ROMAN ANTIQUITIES. By Prof. WILKINS.

CLASSICAL GEOGRAPHY. By H. F. TOZER.

FRANCE. By CHARLOTTE M. YONGE.

GEOGRAPHY. By Sir GEO. GROVE, D.C.L.

INDIAN HISTORY, ASIATIC AND EUROPEAN. By J. TALBOYS WHEELER.

ANALYSIS OF ENGLISH HISTORY. By T. F. TOUT, M.A.

PRIMERS.—LITERATURE. Edited by JOHN R. GREEN, M.A., LL.D. 18mo. 1s. each:

ENGLISH GRAMMAR. By Rev. R. MORRIS.

ENGLISH GRAMMAR EXERCISES. By Rev. R. MORRIS and H. C. BOWEN.

EXERCISES ON MORRIS'S PRIMER OF ENGLISH GRAMMAR. By J. WETHERELL, M.A.

ENGLISH COMPOSITION. By Prof. NICHOL.

QUESTIONS AND EXERCISES IN ENGLISH COMPOSITION. By Prof. NICHOL and W. S. M'CORMICK.

PRIMERS (LITERATURE)—continued.

PHILOLOGY. By J. PEILE, M.A.

ENGLISH LITERATURE. By Rev. STOPFORD BROOKE, M.A.

CHILDREN'S TREASURY OF LYRICAL POETRY. Selected by Prof. F. T. PALGRAVE. In 2 parts. 1s. each.

SHAKSPERE. By Prof. DOWDEN.

GREEK LITERATURE. By Prof. JEBB.

HOMER. By Right Hon. W. E. GLADSTONE.

ROMAN LITERATURE. By A. S. WILKINS.

PRIMERS.—SCIENCE. Under the joint Editorship of Prof. HUXLEY, Sir H. E. ROSCOE, and Prof. BALFOUR STEWART. 18mo. 1s. each:

INTRODUCTORY. By Prof. HUXLEY.

CHEMISTRY. By Sir HENRY ROSCOE, F.R.S. With Illustrations, and Questions.

PHYSICS. By BALFOUR STEWART, F.R.S. With Illustrations, and Questions.

PHYSICAL GEOGRAPHY. By A. GEIKIE, F.R.S. With Illustrations, and Questions.

GEOLOGY. By ARCHIBALD GEIKIE, F.R.S.

PHYSIOLOGY. By MICHAEL FOSTER, F.R.S.

ASTRONOMY. By J. N. LOCKYER, F.R.S.

BOTANY. By Sir J. D. HOOKER, C.B.

LOGIC. By W. STANLEY JEVONS, F.R.S.

POLITICAL ECONOMY. By W. STANLEY JEVONS, LL.D., M.A., F.R.S.

Also Uniform with the above. 18mo. 1s. each.

ARNOLD (M.). — A BIBLE-READING FOR SCHOOLS: The Great Prophecy of Israel's Restoration (Isai. xl.-lxvi). Arranged and Edited for Young Beginners. 4th Edition.

BARKER (Lady).—FIRST LESSONS IN THE PRINCIPLES OF COOKING. 3rd Edition.

BERNERS (J.).—FIRST LESSONS ON HEALTH.

BETTANY (G. T.). — FIRST LESSONS IN PRACTICAL BOTANY.

BUCKLAND (Anna).—OUR NATIONAL INSTITUTIONS.

COLLIER-(Hon. John).—A PRIMER OF ART.

ELDERTON (W. A.). — MAPS AND MAP DRAWING.

FIRST LESSONS IN BUSINESS MATTERS. By A BANKER'S DAUGHTER. 2nd Edition.

GASKOIN (Mrs. Herman). — CHILDREN'S TREASURY OF BIBLE STORIES.—Part I. Old Testament; II. New Testament; III. Three Apostles. 1s. each.

GEIKIE (A.).—GEOGRAPHY OF THE BRITISH ISLES.

GRAND'HOMME.—CUTTING OUT AND DRESSMAKING. From the French of Mdlle. GRAND'HOMME.

JEX-BLAKE (Dr. Sophia).—THE CARE OF INFANTS: A Manual for Mothers and Nurses.

MACLEAR (Rev. Canon).—A SHILLING BOOK OF OLD TESTAMENT HISTORY.

— A SHILLING BOOK OF NEW TESTAMENT HISTORY.

PRIMERS—*continued*.

TANNER (Prof. Henry).—FIRST PRINCIPLES OF AGRICULTURE.

TAYLOR (Franklin).— PRIMER OF PIANO-FORTE PLAYING.

TEGETMEIER (W. B.).—HOUSEHOLD MAN-AGEMENT AND COOKERY.

THORNTON (J.). — PRIMER OF BOOK-KEEPING.

WRIGHT (Miss Guthrie). — THE SCHOOL COOKERY BOOK.

PROCTER (Rev. F.).—A HISTORY OF THE BOOK OF COMMON PRAYER. 18th Edition. Crown 8vo. 10s. 6d.

PROCTER (Rev. F.) and MACLEAR (Rev. Canon).—AN ELEMENTARY INTRODUCTION TO THE BOOK OF COMMON PRAYER. 18mo. 2s. 6d.

PROPERT (J. Lumsden).—A HISTORY OF MINIATURE ART. With Illustrations. Super royal 4to. 3l. 13s. 6d.
Also bound in vellum. 4l. 14s. 6d.

PSALMS (THE). With Introductions and Critical Notes. By A. C. JENNINGS, M.A., and W. H. LOWE, M.A. In 2 vols. 2nd Edition. Crown 8vo. 10s. 6d. each.

PUCKLE (G. H.).—AN ELEMENTARY TREA-TISE ON CONIC SECTIONS AND ALGEBRAIC GEOMETRY. 6th Edit. Crn. 8vo. 7s. 6d.

PYLODET (L.).—NEW GUIDE TO GERMAN CONVERSATION. 18mo. 2s. 6d.

RADCLIFFE (Charles B.).—BEHIND THE TIDES. 8vo. 4s. 6d.

RAMSAY (Prof. William).—EXPERIMENTAL PROOFS OF CHEMICAL THEORY. 18mo. 2s.6d.

RANSOME (Prof. Cyril).—SHORT STUDIES OF SHAKESPEARE'S PLOTS. Cr.8vo. 3s.6d.

RATHBONE (Wm.).—THE HISTORY AND PROGRESS OF DISTRICT NURSING, FROM ITS COMMENCEMENT IN THE YEAR 1859 TO THE PRESENT DATE. Crown 8vo. 2s. 6d.

RAWNSLEY (H. D.).—POEMS, BALLADS, AND BUCOLICS. Fcp. 8vo. 5s.

RAY (Prof. P. K.).—A TEXT-BOOK OF DE-DUCTIVE LOGIC. 4th Ed. Globe 8vo. 4s. 6d.

RAYLEIGH (Lord).—THEORY OF SOUND. 8vo. Vol. I. 12s. 6d.—Vol. II. 12s. 6d.—Vol. III. (*in preparation*.)

RAYS OF SUNLIGHT FOR DARK DAYS. With a Preface by C. J. VAUGHAN, D.D. New Edition. 18mo. 3s. 6d.

REALMAH. By the Author of " Friends in Council." Crown 8vo. 6s.

REASONABLE FAITH: A SHORT RELI-GIOUS ESSAY FOR THE TIMES. By "THREE FRIENDS." Crown 8vo. 1s.

RECOLLECTIONS OF A NURSE. By E. D. Crown 8vo. 2s.

REED.—MEMOIR OF SIR CHARLES REED. By his Son, CHARLES E. B. REED, M.A. With Portrait. Crown 8vo. 4s. 6d.

REICHEL (Rt. Rev. Bishop).—CATHEDRAL AND UNIVERSITY SERMONS. Crn. 8vo. 6s.

REMSEN (Prof. Ira).—AN INTRODUCTION TO THE STUDY OF ORGANIC CHEMISTRY. Crown 8vo. 6s. 6d.

—— AN INTRODUCTION TO THE STUDY OF CHEMISTRY (INORGANIC CHEMISTRY). Cr. 8vo. 6s. 6d.

—— THE ELEMENTS OF CHEMISTRY. A Text-Book for Beginners. Fcp. 8vo. 2s. 6d.

—— TEXT-BOOK OF INORGANIC CHEMISTRY. 8vo. 16s.

RENDALL (Rev. Frederic).—THE EPISTLE TO THE HEBREWS IN GREEK AND ENGLISH. With Notes. Crown 8vo. 6s.

—— THE THEOLOGY OF THE HEBREW CHRIS-TIANS. Crown 8vo. 5s.

—— THE EPISTLE TO THE HEBREWS. Eng-lish Text, with Commentary. Crown 8vo. 7s. 6d.

RENDU—WILLS.—THE THEORY OF THE GLACIERS OF SAVOY. By M. LE CHANOINE RENDU. Translated by A. WILLS, Q.C. 8vo. 7s. 6d.

REULEAUX — KENNEDY. — THE KINE-MATICS OF MACHINERY. By Prof. F. REU-LEAUX. Translated by Prof. A. B. W. KEN-NEDY, F.R.S., C.E. Medium 8vo. 21s.

REYNOLDS (J. R.).—A SYSTEM OF MEDI-CINE. Edited by J. RUSSELL REYNOLDS, M.D., F.R.C.P. London. In 5 vols. Vols. I. II. III. and V. 8vo. 25s. each.—Vol. IV. 21s.

REYNOLDS (Prof. Osborne).—SEWER GAS, AND HOW TO KEEP IT OUT OF HOUSES. 3rd Edition. Crown 8vo. 1s. 6d.

RICE (Prof. J. M.) and JOHNSON (W.W.).—AN ELEMENTARY TREATISE ON THE DIF-FERENTIAL CALCULUS. New Edition. 8vo. 18s. Abridged Edition. 9s.

RICHARDSON (A. T.).—THE " PROGRES-SIVE" EUCLID. Books I. and II. Globe 8vo. 2s. 6d.

RICHARDSON (Dr. B. W.).—ON ALCOHOL. Crown 8vo. 1s.

—— DISEASES OF MODERN LIFE. Crown 8vo. (*Reprinting.*)

—— HYGEIA: A CITY OF HEALTH. Crown 8vo. 1s.

—— THE FUTURE OF SANITARY SCIENCE. Crown 8vo. 1s.

—— THE FIELD OF DISEASE. A Book of Preventive Medicine. 8vo. 25s.

RICHEY (Alex. G.).—THE IRISH LAND LAWS. Crown 8vo. 3s. 6d.

ROBINSON (Prebendary H. G.).—MAN IN THE IMAGE OF GOD, AND OTHER SERMONS. Crown 8vo. 7s. 6d.

ROBINSON (Rev. J. L.).—MARINE SURVEY-ING: AN ELEMENTARY TREATISE ON. Pre-pared for the Use of Younger Naval Officers. With Illustrations. Crown 8vo. 7s. 6d.

ROBY (H. J.).—A GRAMMAR OF THE LATIN LANGUAGE FROM PLAUTUS TO SUETONIUS. In Two Parts.—Part I. containing Sounds, Inflexions, Word Formation, Appendices, etc. 5th Edition. Crown 8vo. 9s.—Part II. Syntax, Prepositions, etc. 6th Edition. Crown 8vo. 10s. 6d.

—— A LATIN GRAMMAR FOR SCHOOLS. Cr. 8vo. 5s.

—— EXERCISES IN LATIN SYNTAX AND IDIOM. Arranged with reference to Roby's School Latin Grammar. By E. B. ENGLAND, M.A. Crown 8vo. 2s. 6d.—Key, 2s. 6d.

ROCKSTRO (W. S.).—LIFE OF GEORGE FREDERICK HANDEL. Crown 8vo. 10s. 6d.

ROGERS (Prof. J. E. T.). — HISTORICAL GLEANINGS.—First Series. Cr. 8vo. 4s. 6d. —Second Series. Crown 8vo. 6s.

—— COBDEN AND POLITICAL OPINION. 8vo. 10s. 6d.

ROMANES (George J.).—THE SCIENTIFIC EVIDENCES OF ORGANIC EVOLUTION. Cr. 8vo. 2s. 6d.

ROSCOE (Sir Henry E., M.P., F.R.S.).— LESSONS IN ELEMENTARY CHEMISTRY. With Illustrations. Fcp. 8vo. 4s. 6d.

—— PRIMER OF CHEMISTRY. With Illustrations. 18mo. With Questions. 1s.

ROSCOE (Sir H. E.) and SCHORLEMMER (C.).—A TREATISE ON CHEMISTRY. With Illustrations. 8vo.—Vols. I. and II. INORGANIC CHEMISTRY: Vol. I. THE NON-METALLIC ELEMENTS. With a Portrait of DALTON. 21s.—Vol. II. Part I. METALS. 18s.; Part II. METALS. 18s.—Vol. III. ORGANIC CHEMISTRY: Parts I. II. and IV. 21s. each; Parts III. and V. 18s. each.

ROSCOE—SCHUSTER.—SPECTRUM ANALYSIS. By Sir HENRY E. ROSCOE, LL.D., F.R.S. 4th Edition, revised by the Author and A. SCHUSTER, Ph.D., F.R.S. Medium 8vo. 21s.

ROSENBUSCH—IDDINGS.—MICROSCOPICAL PHYSIOGRAPHY OF THE ROCK-MAKING MINERALS. By Prof. H. ROSENBUSCH. Translated by J. P. IDDINGS. Illustrated. 8vo. 24s.

ROSS (Percy).—A MISGUIDIT LASSIE. Crown 8vo. 4s. 6d.

ROSSETTI (Dante Gabriel). — A RECORD AND A STUDY. By W. SHARP. Crown 8vo. 10s. 6d.

ROSSETTI (Christina).—POEMS. New and Enlarged Edition. Globe 8vo. 7s. 6d.

—— SPEAKING LIKENESSES. Illustrated by ARTHUR HUGHES. Crown 8vo. 4s. 6d.

ROUSSEAU. By JOHN MORLEY. 2 vols. Globe 8vo. 10s.

ROUTH (E. J.). — A TREATISE ON THE DYNAMICS OF A SYSTEM OF RIGID BODIES. 8vo.—Part I. ELEMENTARY. 5th Edition. 14s.—Part II. ADVANCED. 4th Edit. 14s.

—— STABILITY OF A GIVEN STATE OF MOTION, PARTICULARLY STEADY MOTION. 8vo. 8s. 6d.

ROUTLEDGE (James).—POPULAR PROGRESS IN ENGLAND. 8vo. 16s.

RUMFORD (Count).—COMPLETE WORKS OF COUNT RUMFORD. With Memoir by GEORGE ELLIS, and Portrait. 5 vols. 8vo. 4l. 14s. 6d.

RUNAWAY (THE). By the Author of "Mrs. Jerningham's Journal." Gl. 8vo. 2s. 6d.

RUSH (Edward).—THE SYNTHETIC LATIN DELECTUS. A First Latin Construing Book. Extra fcp. 8vo. 2s. 6d.

RUSHBROOKE (W. G.).—SYNOPTICON: AN EXPOSITION OF THE COMMON MATTER OF THE SYNOPTIC GOSPELS. Printed in Colours. In Six Parts, and Appendix. 4to.—Part I. 3s. 6d.—Parts II. and III. 7s.—Parts IV. V. and VI., with Indices. 10s. 6d.—Appendices. 10s. 6d.—Complete in 1 vol. 35s.

RUSSELL (Sir Charles).—NEW VIEWS ON IRELAND. Crown 8vo. 6s.

—— THE PARNELL COMMISSION: THE OPENING SPEECH FOR THE DEFENCE. 8vo. 10s. 6d.—Cheap Edition. Sewed. 2s.

RUSSELL (Dean). -- THE LIGHT THAT LIGHTETH EVERY MAN : Sermons. With an Introduction by Dean PLUMPTRE, D.D. Crown 8vo. 6s.

RUST (Rev. George).—FIRST STEPS TO LATIN PROSE COMPOSITION. 18mo. 1s. 6d.

—— A KEY TO RUST'S FIRST STEPS TO LATIN PROSE COMPOSITION. By W. YATES. 18mo. 3s. 6d.

RUTHERFORD (W. Gunion, M.A., LL.D.). —FIRST GREEK GRAMMAR. Part I. Accidence, 2s.; Part II. Syntax, 2s.; or in 1 vol. 3s. 6d.

—— THE NEW PHRYNICHUS. Being a revised Text of the Ecloga of the Grammarian Phrynichus, with Introduction and Commentary. 8vo. 18s.

—— BABRIUS. With Introductory Dissertations, Critical Notes, Commentary, and Lexicon. 8vo. 12s. 6d.

—— THUCYDIDES. Book IV. A Revision of the Text, illustrating the Principal Causes of Corruption in the Manuscripts of this Author. 8vo. 7s. 6d.

RYLAND (F.).—CHRONOLOGICAL OUTLINES OF ENGLISH LITERATURE. Crn. 8vo. 6s.

ST. JOHNSTON (A.).—CAMPING AMONG CANNIBALS. Crown 8vo. 4s. 6d.

—— A SOUTH SEA LOVER : A Romance. Cr. 8vo. 6s.

—— CHARLIE ASGARDE : THE STORY OF A FRIENDSHIP. Crown 8vo. 5s.

SAINTSBURY (George).—A HISTORY OF ELIZABETHAN LITERATURE. Cr. 8vo. 7s. 6d.

SALLUST.—THE CONSPIRACY OF CATILINE AND THE JUGURTHINE WAR. Translated by A. W. POLLARD, B.A. Crn. 8vo. 6s. CATILINE separately. Crown 8vo. 3s.

See also p. 33.

SALMON (Rev. Prof. George). — NON-MIRACULOUS CHRISTIANITY, AND OTHER SERMONS. 2nd Edition. Crown 8vo. 6s.

—— GNOSTICISM AND AGNOSTICISM, AND OTHER SERMONS. Crown 8vo. 7s. 6d.

SANDERSON (F. W.).—HYDROSTATICS FOR BEGINNERS. Globe 8vo. 4s. 6d.

SANDHURST MATHEMATICAL PA-PERS, FOR ADMISSION INTO THE ROYAL MILITARY COLLEGE, 1881—89. Edited by E. J. BROOKSMITH, B.A. Cr. 8vo. 3s. 6d.

SANDYS (J. E.).—AN EASTER VACATION IN GREECE. Crown 8vo. 3s. 6d.

SAYCE (Prof. A. H.).—THE ANCIENT EM-PIRES OF THE EAST. Crown 8vo. 6s.

—— HERODOTOS. Books I.—III. The An-cient Empires of the East. Edited, with Notes, and Introduction. 8vo. 16s.

SCHILLER.—See p. 35.

SCHILLER'S LIFE. By Prof. HEINRICH DÜNTZER. Translated by PERCY E. PIN-KERTON. Crown 8vo. 10s. 6d.

SCHMID. — HEINRICH VON EICHENFELS. Edited by G. E. FASNACHT. 2s. 6d.

SCHMIDT—WHITE.—AN INTRODUCTION TO THE RHYTHMIC AND METRIC OF THE CLASSICAL LANGUAGES. By Dr. J. H. HEINRICH SCHMIDT. Translated by JOHN WILLIAMS WHITE, Ph.D. 8vo. 10s. 6d.

SCIENCE LECTURES AT SOUTH KEN-SINGTON. With Illustrations.—Vol. I. Containing Lectures by Capt. ABNEY, R.E., F.R.S.; Prof. STOKES; Prof. A. B. W. KENNEDY, F.R.S., C.E.; F. J. BRAMWELL, C.E., F.R.S.; Prof. F. FORBES; H. C. SORBY, F.R.S.; J. T. BOTTOMLEY, F.R.S.E.; S. H. VINES, D.Sc.; Prof. CAREY FOSTER. Crown 8vo. 6s.

Vol. II. Containing Lectures by W. SPOT-TISWOODE, F.R.S.; Prof. FORBES; H. W. CHISHOLM; Prof. T. F. PIGOT; W. FROUDE, LL.D., F.R.S.; Dr. SIEMENS; Prof. BAR-RETT; Dr. BURDON-SANDERSON; Prof. LAUDER BRUNTON, F.R.S.; Prof. McLEOD; Sir H. E. ROSCOE, F.R.S. Illust. Cr.8vo. 6s.

SCOTCH SERMONS, 1880. By Principal CAIRD and others. 3rd Edit. 8vo. 10s. 6d.

SCOTT. See ENGLISH CLASSICS, p. 12, and GLOBE READINGS, p. 17.

SCRATCHLEY — KINLOCH COOKE.—AUSTRALIAN DEFENCES AND NEW GUINEA. Compiled from the Papers of the late Major-General Sir PETER SCRATCHLEY, R.E., by C. KINLOCH COOKE. 8vo. 14s.

SCULPTURE, SPECIMENS OF AN-CIENT. Egyptian, Etruscan, Greek, and Roman. Selected from different Collections in Great Britain by the SOCIETY OF DILET-TANTI. Vol. II. 5l. 5s.

SEATON (Dr. Edward C.).—A HANDBOOK OF VACCINATION. Extra fcp. 8vo. 8s. 6d.

SEELEY (Prof. J. R.). — LECTURES AND ESSAYS. 8vo. 10s. 6d.

—— THE EXPANSION OF ENGLAND. Two Courses of Lectures. Crown 8vo. 4s. 6d.

—— OUR COLONIAL EXPANSION. Extracts from "The Expansion of England." Crown 8vo. 1s.

SEILER (Carl, M.D.)—MICRO-PHOTOGRAPHS IN HISTOLOGY, NORMAL AND PATHOLOGI-CAL. 4to. 31s. 6d.

SELBORNE (Roundell, Earl of).—A DE-FENCE OF THE CHURCH OF ENGLAND AGAINST DISESTABLISHMENT. Crown 8vo. 2s. 6d.

—— ANCIENT FACTS AND FICTIONS CONCERN-ING CHURCHES AND TITHES. Cr. 8vo. 7s. 6d.

—— THE BOOK OF PRAISE. From the Best English Hymn Writers. 18mo. 4s. 6d.

——A HYMNAL. Chiefly from "The Book of Praise." In various sizes.—A. In Royal 32mo, cloth limp. 6d.—B. Small 18mo, larger type, cloth limp. 1s.—C. Same Edition, fine paper, cloth. 1s. 6d.—An Edition with Music, Selected, Harmonised, and Composed by JOHN HULLAH. Square 18mo. 3s. 6d.

SERVICE (Rev. John).—SERMONS. With Portrait. Crown 8vo. 6s.

—— PRAYERS FOR PUBLIC WORSHIP. Crown 8vo. 4s. 6d.

SHAIRP (John Campbell).—GLEN DESSERAY, AND OTHER POEMS, LYRICAL AND ELEGIAC. Ed. by F. T. PALGRAVE. Crown 8vo. 6s.

SHAKESPEARE.—THE WORKS OF WILLIAM SHAKESPEARE. Cambridge Edition. New and Revised Edition, by W. ALDIS WRIGHT, M.A. 9 vols. 8vo. 10s. 6d. each.—Vol. I. Jan. 1891.

—— SHAKESPEARE. Edited by W. G. CLARK and W. A. WRIGHT. Globe Edition. Globe 8vo. 3s. 6d.

—— THE WORKS OF WILLIAM SHAKESPEARE. Victoria Edition.—Vol. I. Comedies.—Vol. II. Histories.—Vol. III. Tragedies. In Three Vols. Crown 8vo. 6s. each.

—— CHARLES LAMB'S TALES FROM SHAK-SPEARE. Edited, with Preface, by the Rev. A. AINGER, M.A. 18mo. 4s. 6d. *Globe Readings Edition.* For Schools. Globe 8vo. 2s.—*Library Edition.* Globe 8vo. 5s.

See also ENGLISH CLASSICS, p. 12.

SHANN (G.).—AN ELEMENTARY TREATISE ON HEAT IN RELATION TO STEAM AND THE STEAM-ENGINE. Illustrated. Crown 8vo. 4s. 6d.

SHELBURNE. LIFE OF WILLIAM, EARL OF SHELBURNE. By Lord EDMOND FITZ-MAURICE. In 3 vols.—Vol. I. 8vo. 12s.— Vol. II. 8vo. 12s.—Vol. III. 8vo. 16s.

SHELLEY. COMPLETE POETICAL WORKS. Edited by Prof. DOWDEN. With Portrait. Crown 8vo. 7s. 6d.

SHIRLEY (W. N.).—ELIJAH: FOUR UNI-VERSITY SERMONS. Fcp. 8vo. 2s. 6d.

SHORTHOUSE (J. H.).—JOHN INGLESANT: A ROMANCE. Crown 8vo. 6s.

—— THE LITTLE SCHOOLMASTER MARK: A SPIRITUAL ROMANCE. Two Parts. Crown 8vo. 2s. 6d. each : complete, 4s. 6d.

—— SIR PERCIVAL: A STORY OF THE PAST AND OF THE PRESENT. Crown 8vo. 6s.

—— A TEACHER OF THE VIOLIN, AND OTHER TALES. Crown 8vo. 6s.

—— THE COUNTESS EVE. Crown 8vo. 6s.

SHORTLAND (Admiral).—NAUTICAL SURVEYING. 8vo. 21s.

SHUCKBURGH (E. S.).—PASSAGES FROM LATIN AUTHORS FOR TRANSLATION INTO ENGLISH. Crown 8vo. 2s.

SHUCHHARDT(Carl).—DR. SCHLIEMANN'S EXCAVATIONS AT TROY, TIRYNS, MYCENAE, ORCHOMENOS, ITHACA PRESENTED IN THE LIGHT OF RECENT KNOWLEDGE. Translated by EUGENIE SELLERS. With Introduction by WALTER LEAF, Litt.D. Illustrated. 8vo. [In the Press.

SHUFELDT (R. W.).—THE MYOLOGY OF THE RAVEN (Corvus corax Sinuatus). A Guide to the Study of the Muscular System in Birds. Illustrated. 8vo. 13s. net.

SIBSON. — DR. FRANCIS SIBSON'S COLLECTED WORKS. Edited by W. M. ORD, M.D. Illustrated. 4 vols. 8vo. 3l. 3s.

SIDGWICK (Prof. Henry).—THE METHODS OF ETHICS. 4th Edit., revised. 8vo. 14s.

—— A SUPPLEMENT TO THE SECOND EDITION. Containing all the important Additions and Alterations in the 4th Edit. 8vo. 6s.

—— THE PRINCIPLES OF POLITICAL ECONOMY. 2nd Edition. 8vo. 16s.

—— OUTLINES OF THE HISTORY OF ETHICS FOR ENGLISH READERS. Cr. 8vo. 3s. 6d.

—— ELEMENTS OF POLITICS. 8vo.

SIMPSON (F. P.).—LATIN PROSE AFTER THE BEST AUTHORS.—Part I. CÆSARIAN PROSE. Extra fcp. 8vo. 2s. 6d. KEY (for Teachers only). Ex. fcp. 8vo. 5s.

SIMPSON (W.).—AN EPITOME OF THE HISTORY OF THE CHRISTIAN CHURCH. Fcp. 8vo. 3s. 6d.

SKRINE (J. H.).—UNDER TWO QUEENS. Crown 8vo. 3s.

—— A MEMORY OF EDWARD THRING. Crown 8vo. 6s.

SMALLEY (George W.).—LONDON LETTERS AND SOME OTHERS. 2 vols. 8vo. 32s.

SMITH (Barnard).—ARITHMETIC AND ALGEBRA. New Edition. Crown 8vo. 10s. 6d.

—— ARITHMETIC FOR THE USE OF SCHOOLS. New Edition. Crown 8vo. 4s. 6d.

—— KEY TO ARITHMETIC FOR SCHOOLS. New Edition. Crown 8vo. 8s. 6d.

—— EXERCISES IN ARITHMETIC. Crown 8vo, 2 Parts, 1s. each, or complete, 2s.—With Answers, 2s. 6d.—Answers separately, 6d.

—— SCHOOL CLASS-BOOK OF ARITHMETIC. 18mo. 3s.—Or, sold separately, in Three Parts. 1s. each.

—— KEY TO SCHOOL CLASS-BOOK OF ARITHMETIC. In Parts, I. II. and III. 2s. 6d. each.

—— SHILLING BOOK OF ARITHMETIC FOR NATIONAL AND ELEMENTARY SCHOOLS. 18mo, cloth.—Or separately, Part I. 2d. ; II. 3d. ; III. 7d.—With Answers, 1s. 6d.

—— ANSWERS TO THE SHILLING BOOK OF ARITHMETIC. 18mo. 6d.

—— KEY TO THE SHILLING BOOK OF ARITHMETIC. 18mo. 4s. 6d.

SMITH (Barnard).—EXAMINATION PAPERS IN ARITHMETIC. In Four Parts. 18mo. 1s. 6d.—With Answers, 2s.—Answers, 6d.

—— KEY TO EXAMINATION PAPERS IN ARITHMETIC. 18mo. 4s. 6d.

—— THE METRIC SYSTEM OF ARITHMETIC. 3d.

—— A CHART OF THE METRIC SYSTEM OF ARITHMETIC. On a Sheet, size 42 by 34 in., on Roller mounted and varnished. 3s. 6d.

—— EASY LESSONS IN ARITHMETIC. Combining Exercises in Reading, Writing, Spelling, and Dictation. Part I. for Standard I. in National Schools. Crown 8vo. 9d.

—— EXAMINATION CARDS IN ARITHMETIC. With Answers and Hints. Standards I. and II. In box. 1s.—Standards III. IV. and V. In boxes. 1s. each.—Standard VI. in Two Parts. In boxes. 1s. each.

SMITH (Catherine Barnard).—POEMS. Fcp. 8vo. 5s.

SMITH (Charles).—AN ELEMENTARY TREATISE ON CONIC SECTIONS. 7th Edition. Crown 8vo. 7s. 6d.

—— SOLUTIONS OF THE EXAMPLES IN "AN ELEMENTARY TREATISE ON CONIC SECTIONS." Crown 8vo. 10s. 6d.

—— AN ELEMENTARY TREATISE ON SOLID GEOMETRY. 2nd Edition. Cr. 8vo. 9s. 6d.

—— ELEMENTARY ALGEBRA. 2nd Edition. Globe 8vo. 4s. 6d.

—— A TREATISE ON ALGEBRA. 2nd Edition. Crown 8vo. 7s. 6d.

—— SOLUTIONS OF THE EXAMPLES IN "A TREATISE ON ALGEBRA." Cr. 8vo. 10s. 6d.

SMITH (Goldwin).—THREE ENGLISH STATESMEN. New Edition. Crown 8vo. 5s.

—— CANADA AND THE CANADIAN QUESTION. 8vo. 8s net.

—— PROHIBITIONISM IN CANADA AND THE UNITED STATES. 8vo, sewed. 6d.

SMITH (Horace).—POEMS. Globe 8vo. 5s.

SMITH (J.).—ECONOMIC PLANTS, DICTIONARY OF POPULAR NAMES OF: THEIR HISTORY, PRODUCTS, AND USES. 8vo. 14s.

SMITH (Rev. Travers).—MAN'S KNOWLEDGE OF MAN AND OF GOD. Crown 8vo. 6s.

SMITH (W. G.).—DISEASES OF FIELD AND GARDEN CROPS, CHIEFLY SUCH AS ARE CAUSED BY FUNGI. With 143 new Illustrations. Fcp. 8vo. 4s. 6d.

SMITH (W. Saumarez).—THE BLOOD OF THE NEW COVENANT: A THEOLOGICAL ESSAY. Crown 8vo. 2s. 6d.

SNOWBALL (J. C.).—THE ELEMENTS OF PLANE AND SPHERICAL TRIGONOMETRY. 14th Edition. Crown 8vo. 7s. 6d.

SONNENSCHEIN (A.) and MEIKLEJOHN (J. M. D.).—THE ENGLISH METHOD OF TEACHING TO READ. Fcp. 8vo. Comprising—

THE NURSERY BOOK, containing all the Two Letter Words in the Language. 1d.—Also in Large Type on Four Sheets, with Roller. 5s.

THE FIRST COURSE, consisting of Short Vowels with Single Consonants. 7d.

SONNENSCHEIN (A.) and MEIKLE-JOHN (J. M. D.).—The English Method of Teaching to Read : Second Course, with Combinations and Bridges consisting of Short Vowels with Double Consonants. 7*d.*

The Third and Fourth Courses, consisting of Long Vowels and all the Double Vowels in the Language. 7*d.*

SOPHOCLES.—Œdipus the King. Translated from the Greek into English Verse by E. D. A. Morshead, M.A. Fcp. 8vo. 3*s.*6*d.*

—— Œdipus Tyrannus. A Record by L. Speed and F. R. Pryor of the performance at Cambridge. Illustr. Folio. 12*s.* 6*d.* net.

SPENDER (J. Kent).—Therapeutic Means for the Relief of Pain. 8vo. 8*s.* 6*d.*

SPINOZA : A Study of. By James Martineau, LL.D. 2nd Ed. Cr. 8vo. 6*s.*

STANLEY (Very Rev. A. P.).—The Athanasian Creed. Crown 8vo. 2*s.*

—— The National Thanksgiving. Sermons preached in Westminster Abbey. 2nd Ed. Crown 8vo. 2*s.* 6*d.*

—— Addresses and Sermons delivered at St. Andrews in 1872-75 and 1877. Crown 8vo. 5*s.*

—— Addresses and Sermons delivered during a Visit to the United States and Canada in 1878. Crown 8vo. 6*s.*

STANLEY (Hon. Maude).—Clubs for Working Girls. Crown 8vo. 6*s.*

STATESMAN'S YEAR-BOOK (THE). A Statistical and Historical Annual of the States of the Civilised World for the year 1891. Twenty-seventh Annual Publication. Revised after Official Returns. Edited by J. Scott Keltie. Crown 8vo. 10*s.* 6*d.*

STEPHEN (Caroline E.).—The Service of the Poor. Crown 8vo. 6*s.* 6*d.*

STEPHEN (Sir J. Fitzjames, K.C.S.I.).—A Digest of the Law of Evidence. 5th Edition. Crown 8vo. 6*s.*

—— A Digest of the Criminal Law : Crimes and Punishments. 4th Edition. 8vo. 16*s.*

—— A Digest of the Law of Criminal Procedure in Indictable Offences. By Sir James F. Stephen, K.C.S.I., etc., and Herbert Stephen, LL.M. 8vo. 12*s.* 6*d.*

—— A History of the Criminal Law of England. 3 vols. 8vo. 48*s.*

—— The Story of Nuncomar and the Impeachment of Sir Elijah Impey. 2 vols. Crown 8vo. 15*s.*

—— A General View of the Criminal Law of England. 2nd Edition. 8vo. 14*s.*

STEPHEN (J. K.).—International Law and International Relations. Crown 8vo. 6*s.*

STEPHENS (J. B.).—Convict Once, and other Poems. Crown 8vo. 7*s.* 6*d.*

STEVENSON (J. J.).—House Architecture. With Illustrations. 2 vols. Royal 8vo. 18*s.* each. Vol. I. Architecture. Vol. II. House Planning.

STEWART (Aubrey).—The Tale of Troy. Done into English. Globe 8vo. 3*s.* 6*d.*

STEWART (Prof. Balfour).—Lessons in Elementary Physics. With Illustrations and Coloured Diagram. Fcp. 8vo. 4*s.* 6*d.*

—— Primer of Physics. Illustrated. New Edition, with Questions. 18mo. 1*s.*

—— Questions on Stewart's Lessons on Elementary Physics. By T. H. Core. 12mo. 2*s.*

STEWART (Prof. Balfour) and GEE (W. W. Haldane).—Lessons in Elementary Practical Physics. Crown 8vo. Illustrated. Vol. I. General Physical Processes. 6*s.* —Vol. II. Electricity and Magnetism. Cr. 8vo. 7*s.* 6*d.*—Vol. III. Optics, Heat, and Sound.

—— Practical Physics for Schools and the Junior Students of Colleges. Globe 8vo. Vol. I. Electricity and Magnetism. 2*s.* 6*d.*—Vol. II. Heat, Light, and Sound.

STEWART (Prof. Balfour) and TAIT (P. G.).—The Unseen Universe ; or, Physical Speculations on a Future State. 15th Edition. Crown 8vo. 6*s.*

STEWART (S. A.) and CORRY (T. H.).—A Flora of the North-East of Ireland. Crown 8vo. 5*s.* 6*d.*

STOKES (Sir George G.).—On Light. The Burnett Lectures. Crown 8vo. 7*s.* 6*d.*

STONE (W. H.).—Elementary Lessons on Sound. Illustrated. Fcap. 8vo. 3*s.* 6*d.*

STRACHAN (J. S.) and WILKINS (A. S.).—Analecta. Passages for Translation. Cr. 8vo. 5*s.*—Key to Latin Passages. Crn. 8vo. 6*d.*

STRACHEY (Lieut.-Gen. R.).—Lectures on Geography. Crown 8vo. 4*s.* 6*d.*

STRANGFORD (Viscountess). — Egyptian Sepulchres and Syrian Shrines. New Edition. Crown 8vo. 7*s.* 6*d.*

STRETTELL (Alma).—Spanish and Italian Folk Songs. Illustrated. Royal 16mo. 12*s.* 6*d.*

STUART, THE ROYAL HOUSE OF Illustrated by Forty Plates in Colours drawn from Relics of the Stuarts by William Gibb. With Introduction by J. Skelton, C.B., LL.D., and Descriptive Notes by W. St. J. Hope. Folio, half morocco, gilt edges. 7*l.* 7*s.* net.

STUBBS (Rev. C. W.).—For Christ and City. Sermons and Addresses. Cr. 8vo. 6*s.*

SURGERY, THE INTERNATIONAL ENCYCLOPAEDIA OF. A Systematic Treatise on the Theory and Practice of Surgery by Authors of Various Nations. Edited by John Ashhurst, Jun., M.D., Professor of Clinical Surgery in the University of Pennsylvania. 6 vols. Royal 8vo. 31*s.* 6*d.* each.

SYMONS (Arthur).—Days and Nights : Poems. Globe 8vo. 6*s.*

TACITUS, The Works of. Transl. by A. J. Church, M.A., and W. J. Brodribb, M.A. The History of Tacitus. Translated. 4th Edition. Crown 8vo. 6*s.*

The Agricola and Germania. With the Dialogue on Oratory. Trans. Cr. 8vo. 4*s* 6*d.*

TACITUS. ANNALS OF TACITUS. Translated. 5th Edition. Crown 8vo. 7s. 6d.

—— THE ANNALS. Edited by Prof. G. O. HOLBROOKE, M.A. 8vo. 16s.

—— THE HISTORIES. Edited, with Introduction and Commentary, by Rev. W. A. SPOONER, M.A. 8vo. 16s.
See also p. 33.

TAIT (Archbishop).—THE PRESENT POSITION OF THE CHURCH OF ENGLAND. Being the Charge delivered at his Primary Visitation. 3rd Edition. 8vo. 3s. 6d.

—— DUTIES OF THE CHURCH OF ENGLAND. Being Seven Addresses delivered at his Second Visitation. 8vo. 4s. 6d.

—— THE CHURCH OF THE FUTURE. Charges delivered at his Third Quadrennial Visitation. 2nd Edition. Crown 8vo. 3s. 6d.

TAIT.—THE LIFE OF ARCHIBALD CAMPBELL TAIT, ARCHBISHOP OF CANTERBURY. By the Rt. Rev. the BISHOP OF ROCHESTER and Rev. W. BENHAM, B.D. 2 vols 8vo.

TAIT.—CATHARINE AND CRAWFURD TAIT, WIFE AND SON OF ARCHIBALD CAMPBELL, ARCHBISHOP OF CANTERBURY: A MEMOIR. Edited by the Rev. W. BENHAM, B.D. Crown 8vo. 6s.
Popular Edition, abridged. Cr. 8vo. 2s. 6d.

TAIT (C. W. A.).—ANALYSIS OF ENGLISH HISTORY, BASED ON GREEN'S "SHORT HISTORY OF THE ENGLISH PEOPLE." Revised and Enlarged Edition. Crown 8vo. 4s. 6d.

TAIT (Prof. P. G.).—LECTURES ON SOME RECENT ADVANCES IN PHYSICAL SCIENCE. 3rd Edition. Crown 8vo. 9s.

—— HEAT. With Illustrations. Cr. 8vo. 6s.

TAIT (P. G.) and STEELE (W. J.).—A TREATISE ON DYNAMICS OF A PARTICLE. 6th Edition. Crown 8vo. 12s.

TANNER (Prof. Henry).—FIRST PRINCIPLES OF AGRICULTURE. 18mo. 1s.

—— THE ABBOTT'S FARM; OR, PRACTICE WITH SCIENCE. Crown 8vo. 3s. 6d.

—— THE ALPHABET OF THE PRINCIPLES OF AGRICULTURE. Extra fcp. 8vo. 6d.

—— FURTHER STEPS IN THE PRINCIPLES OF AGRICULTURE. Extra fcp. 8vo. 1s.

—— ELEMENTARY SCHOOL READINGS IN THE PRINCIPLES OF AGRICULTURE FOR THE THIRD STAGE. Extra fcp. 8vo. 1s.

—— ELEMENTARY LESSONS IN THE SCIENCE OF AGRICULTURAL PRACTICE. Fcp. 8vo. 3s. 6d.

TAVERNIER (Baron): TRAVELS IN INDIA OF JEAN BAPTISTE TAVERNIER, BARON OF AUBONNE. Translated by V. BALL, LL.D. Illustrated. 2 vols. 8vo. 2l. 2s.

TAYLOR (Franklin).— PRIMER OF PIANOFORTE PLAYING. 18mo. 1s.

TAYLOR (Isaac).—THE RESTORATION OF BELIEF. Crown 8vo. 8s. 6d.

TAYLOR (Isaac). — WORDS AND PLACES. 9th Edition. Maps. Globe 8vo. 6s.

—— ETRUSCAN RESEARCHES. With Woodcuts. 8vo. 14s.

—— GREEKS AND GOTHS: A STUDY OF THE RUNES. 8vo. 9s.

TAYLOR (Sedley).—SOUND AND MUSIC. 2nd Edition. Extra Crown 8vo. 8s. 6d.

—— A SYSTEM OF SIGHT-SINGING FROM THE ESTABLISHED MUSICAL NOTATION. 8vo. 5s. net.

TEBAY (S.).—ELEMENTARY MENSURATION FOR SCHOOLS. Extra fcp. 8vo. 3s. 6d.

TEGETMEIER (W. B.).—HOUSEHOLD MANAGEMENT AND COOKERY. 18mo. 1s.

TEMPLE (Right Rev. Frederick, D.D., Bishop of London).—SERMONS PREACHED IN THE CHAPEL OF RUGBY SCHOOL. 3rd and Cheaper Edition. Extra fcp. 8vo. 4s. 6d.

—— SECOND SERIES. 3rd Ed. Ex. fcp. 8vo. 6s.

—— THIRD SERIES. 4th Ed. Ex. fcp. 8vo. 6s.

—— THE RELATIONS BETWEEN RELIGION AND SCIENCE. Bampton Lectures, 1884. 7th and Cheaper Edition. Crown 8vo. 6s.

TENNYSON (Lord). — COMPLETE WORKS. New and enlarged Edition, with Portrait. Crown 8vo. 7s. 6d.
School Edition. In Four Parts. Crown 8vo. 2s. 6d. each.

—— POETICAL WORKS. *Pocket Edition.* 18mo, morocco, gilt edges. 7s. 6d. net.

—— WORKS. *Library Edition.* In 8 vols. Globe 8vo. 5s. each. Each volume may be had separately.—POEMS. 2 vols.—IDYLLS OF THE KING.—THE PRINCESS, AND MAUD. —ENOCH ARDEN, AND IN MEMORIAM.— BALLADS, AND OTHER POEMS. — QUEEN MARY, AND HAROLD.—BECKET, AND OTHER PLAYS.

—— WORKS. *Extra Fcp. 8vo. Edition*, on Hand-made Paper. In 7 volumes (supplied in sets only). 3l. 13s. 6d.

—— WORKS. *Miniature Edition*, in 14 vols., viz. THE POETICAL WORKS, 10 vols. in a box. 21s.—THE DRAMATIC WORKS, 4 vols. in a box. 10s. 6d.

—— *The Original Editions.* Fcp. 8vo.
POEMS. 6s.
MAUD, AND OTHER POEMS. 3s. 6d.
THE PRINCESS. 3s. 6d.
ENOCH ARDEN, etc. 3s. 6d.
THE HOLY GRAIL, AND OTHER POEMS. 4s. 6d.
BALLADS, AND OTHER POEMS. 5s.
HAROLD: A DRAMA. 6s.
QUEEN MARY: A DRAMA. 6s.
THE CUP, AND THE FALCON. 5s.
BECKET. 6s.
TIRESIAS, AND OTHER POEMS. 6s.
LOCKSLEY HALL SIXTY YEARS AFTER, etc. 6s.
DEMETER, AND OTHER POEMS. 6s.

—— LYRICAL POEMS. Selected and Annotated by Prof. F. T. PALGRAVE. 18mo. 4s. 6d.
Large Paper Edition. 8vo. 9s.

—— IN MEMORIAM. 18mo. 4s. 6d.
Large Paper Edition. 8vo. 9s.

—— THE TENNYSON BIRTHDAY BOOK. Edit. by EMILY SHAKESPEAR. 18mo. 2s. 6d.

TENNYSON (Lord).—*The Original Editions —continued.*

THE HOLY GRAIL, AND OTHER POEMS. 4s. 6d.
BALLADS, AND OTHER POEMS. 5s.
HAROLD : A DRAMA. 6s.
QUEEN MARY : A DRAMA. 6s.
THE CUP, AND THE FALCON. 5s.
BECKET. 6s.
TIRESIAS, AND OTHER POEMS. 6s.
LOCKSLEY HALL SIXTY YEARS AFTER, etc. 6s.
DEMETER, AND OTHER POEMS. 6s.

—— *The Royal Edition.* 1 vol. 8vo. 16s.

—— SELECTIONS FROM TENNYSON'S WORKS. Square 8vo. 3s. 6d.

—— SONGS FROM TENNYSON'S WRITINGS. Square 8vo. 2s. 6d.

TENNYSON FOR THE YOUNG. Selections from Lord TENNYSON'S Poems. Edited with Notes, by the Rev. ALFRED AINGER, M.A. 18mo. 1s. net.

TENNYSON (Frederick).—THE ISLES OF GREECE : SAPPHO AND ALCAEUS. Crown 8vo. 7s. 6d.

TENNYSON (Hallam). — JACK AND THE BEAN-STALK. With 40 Illustrations by RANDOLPH CALDECOTT. Fcp. 4to. 3s. 6d.

TERENCE.—*See* pp. 32, 33.

TERESA (ST.) : LIFE OF. By the Author of "Devotions before and after Holy Communion." Crown 8vo. 8s. 6d.

THEOCRITUS, BION, AND MOSCHUS. Rendered into English Prose, with Introductory Essay, by A. LANG, M.A. 18mo. 4s. 6d. Large Paper Edition. 8vo. 9s.

THOMPSON (Edith).—HISTORY OF ENGLAND. New Edit., with Maps. 18mo, 2s. 6d.

THOMPSON (Prof. Silvanus P.).—ELEMENTARY ELECTRICITY AND MAGNETISM. Illustrated. New Edition. Fcp. 8vo. 4s. 6d.

THOMSON (Hugh).—DAYS WITH SIR ROGER DE COVERLEY. Illustrated. Fcp. 4to. 6s.

THOMSON (J. J.).—A TREATISE ON THE MOTION OF VORTEX RINGS. 8vo. 6s.

—— APPLICATIONS OF DYNAMICS TO PHYSICS AND CHEMISTRY. Crown 8vo. 7s. 6d.

THOMSON (Sir Wm.).—REPRINT OF PAPERS ON ELECTROSTATICS AND MAGNETISM. 2nd Edition. 8vo. 18s.

—— POPULAR LECTURES AND ADDRESSES. In 3 vols.—Vol. I. CONSTITUTION OF MATTER. Illustrated. Crown 8vo. 6s.—Vol. III. PAPERS ON NAVIGATION.

THOMSON (Sir C. Wyville).—THE DEPTHS OF THE SEA. An Account of the General Results of the Dredging Cruises of H.M.SS. "Lightning" and "Porcupine" during the Summers of 1868-69-70. With Illustrations, Maps, and Plans. 2nd Edit. 8vo. 31s. 6d.

—— THE VOYAGE OF THE "CHALLENGER" : THE ATLANTIC. With Illustrations, Coloured Maps, Charts, etc. 2 vols. 8vo. 45s.

THORNTON (J.).—FIRST LESSONS IN BOOK-KEEPING. New Edition. Crown 8vo. 2s. 6d.

—— KEY. Containing all the Exercises fully worked out, with brief Notes. Oblong 4to. 10s. 6d.

—— PRIMER OF BOOK-KEEPING. 18mo. 1s.

—— KEY. Demy 8vo. 2s. 6d.

THORPE (Prof. T. E.) and TATE (W.).—A SERIES OF PROBLEMS, FOR USE IN COLLEGES AND SCHOOLS. New Edition, with Key. 18mo. 2s.

THRING (Rev. Edward).—A CONSTRUING BOOK. Fcp. 8vo. 2s. 6d.

—— A LATIN GRADUAL. 2nd Ed. 18mo. 2s. 6d.

—— THE ELEMENTS OF GRAMMAR TAUGHT IN ENGLISH. 5th Edition. 18mo. 2s.

—— EDUCATION AND SCHOOL. 2nd Edition. Crown 8vo. 6s.

—— A MANUAL OF MOOD CONSTRUCTIONS. Extra fcp. 8vo. 1s. 6d.

—— THOUGHTS ON LIFE SCIENCE. 2nd Edit. Crown 8vo. 7s. 6d.

—— A MEMORY OF EDWARD THRING. By J. H. SKRINE. Portrait. Crown 8vo. 6s.

THROUGH THE RANKS TO A COMMISSION. New Edit. Cr. 8vo. 2s. 6d.

THRUPP (Rev. J. F.).—INTRODUCTION TO THE STUDY AND USE OF THE PSALMS. 2nd Edition. 2 vols. 8vo. 21s.

THUCYDIDES.—BOOK IV. A Revision of the Text, illustrating the Principal Causes of Corruption in the Manuscripts of this Author. By WILLIAM G. RUTHERFORD, M.A., LL.D. 8vo. 7s. 6d.

—— Book VIII. Edited, with Introduction and Commentary, by H. C. GOODHART, M.A. 8vo.

See also pp. 32, 33.

THUDICHUM (J. L. W.) and DUPRÉ (A.).—TREATISE ON THE ORIGIN, NATURE, AND VARIETIES OF WINE. Medium 8vo. 25s.

TODHUNTER (Isaac).—EUCLID FOR COLLEGES AND SCHOOLS. 18mo. 3s. 6d.

—— BOOKS I. AND II. [*In the Press.*

—— KEY TO EXERCISES IN EUCLID. Crown 8vo. 6s. 6d.

—— MENSURATION FOR BEGINNERS. With Examples. 18mo. 2s. 6d.

—— KEY TO MENSURATION FOR BEGINNERS. By Rev. FR. L. MCCARTHY. Cr. 8vo. 7s. 6d.

—— ALGEBRA FOR BEGINNERS. With numerous Examples. 18mo. 2s. 6d.

—— KEY TO ALGEBRA FOR BEGINNERS. Cr. 8vo. 6s. 6d.

—— ALGEBRA FOR THE USE OF COLLEGES AND SCHOOLS. Crown 8vo. 7s. 6d.

—— KEY TO ALGEBRA FOR COLLEGES AND SCHOOLS. Crown 8vo. 10s. 6d.

—— TRIGONOMETRY FOR BEGINNERS. With numerous Examples. 18mo. 2s. 6d.

—— KEY TO TRIGONOMETRY FOR BEGINNERS. Crown 8vo. 8s. 6d.

—— PLANE TRIGONOMETRY FOR COLLEGES AND SCHOOLS. Crown 8vo. 5s.

4

TODHUNTER (Isaac).— KEY TO PLANE TRIGONOMETRY. Crown 8vo. 10s. 6d.

—— A TREATISE ON SPHERICAL TRIGONOMETRY FOR THE USE OF COLLEGES AND SCHOOLS. Crown 8vo. 4s. 6d.

—— MECHANICS FOR BEGINNERS. With numerous Examples. 18mo. 4s. 6d.

—— KEY TO MECHANICS FOR BEGINNERS. 6s. 6d.

—— A TREATISE ON THE THEORY OF EQUATIONS. Crown 8vo. 7s. 6d.

—— A TREATISE ON PLANE CO-ORDINATE GEOMETRY. Crown 8vo. 7s. 6d.

—— SOLUTIONS AND PROBLEMS CONTAINED IN A TREATISE ON PLANE CO-ORDINATE GEOMETRY. By C. W. BOURNE, M.A. Crown 8vo. 10s. 6d.

—— A TREATISE ON THE DIFFERENTIAL CALCULUS. Crown 8vo 10s. 6d.

—— KEY TO TREATISE ON THE DIFFERENTIAL CALCULUS. By H. ST. J. HUNTER, M.A. Crown 8vo. 10s. 6d.

—— A TREATISE ON THE INTEGRAL CALCULUS. Crown 8vo. 10s. 6d.

—— KEY TO TREATISE ON THE INTEGRAL CALCULUS AND ITS APPLICATIONS. By H. ST. J. HUNTER, M.A. Cr. 8vo. 10s. 6d.

—— EXAMPLES OF ANALYTICAL GEOMETRY OF THREE DIMENSIONS. Crown 8vo. 4s.

—— THE CONFLICT OF STUDIES. 8vo. 10s. 6d.

—— AN ELEMENTARY TREATISE ON LAPLACE'S, LAMÉ'S, AND BESSEL'S FUNCTIONS. Crown 8vo. 10s. 6d.

—— A TREATISE ON ANALYTICAL STATICS. Edited by J. D. EVERETT, M.A., F.R.S. 5th Edition. Crown 8vo. 10s. 6d.

TOM-BROWN'S SCHOOL DAYS. By AN OLD BOY.

Golden Treasury Edition. 18mo. 4s. 6d.

Illustrated Edition. Crown 8vo. 6s.

Uniform Edition. Crown 8vo. 3s. 6d.

People's Edition. 18mo. 2s.

People's Sixpenny Edition. With Illustrations. Medium 4to. 6d.—Also uniform with the Sixpenny Edition of Charles Kingsley's Novels. Medium 8vo. 6d.

TOM BROWN AT OXFORD. By the Author of "Tom Brown's School Days." Illustrated. Crown 8vo. 6s.

Uniform Edition. Crown 8vo. 3s. 6d.

TRENCH (R. Chenevix).— HULSEAN LECTURES. 8vo. 7s. 6d.

TRENCH (Capt. F.).—THE RUSSO-INDIAN QUESTION. Crown 8vo. 7s. 6d.

TREVELYAN (Sir Geo. Otto).—CAWNPORE. Crown 8vo. 6s.

TRISTRAM (W. Outram).—COACHING DAYS AND COACHING WAYS. Illustrated by HERBERT RAILTON and HUGH THOMSON. Extra Crown 4to. 21s.

TRUMAN (Jos.).—AFTER-THOUGHTS: POEMS. Crown 8vo. 3s. 6d.

TULLOCH (Principal).—THE CHRIST OF THE GOSPELS AND THE CHRIST OF MODERN CRITICISM. Extra fcp. 8vo. 4s. 6d.

TURNER'S LIBER STUDIORUM. A Description and a Catalogue. By W. G. RAWLINSON. Medium 8vo. 12s. 6d.

TURNER (Charles Tennyson).—COLLECTED SONNETS, OLD AND NEW. Ex. fcp. 8vo. 7s. 6d.

TURNER (Rev. Geo.).—SAMOA, A HUNDRED YEARS AGO AND LONG BEFORE. Preface by E. B. TYLOR, F.R.S. Crown 8vo. 9s.

TURNER (H. H.).—A COLLECTION OF EXAMPLES ON HEAT AND ELECTRICITY. Cr. 8vo. 2s. 6d.

TYLOR (E. B.).—ANTHROPOLOGY. With Illustrations. Crown 8vo. 7s. 6d.

TYRWHITT (Rev. R. St. John).— OUR SKETCHING CLUB. 4th Ed. Cr. 8vo. 7s. 6d.

—— FREE FIELD. Lyrics, chiefly Descriptive. Globe 8vo. 3s. 6d.

—— BATTLE AND AFTER: Concerning Sergt. Thomas Atkins, Grenadier Guards; and other Verses. Globe 8vo. 3s. 6d.

UNDERHILL (H. G.).—EASY EXERCISES IN GREEK ACCIDENCE. Globe 8vo. 2s.

UPPINGHAM BY THE SEA. By J. H. S. Crown 8vo. 3s. 6d.

VAUGHAN (Very Rev. Charles J.).—NOTES FOR LECTURES ON CONFIRMATION. 14th Edition. Fcp. 8vo. 1s. 6d.

—— MEMORIALS OF HARROW SUNDAYS. 5th Edition. Crown 8vo. 10s. 6d.

—— LECTURES ON THE EPISTLE TO THE PHILIPPIANS. 4th Edition. Cr. 8vo. 7s. 6d.

—— LECTURES ON THE REVELATION OF ST. JOHN. 5th Edition. Crown 8vo. 10s. 6d.

—— EPIPHANY, LENT, AND EASTER. 3rd Edition. Crown 8vo. 10s. 6d.

—— HEROES OF FAITH. 2nd Ed. Cr. 8vo. 6s.

—— THE BOOK AND THE LIFE, AND OTHER SERMONS. 3rd Edition. Fcp. 8vo. 4s. 6d.

—— ST. PAUL'S EPISTLE TO THE ROMANS. The Greek Text with English Notes. 7th Edition. Crown 8vo. 7s. 6d.

—— TWELVE DISCOURSES ON SUBJECTS CONNECTED WITH THE LITURGY AND WORSHIP OF THE CHURCH OF ENGLAND. 4th Edition Fcp. 8vo. 6s.

—— WORDS FROM THE GOSPELS. 3rd Edition. Fcp. 8vo. 4s. 6d.

—— THE EPISTLES OF ST. PAUL. For English Readers. Part I. containing the First Epistle to the Thessalonians. 2nd Ed. 8vo. 1s. 6d.

—— THE CHURCH OF THE FIRST DAYS. New Edition. Crown 8vo. 10s. 6d.

—— LIFE'S WORK AND GOD'S DISCIPLINE. 3rd Edition. Extra fcp. 8vo. 2s. 6d.

—— THE WHOLESOME WORDS OF JESUS CHRIST. 2nd Edition. Fcp. 8vo. 3s. 6d.

—— FOES OF FAITH. 2nd Ed. Fcp. 8vo. 3s. 6d.

VAUGHAN (Very Rev. Charles J.).—CHRIST SATISFYING THE INSTINCTS OF HUMANITY. 2nd Edition. Ext. fcp. 8vo. 3s. 6d.

—— COUNSELS FOR YOUNG STUDENTS. Fcp. 8vo. 2s. 6d.

—— THE TWO GREAT TEMPTATIONS. 2nd Edition. Fcp. 8vo. 3s. 6d.

—— ADDRESSES FOR YOUNG CLERGYMEN. Extra fcp. 8vo. 4s. 6d.

—— "MY SON, GIVE ME THINE HEART." Extra fcp. 8vo. 5s.

—— REST AWHILE. Addresses to Toilers in the Ministry. Extra fcp. 8vo. 5s.

—— TEMPLE SERMONS. Crown 8vo. 10s. 6d.

—— AUTHORISED OR REVISED? Sermons on some of the Texts in which the Revised Version differs from the Authorised. Crown 8vo. 7s. 6d.

—— ST. PAUL'S EPISTLE TO THE PHILIPPIANS. With Translation, Paraphrase, and Notes for English Readers. Crown 8vo. 5s.

—— LESSONS OF THE CROSS AND PASSION. WORDS FROM THE CROSS. THE REIGN OF SIN. THE LORD'S PRAYER. Four Courses of Lent Lectures. Crown 8vo. 10s. 6d.

—— UNIVERSITY SERMONS, NEW AND OLD. Crown 8vo. 10s. 6d.

—— THE EPISTLE TO THE HEBREWS. With Notes. Crown 8vo. 7s. 6d.

VAUGHAN (D. J.).—THE PRESENT TRIAL OF FAITH. Crown 8vo. 9s.

VAUGHAN (E. T.).—SOME REASONS OF OUR CHRISTIAN HOPE. Hulsean Lectures for 1875. Crown 8vo. 6s. 6d.

VAUGHAN (Robert).—STONES FROM THE QUARRY: Sermons. Crown 8vo. 5s.

VELEY (Marg.).—A GARDEN OF MEMORIES; MRS. AUSTIN; LIZZIE'S BARGAIN. Three Stories. 2 vols. Globe 8vo. 12s.

VENN (John). — ON SOME CHARACTER-ISTICS OF BELIEF, SCIENTIFIC AND RELI-GIOUS. Hulsean Lectures, 1869. 8vo. 7s. 6d.

—— THE LOGIC OF CHANCE. 2nd Edition. Crown 8vo. 10s. 6d.

—— SYMBOLIC LOGIC. Crown 8vo. 10s. 6d.

—— THE PRINCIPLES OF EMPIRICAL OR IN-DUCTIVE LOGIC. 8vo. 18s.

VERRALL (A. W.).—STUDIES, LITERARY AND HISTORICAL, IN THE ODES OF HORACE. 8vo. 8s. 6d.

VERRALL (Mrs. M. de G.) and HARRISON (Miss Jane E.).—MYTHOLOGY AND MONU-MENTS OF ANCIENT ATHENS. Illustrated. Crown 8vo. 16s.

VICTORIA UNIVERSITY CALENDAR, 1890. Crown 8vo. 1s. net.

VICTOR EMMANUEL II., FIRST KING OF ITALY. By G. S. GODKIN. 2nd Edi-tion. Crown 8vo. 6s.

VIDA: STUDY OF A GIRL. By AMY DUNS-MUIR. 3rd Edition. Crown 8vo. 6s.

VINCENT (Sir E.) and DICKSON (T. G.).— HANDBOOK TO MODERN GREEK. 3rd Ed. Crown 8vo. 6s.

VIRGIL.—THE WORKS OF VIRGIL RENDERED INTO ENGLISH PROSE. By JAS. LONSDALE, M.A., and S. LEE, M.A. Globe 8vo. 3s. 6d.

—— THE ÆNEID. Transl. into English Prose by J. W. MACKAIL, M.A. Cr. 8vo. 7s. 6d.

See also pp. 31, 33.

VOICES CRYING IN THE WILDER-NESS. A Novel. Crown 8vo. 7s. 6d.

WALDSTEIN (C.).—CATALOGUE OF CASTS IN THE MUSEUM OF CLASSICAL ARCHÆO-LOGY, CAMBRIDGE. Crown 8vo. 1s. 6d.

Large Paper Edition. Small 4to. 5s.

WALKER (Prof. Francis A.).—THE WAGES QUESTION. 8vo. 14s.

—— MONEY. 8vo. 16s.

—— MONEY IN ITS RELATION TO TRADE AND INDUSTRY. Crown 8vo. 7s. 6d.

—— POLITICAL ECONOMY. 2nd Edition. 8vo. 12s. 6d.

—— A BRIEF TEXT-BOOK OF POLITICAL ECO-NOMY. Crown 8vo. 6s. 6d.

—— LAND AND ITS RENT. Fcp. 8vo. 3s. 6d.

—— FIRST LESSONS IN POLITICAL ECONOMY. Crown 8vo. 5s.

WALLACE (Alfred Russel).—THE MALAY ARCHIPELAGO: THE LAND OF THE ORANG UTANG AND THE BIRD OF PARADISE. Maps and Illustrations. 10th Edition. Crown 8vo. 6s.

—— THE GEOGRAPHICAL DISTRIBUTION OF ANIMALS. With Illustrations and Maps. 2 vols. Medium 8vo. 42s.

—— ISLAND LIFE. With Illustrations and Maps. Crown 8vo. 6s.

—— BAD TIMES. An Essay on the present Depression of Trade. Crown 8vo. 2s. 6d.

—— DARWINISM. An Exposition of the Theory of Natural Selection, with some of its Appli-cations. Illustrated. 3rd Edition. Crown 8vo. 9s.

—— CONTRIBUTIONS TO THE THEORY OF NATURAL SELECTION; AND TROPICAL NA-TURE AND OTHER ESSAYS. New Edition. Crown 8vo. 6s.

WALLACE (Sir D. Mackenzie).—EGYPT AND THE EGYPTIAN QUESTION. 8vo. 14s.

WALTON and COTTON—LOWELL.—THE COMPLETE ANGLER. With an Introduc-tion by JAS. RUSSELL LOWELL. Illustrated. Extra crown 8vo. 2l. 12s. 6d. net.

Also an Edition on large paper, Proofs on Japanese paper. 3l. 13s. 6d. net.

WARD (Prof. A. W.).—A HISTORY OF ENG-LISH DRAMATIC LITERATURE, TO THE DEATH OF QUEEN ANNE. 2 vols. 8vo. 32s.

WARD (Prof. H. M.).—TIMBER AND SOME OF ITS DISEASES. Illustrated. Cr. 8vo. 6s.

WARD (John).—EXPERIENCES OF A DIPLO-MATIST. 8vo. 10s. 6d.

WARD(T. H.).—ENGLISH POETS. Selections, with Critical Introductions by various Writers, and a General Introduction by MATTHEW ARNOLD. Edited by T. H. WARD, M.A. 4 vols. 2nd Ed. Crown 8vo. 7s. 6d. each.— Vol. I. CHAUCER TO DONNE. — II. BEN JONSON TO DRYDEN. — III. ADDISON TO BLAKE.—IV. WORDSWORTH TO ROSSETTI.

WARD (Mrs. T. Humphry).—MILLY AND OLLY. With Illustrations by Mrs. ALMA TADEMA. Globe 8vo. 2s. 6d.

—— MISS BRETHERTON. Crown 8vo. 3s. 6d.

—— THE JOURNAL INTIME OF HENRI-FRÉDÉRIC AMIEL. Translated, with an Introduction and Notes. 2nd Ed. Cr. 8vo. 6s.

WARD (W.).—WILLIAM GEORGE WARD AND THE OXFORD MOVEMENT. Portrait. 8vo. 14s.

WATERTON (Charles).—WANDERINGS IN SOUTH AMERICA, THE NORTH-WEST OF THE UNITED STATES, AND THE ANTILLES. Edited by Rev. J. G. WOOD. With 100 Illustrations. Crown 8vo. 6s.

People's Edition. With 100 Illustrations. Medium 4to. 6d.

WATSON. A RECORD OF ELLEN WATSON. By ANNA BUCKLAND. Crown 8vo. 6s.

WATSON (R. Spence).—A VISIT TO WAZAN, THE SACRED CITY OF MOROCCO. 8vo. 10s.6d.

WEBSTER (Augusta).—DAFFODIL AND THE CROÄXAXICANS. Crown 8vo. 6s.

WELBY-GREGORY (The Hon. Lady).— LINKS AND CLUES. 2nd Edition. Crown 8vo. 6s.

WELCH (Wm.) and DUFFIELD (C. G.).— LATIN ACCIDENCE AND EXERCISES ARRANGED FOR BEGINNERS. 18mo. 1s. 6d.

WELLDON (Rev. J. E. C.).—THE SPIRITUAL LIFE, AND OTHER SERMONS. Cr. 8vo. 6s.

WESTCOTT (The Rt. Rev. Bishop.)—A GENERAL SURVEY OF THE HISTORY OF THE CANON OF THE NEW TESTAMENT DURING THE FIRST FOUR CENTURIES. 6th Edition. Crown 8vo. 10s. 6d.

—— INTRODUCTION TO THE STUDY OF THE FOUR GOSPELS. 7th Ed. Cr. 8vo. 10s. 6d.

—— THE GOSPEL OF THE RESURRECTION. 6th Edition. Crown 8vo. 6s.

—— THE BIBLE IN THE CHURCH. 10th Edit. 18mo. 4s. 6d.

—— THE CHRISTIAN LIFE, MANIFOLD AND ONE. Crown 8vo. 2s. 6d.

—— ON THE RELIGIOUS OFFICE OF THE UNIVERSITIES. Sermons. Cr. 8vo. 4s. 6d.

—— THE REVELATION OF THE RISEN LORD. 4th Edition. Crown 8vo. 6s.

—— THE HISTORIC FAITH. 3rd Edition. Cr. 8vo. 6s.

—— THE EPISTLES OF ST. JOHN. The Greek Text, with Notes. 2nd Edition. 8vo. 12s. 6d

—— THE REVELATION OF THE FATHER. Cr. 8vo. 6s.

WESTCOTT (Bishop).—CHRISTUS CONSUMMATOR. 2nd Edition. Crown 8vo. 6s.

—— SOME THOUGHTS FROM THE ORDINAL. Crown 8vo. 1s. 6d.

—— SOCIAL ASPECTS OF CHRISTIANITY. Cr. 8vo. 6s.

—— GIFTS FOR MINISTRY. Addresses to Candidates for Ordination. Crown 8vo. 1s. 6d.

—— THE EPISTLE TO THE HEBREWS. The Greek Text, with Notes and Essays. 8vo. 14s.

—— THE VICTORY OF THE CROSS. Sermons preached during Holy Week, 1888, in Hereford Cathedral. Crown 8vo. 3s. 6d.

—— FROM STRENGTH TO STRENGTH. Three Sermons (In Memoriam J. B. D.) Crown 8vo. 2s.

—— ESSAYS IN THE HISTORY OF RELIGIOUS THOUGHT IN THE WEST. Globe 8vo. 6s.

—— THOUGHTS ON REVELATION AND LIFE. Selections from the Writings of Bp. WESTCOTT. Edited by Rev. S. PHILLIPS. Crown 8vo. 6s.

WESTCOTT (Bishop) and HORT (Prof.).— THE NEW TESTAMENT IN THE ORIGINAL GREEK. Revised Text. 2 vols. Crown 8vo. 10s. 6d. each.—Vol. I. Text.—Vol. II. The Introduction and Appendix.

—— THE NEW TESTAMENT IN THE ORIGINAL GREEK. An Edition for Schools. The Text revised by Bishop WESTCOTT and Dr. HORT. 18mo, 4s. 6d.; roan, 5s. 6d.; morocco, 6s. 6d.

WHEELER (J. Talboys).—A SHORT HISTORY OF INDIA. With Maps. Crown 8vo. 12s.

—— INDIA UNDER BRITISH RULE. 8vo. 12s.6d.

—— COLLEGE HISTORY OF INDIA. Asiatic and European. Crown 8vo. 3s.; sewed, 2s. 6d.

—— PRIMER OF INDIAN HISTORY, ASIATIC AND EUROPEAN. 18mo. 1s.

WHEN PAPA COMES HOME. By the Author of "When I was a Little Girl." With Illustrations. Globe 8vo. 4s. 6d.

WHEWELL. DR. WILLIAM WHEWELL, late Master of Trinity College. Cambridge. An Account of his Writings, with Selections from his Literary and Scientific Correspondence. By I. TODHUNTER, M.A. 2 vols. 8vo. 25s.

WHITE (Gilbert).—NATURAL HISTORY AND ANTIQUITIES OF SELBORNE. Edited by FRANK BUCKLAND. With a Chapter on Antiquities by Lord SELBORNE. Cr.8vo. 6s.

WHITE (John Williams).—A SERIES OF FIRST LESSONS IN GREEK. Adapted to GOODWIN'S Greek Grammar. Crown 8vo. 3s. 6d.

WHITE (Dr. W. Hale).—A TEXT-BOOK OF GENERAL THERAPEUTICS. Illustrated. Cr. 8vo. 8s. 6d.

WHITHAM (Prof. J. M.).—STEAM ENGINE DESIGN. Illustrated. 8vo. 25s.

WHITNEY (Prof. W. D.).—A COMPENDIOUS GERMAN GRAMMAR. Crown 8vo. 4s. 6d.

—— A GERMAN READER IN PROSE AND VERSE. With Notes and Vocabulary. Cr. 8vo. 5s.

—— A COMPENDIOUS GERMAN AND ENGLISH DICTIONARY. Crown 8vo. 7s. 6d.—German-English Part separately. 5s.

WHITTIER.—COMPLETE POETICAL WORKS OF JOHN GREENLEAF WHITTIER. With Portrait. 18mo. 4s. 6d.

—— THE COMPLETE WORKS OF JOHN GREENLEAF WHITTIER. 7 vols. Crown 8vo. 6s. each.—Vol. I. NARRATIVE AND LEGENDARY POEMS.—II. POEMS OF NATURE; POEMS SUBJECTIVE AND REMINISCENT; RELIGIOUS POEMS.—III. ANTISLAVERY POEMS; SONGS OF LABOUR AND REFORM.— IV. PERSONAL POEMS; OCCASIONAL POEMS; THE TENT ON THE BEACH; with the Poems of ELIZABETH H. WHITTIER, and an Appendix containing Early and Uncollected Verses. — V. MARGARET SMITH'S JOURNAL; TALES AND SKETCHES. — VI. OLD PORTRAITS AND MODERN SKETCHES; PERSONAL SKETCHES AND TRIBUTES; HISTORICAL PAPERS.—VII. THE CONFLICT WITH SLAVERY, POLITICS AND REFORM; THE INNER LIFE, CRITICISM.

WICKHAM (Rev. E. C.).—WELLINGTON COLLEGE SERMONS. Crown 8vo. 6s.

WICKSTEED (Philip H.).—ALPHABET OF ECONOMIC SCIENCE.—I. ELEMENTS OF THE THEORY OF VALUE OR WORTH. Globe 8vo. 2s. 6d.

WIEDERSHEIM—PARKER.— ELEMENTS OF THE COMPARATIVE ANATOMY OF VERTEBRATES. Adapted from the German of Prof. ROBERT WIEDERSHEIM, by Prof. W. NEWTON PARKER. Illustrated. Medium 8vo. 12s. 6d.

WILBRAHAM (Frances M.).—IN THE SERE AND YELLOW LEAF: THOUGHTS AND RECOLLECTIONS FOR OLD AND YOUNG. Globe 8vo. 3s. 6d.

WILKINS (Prof. A. S.).—THE LIGHT OF THE WORLD: AN ESSAY. 2nd Edition. Crown 8vo. 3s. 6d.

—— ROMAN ANTIQUITIES. Illustr. 18mo. 1s.

—— ROMAN LITERATURE. 18mo. 1s.

WILKINSON (S.). — THE BRAIN OF AN ARMY. A Popular Account of the German General Staff. Crown 8vo. 2s. 6d.

WILLIAMS (Montagu).—LEAVES OF A LIFE. 15th Thousand. Crown 8vo. 3s. 6d.; sewed, 2s. 6d.

—— LATER LEAVES. 8vo. 15s.

WILLOUGHBY (F.).—FAIRY GUARDIANS. Illustrated by TOWNLEY GREEN. Crown 8vo. 5s.

WILSON (Dr. George).—RELIGIO CHEMICI. Crown 8vo. 8s. 6d.

—— THE FIVE GATEWAYS OF KNOWLEDGE. 9th Edition. Extra fcp. 8vo. 2s. 6d.

WILSON. MEMOIR OF PROF. GEORGE WILSON, M.D. By HIS SISTER. With Portrait. 2nd Edition. Crown 8vo. 6s.

WILSON (Rev. Canon).—THE BIBLE STUDENT'S GUIDE. 2nd Edition. 4to. 25s.

WILSON (Sir Daniel, LL. D.).—PREHISTORIC ANNALS OF SCOTLAND. With Illustrations. 2 vols. Demy 8vo. 36s.

—— PREHISTORIC MAN: RESEARCHES INTO THE ORIGIN OF CIVILISATION IN THE OLD AND NEW WORLD. 3rd Edition. With Illustrations. 2 vols. Medium 8vo. 36s.

—— CHATTERTON: A BIOGRAPHICAL STUDY. Crown 8vo. 6s. 6d.

—— CALIBAN: A CRITIQUE ON SHAKESPEARE'S "TEMPEST" AND "A MIDSUMMER NIGHT'S DREAM." 8vo. 10s. 6d.

WILSON (Rev. J. M.).—SERMONS PREACHED IN CLIFTON COLLEGE CHAPEL, 1879—83. Crown 8vo. 6s.

—— ESSAYS AND ADDRESSES. Cr. 8vo. 4s. 6d.

—— SOME CONTRIBUTIONS TO THE RELIGIOUS THOUGHT OF OUR TIME. Crown 8vo. 6s.

—— ELEMENTARY GEOMETRY. Books I.—V. Containing the Subjects of Euclid's First Six Books, following the Syllabus of Geometry prepared by the Geometrical Association. Extra fcp. 8vo. 4s. 6d.

—— SOLID GEOMETRY AND CONIC SECTIONS. Extra fcp. 8vo. 3s. 6d.

WINGATE (Major F. R.).—MAHDIISM AND THE SOUDAN. Being an Account of the Rise and Progress of Mahdiism, and of subsequent Events in the Soudan to the Present Time. With 10 Maps. 8vo.

WINKWORTH (Catherine). — CHRISTIAN SINGERS OF GERMANY. Crown 8vo. 4s. 6d.

WOLSELEY (General Viscount).—THE SOLDIER'S POCKET-BOOK FOR FIELD SERVICE. 5th Edition. 16mo, roan. 5s.

—— FIELD POCKET-BOOK FOR THE AUXILIARY FORCES. 16mo. 1s. 6d.

WOLSTENHOLME (Joseph). — MATHEMATICAL PROBLEMS ON SUBJECTS INCLUDED IN THE FIRST AND SECOND DIVISION OF THE SCHEDULE OF SUBJECTS FOR THE CAMBRIDGE MATHEMATICAL TRIPOS EXAMINATION. 2nd Edition. 8vo. 18s.

—— EXAMPLES FOR PRACTICE IN THE USE OF SEVEN-FIGURE LOGARITHMS. 8vo. 5s.

WOOD (Andrew Goldie).—THE ISLES OF THE BLEST, AND OTHER POEMS. Globe 8vo. 5s.

WOOD (Rev. E. G.).—THE REGAL POWER OF THE CHURCH. 8vo. 4s. 6d.

WOODS (Miss M. A.).—A FIRST POETRY BOOK. Fcp. 8vo. 2s. 6d.

—— A SECOND POETRY BOOK. 2 Parts. Fcp. 8vo. 2s. 6d. each.

WOODS (Miss M. A.).—A THIRD POETRY BOOK. Fcp. 8vo. 4s. 6d.

—— HYMNS FOR SCHOOL WORSHIP. 18mo. 1s. 6d.

WOODWARD (C. M.).—A HISTORY OF THE ST. LOUIS BRIDGE. 4to. 2l. 2s. net.

WOOLNER (Thomas). — MY BEAUTIFUL LADY. 3rd Edition. Fcp. 8vo. 5s.

—— PYGMALION : A POEM. Cr. 8vo. 7s. 6d.

—— SILENUS : A POEM. Crown 8vo. 6s.

WOOLWICH MATHEMATICAL PAPERS. For Admission in the Royal Military Academy for the Years 1880—88. Edit. by E. J. BROOKSMITH, B.A. Cr. 8vo. 6s.

WORDS FROM THE POETS. With a Vignette and Frontispiece. 12th Edition. 18mo. 1s.

WORDSWORTH.—THE RECLUSE: A POEM. Fcp. 8vo. 2s. 6d.

—— THE COMPLETE POETICAL WORKS. Copyright Edition. With an Introduction by JOHN MORLEY, and Portrait. Cr.8vo. 7s.6d.

WORDSWORTHIANA : A SELECTION OF PAPERS READ TO THE WORDSWORTH SOCIETY. Edited by W. KNIGHT. Crown 8vo. 7s. 6d.

WORSHIP (THE) OF GOD, AND FELLOWSHIP AMONG MEN. By the late Prof. MAURICE and others. Fcp. 8vo. 3s. 6d.

WORTHEY (Mrs.).—THE NEW CONTINENT: A NOVEL. 2 vols. Globe 8vo. 12s.

WRIGHT (Rev. Arthur).—THE COMPOSITION OF THE FOUR GOSPELS. Crown 8vo. 5s.

WRIGHT (Miss Guthrie). — THE SCHOOL COOKERY-BOOK. 18mo. 1s.

WRIGHT (Rev. Josiah).—THE SEVEN KINGS OF ROME. Abridged from the First Book of Livy. 8th Edition. Fcp. 8vo. 3s. 6d.

—— FIRST LATIN STEPS. Crown 8vo. 3s.

—— ATTIC PRIMER. Crown 8vo. 2s. 6d.

—— A COMPLETE LATIN COURSE. Crown 8vo. 2s. 6d.

WRIGHT (Lewis).—LIGHT. A Course of Experimental Optics, chiefly with the Lantern. With Illustrations and Coloured Plates. Crown 8vo. 7s. 6d.

WRIGHT (Miss Romley).—MIDDLE-CLASS COOKERY BOOK. Fcp. 8vo. 1s. 6d.

WRIGHT (W. Aldis).—THE BIBLE WORD-BOOK. 2nd Edition. Crown 8vo. 7s. 6d.

WURTZ.—A HISTORY OF CHEMICAL THEORY. By AD. WURTZ. Translated by HENRY WATTS, F.R.S. Crown 8vo. 6s.

WYATT (Sir M. Digby). — FINE ART : A Sketch of its History, Theory, Practice, and Application to Industry. 8vo. 5s.

XENOPHON. — THE COMPLETE WORKS. Translated by H. G. DAKYNS, M.A. 4 vols. Crown 8vo.—Vol. I. THE ANABASIS AND BOOKS I. AND II. OF THE HELLENICA. 10s. 6d.—Vol. II. HELLENICA III.—VII., and the two Polities—ATHENIAN and LACONIAN, the AGESILAUS, and Tract on REVENUES. With Maps and Plans.

See also pp. 31, 33.

YONGE (Charlotte M.). — NOVELS AND TALES. Crown 8vo. 3s. 6d. each.

1. THE HEIR OF REDCLYFFE.
2. HEARTSEASE.
3. HOPES AND FEARS.
4. DYNEVOR TERRACE.
5. THE DAISY CHAIN.
6. THE TRIAL: MORE LINKS OF THE DAISY CHAIN.
7. PILLARS OF THE HOUSE. Vol. I.
8. PILLARS OF THE HOUSE. Vol. II.
9. THE YOUNG STEPMOTHER.
10. CLEVER WOMAN OF THE FAMILY.
11. THE THREE BRIDES.
12. MY YOUNG ALCIDES.
13. THE CAGED LION.
14. THE DOVE IN THE EAGLE'S NEST.
15. THE CHAPLET OF PEARLS.
16. LADY HESTER: AND THE DANVERS PAPERS.
17. MAGNUM BONUM.
18. LOVE AND LIFE.
19. UNKNOWN TO HISTORY.
20. STRAY PEARLS.
21. THE ARMOURER'S PRENTICES.
22. THE TWO SIDES OF THE SHIELD.
23. NUTTIE'S FATHER.
24. SCENES AND CHARACTERS.
25. CHANTRY HOUSE.
26. A MODERN TELEMACHUS.
27. BYWORDS.
28. BEECHCROFT AT ROCKSTONE.
29. MORE BYWORDS.
30. A REPUTED CHANGELING.
31. THE PRINCE AND THE PAGE.
32. THE LANCES OF LYNWOOD.
33. P's AND Q's.
34. LITTLE LUCY'S WONDERFUL GLOBE.

—— A BOOK OF GOLDEN DEEDS. 18mo. 4s.6d.
Cheap Edition. 18mo. 1s.
Globe Readings Edition. Globe 8vo. 2s.

—— CAMEOS FROM ENGLISH HISTORY. Extra fcp. 8vo. 5s. each.—Vol. I. FROM ROLLO TO EDWARD II.—Vol. II. THE WARS IN FRANCE. —Vol. III. THE WARS OF THE ROSES. —Vol. IV. REFORMATION TIMES.—Vol. V. ENGLAND AND SPAIN. — Vol. VI. FORTY YEARS OF STUART RULE (1603—1643).— Vol. VII. THE REBELLION AND RESTORATION (1642—78).

YONGE (Charlotte M.).—Scripture Read-
ings for Schools and Families. Globe
8vo. 1s. 6d. each; also with Comments,
3s. 6d. each.—Genesis to Deuteronomy.
—Second Series: Joshua to Solomon.—
Third Series: Kings and the Prophets.—
Fourth Series: The Gospel Times.—Fifth
Series: Apostolic Times.

—— The Life of John Coleridge Patteson. 2 vols. Crown 8vo. 12s.

—— The Pupils of St. John. Illustrated.
Crown 8vo. 6s.

—— Pioneers and Founders; or, Recent
Workers in the Mission Field. Crown
8vo. 6s.

—— History of Christian Names. New
Edition, revised. Crown 8vo. 7s. 6d.

—— Two Penniless Princesses. 2 vols.
Crown 8vo. 12s.

YONGE (Charlotte M.).—The Victorian
Half-Century. Crn. 8vo. 1s. 6d.; swd 1s.

—— The Herb of the Field. A New
Edition, revised. Crown 8vo. 5s.

YOUNG (E. W.).—Simple Practical Methods of Calculating Strains on Gir-
ders, Arches, and Trusses. 8vo. 7s. 6d.

ZECHARIAH. The Hebrew Student's
Commentary on Zechariah, Hebrew and
LXX. By W. H. Lowe, M.A. 8vo. 10s. 6d.

ZIEGLER.—A Text-Book of Pathologi-
cal Anatomy and Pathogenesis. By
Ernst Ziegler. Translated and Edited
for English Students by Donald Mac-
Alister, M.A., M.D. With Illustrations.
8vo. — Part I. General Pathological
Anatomy. 2nd Edition. 12s. 6d.—Part II.
Special Pathological Anatomy. Sections
I.—VIII. 2nd Edition. 12s. 6d. Sections
IX.—XII. 8vo. 12s. 6d.

MACMILLAN AND CO., LONDON.

J. PALMER, PRINTER, ALEXANDRA STREET, CAMBRIDGE.

VII/50/2/91